HELL'S GATES

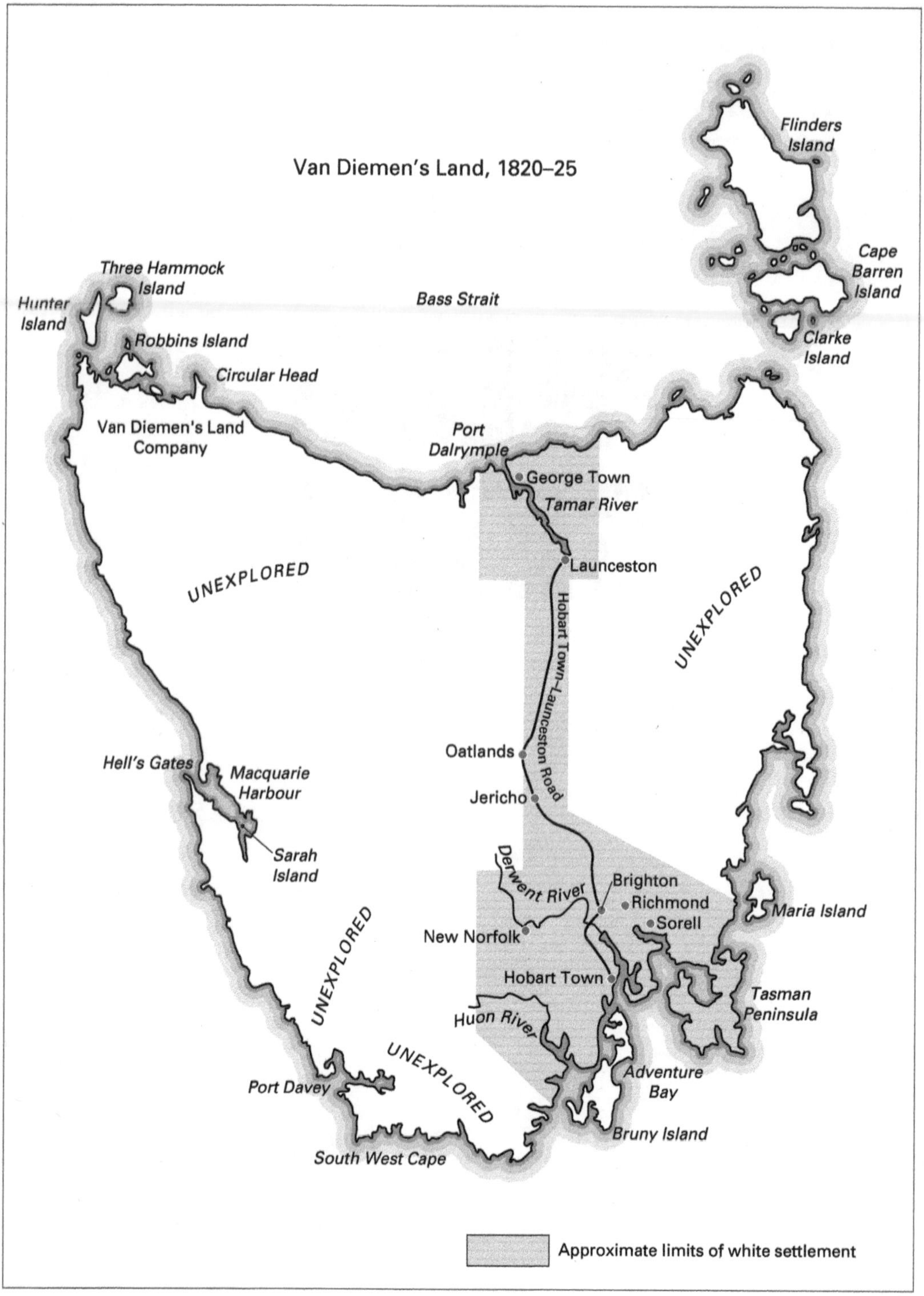

Van Diemen's Land, 1820–25

HELL'S GATES

THE TRUE TASMANIAN STORY OF THE ESCAPED CONVICTS WHO TURNED TO CANNIBALISM TO SURVIVE

PAUL COLLINS

hardie grant books
MELBOURNE • LONDON

This edition published in 2014 by Hardie Grant Books,
an imprint of Hardie Grant Publishing

Hardie Grant Books (Melbourne)
Building 1, 658 Church Street
Richmond, Victoria 3121

Hardie Grant Books (London)
5th & 6th Floors
52–54 Southwark Street
London SE1 1UN

hardiegrant.com/au/books

A catalogue record for this
book is available from the
National Library of Australia

Hell's Gates
ISBN 9781742708652

Cover image courtesy Madman
Text design by Guy Mirabella
Typeset in Joanna 12/15 pt Joanna by J&M Typesetting
Printed in Australia by Opus Group Pty Ltd, an Accredited
ISO AS/NZS 14001 Environmental Management System printer.

MIX
Paper | Supporting responsible forestry
FSC® C018684
FSC www.fsc.org

The paper this book is printed on is certified against the Forest Stewardship Council® Standards. Griffin Press holds chain of custody certification SCS-COC-001185. FSC® promotes environmentally responsible, socially beneficial and economically viable management of the world's forests.

Contents

List of Illustrations

ACKNOWLEDGEMENTS

Anyone who writes history is constantly in the debt of others. This is especially true when Alexander Pearce and his exploits have become the subject of numerous inaccurate books, newspaper and magazine articles, extending over a period of more than 150 years. Within fifty years of his execution, Pearce had metamorphosed into the appalling Gabbett, the convict cannibal of Marcus Clarke's *For the Term of His Natural Life* (London, 1875). Nowadays many Australians have heard of Pearce and know some of the details of the story, but they are often confused between fiction and fact. In sorting it all out I have been helped enormously by a number of people. I want to record here the names of just a few who guided me in the task of trying to get the story right.

Everyone who writes about Pearce is in the debt of Dan Sprod. He was the first researcher to sort out fact from fiction in what we know about Alexander Pearce. His *Alexander Pearce of Macquarie Harbour: Convict – Bushranger – Cannibal* (Hobart, 1977) is thorough, meticulous and reliable. Without his groundwork and careful research my task would have been close to impossible. As well as Dan Sprod, there are a number of other writers whose work has been very helpful and I have tried to acknowledge each of them in the bibliographical essay.

For the Sarah Island penal settlement and for convict remains generally in the Macquarie Harbour area, I am deeply in the debt of Richard Davies. Richard's knowledge and understanding of the history and archaeology of the area is unrivalled, and a tour with him will teach you more in a day than you can learn in weeks of research. He is also extraordinarily generous in sharing all that he knows. He is the writer and usually one of the actors in the comedy-drama *The Ship That Never Was*, which is performed year-round in the theatre next to the Visitor Information Centre in Strahan. I am particularly grateful to Richard and his family for the warm welcome I have always received from them.

Over the years since 1970, when I first went to Tasmania as a resident, I have seen the town of Strahan change from an isolated and quiet fishing village known only to a few Tasmanians and to an even smaller number from the mainland, to something of a national and even international tourist mecca. Not everyone approves of this, but the people of Strahan are always courteous and helpful to visitors. When you have visited the place as often as I have for over thirty years you can speak of local kindness with confidence.

Bushwalkers and those who work for the Tasmanian Parks and Wildlife Service love the bush, and they love talking about it even more. I interviewed several of them to tap into their experience and knowledge of western Tasmania and the World Heritage Area. Terry Reid, Senior Ranger in Queenstown for the Parks and Wildlife Service, is west-coast born and bred, and he shared his knowledge of the Tasmanian west – vast and detailed as it is – with me generously. Geoff Law, campaigner for the Wilderness Society in Hobart, has an immense and intimate knowledge of the Tasmanian bush; he literally seems to have been everywhere on the island. Like Terry, Geoff can speak from personal experience of what it is like to try to penetrate the country traversed by Pearce and the other escapees. Both men also have a thorough understanding of the possible routes taken by the Pearce group.

Two others who helped me enormously in understanding the lay of the land, the vegetation, fire regimen and the route options were Sue Rundle and Dr Jon Marsden-Smedley of the Parks and Wildlife Service in Hobart. Both have an intimate knowledge of the bush. Another who helped me understand the topography and possible routes was Dr Simon Kleinig of Adelaide, a very experienced bushwalker himself, who is at present working on a history of the Frenchman's Cap region. I am deeply indebted to their generosity.

Well-funded public institutions are essential to any working democracy, and especially helpful to independent scholars like myself. The libraries and archives that I have used over the years have constantly had to struggle to make ends meet, and have had to live with the never-ending cuts imposed on them. These institutions still survive on the skill, knowledge and generosity of their staff and the richness of their holdings. Especially helpful in writing this book were the librarians and archivists of the National Library of Australia, and the library system of the Australian National University, both in Canberra; the Tasmaniana Library, the Allport Library and the Archives Office of Tasmania, all in Hobart; the Mitchell Library in Sydney; the National Archives of Ireland in Dublin; and the City of London Archives. The microfilms of the Australian Joint Copying Project were also very helpful; they have made an extraordinary amount of British and Irish archival material available to Australian researchers. Other sources are mentioned in the bibliographical essay.

There are four specific people I must mention. Mary Cunnane is my literary agent and I am deeply indebted to her skill, support and sensible advice. Caroline Williamson and Foong Ling Kong have been real professionals who are dreams to work with, as have been the staff of Hardie Grant.

And finally, my dear friend Marilyn Hatton has listened to endless versions of this book, made pivotal critical comments and accompanied me on several trips to Tasmania, during which we experienced something of the south-west and the country through which Pearce and his cohorts travelled. I deeply appreciate her love and support.

HELL'S GATES

Prologue

Somewhere to the west of the confluence of the Ouse and Shannon rivers, Van Diemen's Land, early November 1822.

It was early morning. Although the air was still cold, when you moved out of the shadows you could feel the sun's heat. The sky was completely cloudless and the sheer clarity of the light illuminated every aspect of the landscape. A tree-covered hill sloped toward a grassy area that bordered a small, reed-filled swamp opening out onto a shallow lake. The source of the lake was a creek that flowed from the higher ground to the north and another creek emptied out of the marsh and lake toward the south. A thin mist hovered above the lake's surface. A group of about twelve light brown, mallard-sized ducks with a black strip across their eyes was grazing beside the swamp. Despite their colouring, they are known in Australia, where they are very common, as Pacific Black ducks. A number of this group were juveniles, but they had already taken on the plumage and colouring of their parents.

The forest on the hill, which was dominated by tall, straight trees, had an understorey that reached from the top of the hill down to the swamp and lake. Most of the trees were manna gums. Their bark peeled off in thin strips from about halfway up their trunks, revealing a greyish-white or pale cream skin underneath. Interspersed among the manna gums were messmates – trees with a long, thick-fibred, stringy bark. They were about the same height as the manna gums and had similar foliage. Some light mist clung to the upper level of the trees, which got thicker further up the hill. The heat of the sun would soon disperse it.

The understorey was almost park-like, with grasses, scattered tree ferns, and small clumps of banksias and wattles. The distinctive smell of the bush was strong, with a pungent freshness from the eucalypts. Their resin exudes a penetrating but cool, aromatic odour that clears the nasal passages and lungs to give a feeling of relaxation. The whole scene was still, but was brought alive by the sounds and movements of the colourful birds: the glossy black and white Australian magpies were warbling their clarinet-like songs, and there was the raucous and penetrating screech of a couple of sulphur-crested white cockatoos perched high in the trees keeping 'cocky' (lookout) for a group that fed on the ground. A smaller flock of even larger yellow-tailed black cockatoos flew slowly through the trees with their plangent, wailing call. It seemed an idyllic setting.

But something was out of place. A short, thin man was staggering rather than walking down the hill through the trees toward the swamp. He was in terrible physical shape. At one stage he tried to step over a fallen log, but missed his footing and fell. It took him a long time to get up again, and even then he was unsteady on his feet. Almost completely naked, he was only wearing the remnants of a pair of dirty canvas trousers. His skin was lacerated, with festering wounds over his torso, arms and legs. It was hard to tell from a distance that he was a European, because he was filthy. He had a scraggly beard, and dirty, dishevelled hair. His body showed signs of starvation – gawking ribs, a bulging collarbone and skin that hung on him like a thin sheet over a bony frame. His sunken eyes had that fixated, slightly crazed look, characteristic of someone who has not eaten properly for many weeks. His legs were swollen and, despite the fact that it was reasonably warm for early November, he was shivering uncontrollably. His name was Alexander Pearce.

As he came down the hill his entire being was dominated by one thought: food. He had lost track of time completely. He could not remember how many days it was since he had killed Bob Greenhill; it was probably three or four. At one stage he had descended into a dark, bleak despair and had decided to kill himself. But when he had tried to focus his mind on the business of hanging himself, he realised he had neither the energy nor the wherewithal to do it. His sneaking feeling of guilt was quickly replaced with the sense that since he had come so far it would be mad to give up now. His one aim was to get to Table Mountain where he had once worked as a shepherd and where he knew there would be food and he would be safe. At Table Mountain there was every chance he would meet another isolated shepherd or, even better, an Irish convict-mate who knew him.

But his sense of direction was completely askew; for all he knew he could have been walking around in circles for days. The truth was that he, like the others, had always been dependent on Greenhill to show him the way. A former sailor, Greenhill was the only one who could read the sun and the stars, and lead them eastward toward the settled districts where there would be food and shelter. After Pearce had killed Greenhill he had tried to keep a sense of direction, and somehow felt he was most likely heading the right way. He was unable to tell by the stars, but he had learned enough to know that he could use the sun. He remembered asking Greenhill one day about how he worked out direction and the sailor had said, 'Just head toward the sun in the early morning, and away from it in the late afternoon and you'll find yourself heading pretty much east, which is the way we want to go'.

After he had killed Greenhill he was exhilarated; at last he was safe from his companions. He felt no sorrow that all of his mates were dead; he was indifferent to them. It was a sense of victory that he was alive and free. But he missed the certainty that Greenhill had brought, the feeling that the man knew where he was going. Certainly, the surrounding country looked very familiar to him, but he was so hungry that food, not direction, dominated most of his waking thoughts. And he'd been in Van Diemen's Land long enough to know how easy it was to get lost in the bush; it all looked so alike. As far as he could remember, the last occasion that he had eaten since abandoning what was left of Greenhill's body had been when he staggered into a small, abandoned Aboriginal camp and had scavenged some cast-off, raw, tasteless pieces of kangaroo and possum from the ground.

He was wrenched from his reverie by the piercing screeches of the cockatoos taking off from their feeding place. Something had disturbed them. When he had first seen them on his arrival in Van Diemen's Land they had seemed funny and amazingly agile in the air, but he had come to hate them and every other living thing in the terrible place to which he had been condemned. He even looked back with nostalgia to the back-breaking labour and grinding poverty of farm-work in Ireland.

Then he saw the ducks and he charged out of the trees. But the Pacific Blacks saw him coming, took off and flew toward the open water of the lake. With a rush of energy he plunged into the swamp, through the weeds and slush, and waded out into the waist-deep cold water. A couple of the ducks flew away, but others were not so quick. As the man lunged at them, some flapped away, treading water, and a couple dived under. Pearce stood up, looked around and was surprised to find one duck surface right beside him. He grabbed it and wrung its neck, dropping its body on the water when another surfaced just in front of him. He caught it also. It was dispatched just as quickly as the first.

He dragged himself out of the lake. Wet through, he sat on the grass, plucked the feathers from the first duck, tore it apart with his bare hands and began to eat the raw flesh ravenously. He had no other choice; he did not have the wherewithal to make a fire. Soon little but feathers were left.

The man was not alone as he sat on the grass tearing off pieces of bleeding flesh. Two young Aboriginal warriors were quietly observing him from the camouflage of the bush. Their skin was a black to reddish-brown colour, and their hair woolly, black and curled in mop-like strands. Their keen eyes took in every aspect of the scene. They stood there, thin, relaxed, stark naked, with a pattern of raised weals on their upper arms, shoulders and chests. Unlike mainland Aborigines, they were uncircumcised. They were leaning on their spears, which were 4 metres long (13 feet). One of the men was standing with one leg bent and his foot resting on his other knee. They had been following the starving man's progress for several days now, ever since he and his mate had first strayed into their country. These were Braylwunyer men and their clan had lived in this land since the Dreaming. They knew every inch of the country and were so well hidden that never once had the starving whites known that they were being watched.

The Braylwunyer people were not the first to observe the strangers. Their closely related clansmen, the Larmairremener, who lived to the west of them, had first sighted three white men coming over the mountains and entering the far western edges of their tribe's country. At first the Larmairremener had decided to wait and see if the whites had the magic sticks that killed people at a distance when the sticks went 'bang'. If they did not have the magic sticks, then the decision was to wait for an opportunity to spear and kill them. For the Larmairremener, like the Braylwunyer, belonged to the Big River tribe, and they and the other three clans that made up the tribe had agreed to defend all of their land vigorously from white invasion. The Big River elders had already heard from other tribes and clans, especially the south-eastern Mouheneenner clan, some of whose land had already been seized by the whites to build their strange dwellings, how violent, cruel, uncivilised and inhumane these men were. They whipped, hung and killed each other, as well as slaughtering the men and cruelly raping and murdering the women of the South-Eastern tribe whose land abutted Big River territory. Quite a number of people from other tribes had learned something of the language of the whites, and there were frequent reports that more and more of them seemed to be coming out of the sea with their strange animals in the giant birds that sailed on the water.

As the Larmairremener warriors observed the three whites, they realised that although the men were starving, they seemed to have no knowledge of the land and could not see any of the food that was around them and there for the taking. The grasslands and open woodlands of the Big River tribe's territory supported large populations of kangaroos that the clans used for both food and clothing. The warriors had seen whites occasionally, but never coming from the west; they usually came from the south and the east. Their observations had convinced the Big River people that these men knew absolutely nothing about the land or the animals and their rhythms and laws. It was this ignorance which had convinced the younger men of the tribe that the elders were mistaken when they said that the whites might be the ghosts of tribespeople who had died. Some of the old men even claimed to recognise long-dead relatives among the strangers. It was true that the colour white signified death, but these people could not be ancestors. The elders tried to explain that death was a terrible process, and that human memory could be easily confused when it passed through this frightening time. Although they kept their disagreement to themselves out of respect, many of the younger men were now convinced that the elders were mistaken, and that these people were really men just like themselves. The time was fast approaching when they would have to be firmly resisted, and any who did penetrate into clan or tribal territory should be killed outright.

But as they observed the three whites who had come over the mountains from the border country between their own land and that of the South-West people, the younger Aboriginal men soon realised that they were not only harmless, but also bewildered and lost. The decision had been taken to let them pass through clan country to see what they would do. Perhaps they would give some indication of the white men's real intentions. As one young warrior had suggested, it was important to observe your enemy and get to know his way of operating and the weaknesses embedded in it.

One day, as the Larmairremener men watched the three strangers, one of them trod on a tiger snake. The white men stopped for several days to look after their companion, but they did not seem to know how to treat the bite and what remedies to use. Then, the two assisted the injured man to continue their journey. The Larmairremener had not seen many white men before; their land was a long way from the country that the new arrivals had invaded with their four-legged animals. Despite white people's reputation for violence among the tribes, they at first seemed kind to their sick companion and posed no threat.

After a couple of days struggling onward, the whites stopped again. The injured man was obviously getting worse. Then the other two did something that utterly shocked the warriors looking on from the bush – one of them took an instrument that they had used to chop trees and killed the man when he was asleep by splitting his head open. They butchered him like a dead kangaroo, and cooked and ate parts of him. The rest of his body they left for the Tasmanian devils to scavenge. There was no ceremony, no burial, no respect for the man's spirit.

The two surviving men then resumed their seemingly purposeless journey through the Big River tribe's country. They eventually crossed out of Larmairremener land and into the territory of the Braylwunyer clan – but not before the elders of the two clans had discussed at length what they should do about the white men. In the end they decided to do nothing; they would simply let the young warriors observe them and make sure that they did not invade or pollute any sacred sites. They felt that these barbarians would eventually either kill each other or die from starvation anyway. Three nights later the shorter of the two men killed his companion in his sleep with the chopping stick. He then butchered, cooked and ate parts of the dead body. Again he abandoned the remains without ceremony, and the Tasmanian devils had another feast.

Eating gave the sole survivor energy for a short time, but it did not sustain him and he was soon hungry again. A day later the Braylwunyer men watched as he stumbled into a camp abandoned by one of their own hearth-families who had moved on that very morning. He ate scraps of food from the ground. The more they watched him the more befuddled they became at the man's actions. They had heard much from the Lennowwenne, the southernmost clan of their own tribe, who lived right on the edge of the area that the whites had taken. The more they saw of these men, the more they were determined to resist such a sub-human species. These creatures seemed to have no law, no custom, no respect for the land, nor its animals and people.

•

After eating the ducks the white man pushed on through the open forest that covered the low, rolling hills. The morning mist gradually lifted and the sun came out. By midday it had become very warm. The man even began to sweat a little. It was the first time that he had felt really warm and dry for months. However, by mid-afternoon he was exhausted again, and when he arrived at a small, clear creek he stopped. It was about two hours before dark.

Somehow he felt that he was no longer under pressure, that he was safe and very close to reaching his goal of Table Mountain. It was his determination to get there that sustained him. As he curled up to sleep that night on soft grass below a rocky outcrop, he tried to think back over all that had happened to him. But if the sequence of events was somewhat confused in his mind, there was one thing he knew for sure: against all the odds, he had survived the nightmare trek across the wilderness. He believed that escape from Van Diemen's Land was still a possibility. He had heard artful and well-travelled men like Bob Greenhill talk about escape to China, or to an island in the vast Pacific Ocean, where there were many beautiful women. He had no idea where any of these places were, or what the people who lived there were like. He hoped that the women were more willing than the screaming Aboriginal woman he had raped when he was on the run after he had bolted a second time. In a way, he wished Greenhill was still around. He was a smart man who had known a lot more about the world than the other filthy dunderheads and thieving bastards with whom he had lived for the last three years.

He did not know where China was, but anywhere in the world would be a lot better than a place of secondary punishment like Macquarie Harbour, where the best he could hope for was a grope in the dark of the dormitory with another convict. He had lost track of the days since he had escaped from the harbour, largely because he could not add up or count; in fact, he could scarcely read or write his own name. He had tried to improve his reading ability on the *Castle Forbes* coming out from Ireland, but lacked application.

He knew he had been on the journey for a long time, and had come a long way through very difficult country. His predominant feeling just before he fell deeply asleep that night was that his luck had, at last, turned. Perhaps, finally, things were going his way. As it panned out, he was both right and wrong.

He was never to know just how remarkable his feat of endurance had been.

1

'I WAS THE CONVICT SENT TO HELL'

The Master of the *Castle Forbes*, Captain Thomas L. Reid, noticed a change in the weather in the early afternoon of the seventh day of January, 1820. It had suddenly become colder, the clouds were growing darker and gloomier, and a light drizzle had started, sure signs that a storm was brewing. For several days now they had been running in a reasonably calm sea with full sail, due east before a west-sou'-westerly wind, and in the previous twenty-four hours they had made good time, sailing just over 100 nautical miles (185 kilometres). They had picked up a lot of speed since Reid had brought the *Castle Forbes* a couple of degrees further south into the Roaring Forties.

This was his first time as a master in these isolated seas. Reid was a careful captain who always knew his position exactly by solar and lunar observation as well as by his own calculations based on the ship's chronometer. The ship was travelling in an easterly direction along latitude 43°25' south, and crossing longitude 99°60' east. The *Castle Forbes* was a newly built merchant ship of 439 tons burthen on her maiden run to New South Wales, having been launched in Aberdeen in 1818. Like most British merchantmen of the time, she was three-masted with square-rigged sails, flat-sided and flat-bottomed, and massively constructed for maximum carrying capacity rather than for speed, with a lot of ballast to prevent her capsizing. A commercial vessel on charter to the British Admiralty, the *Castle Forbes* was car-

Journey of the *Castle Forbes* to New South Wales.

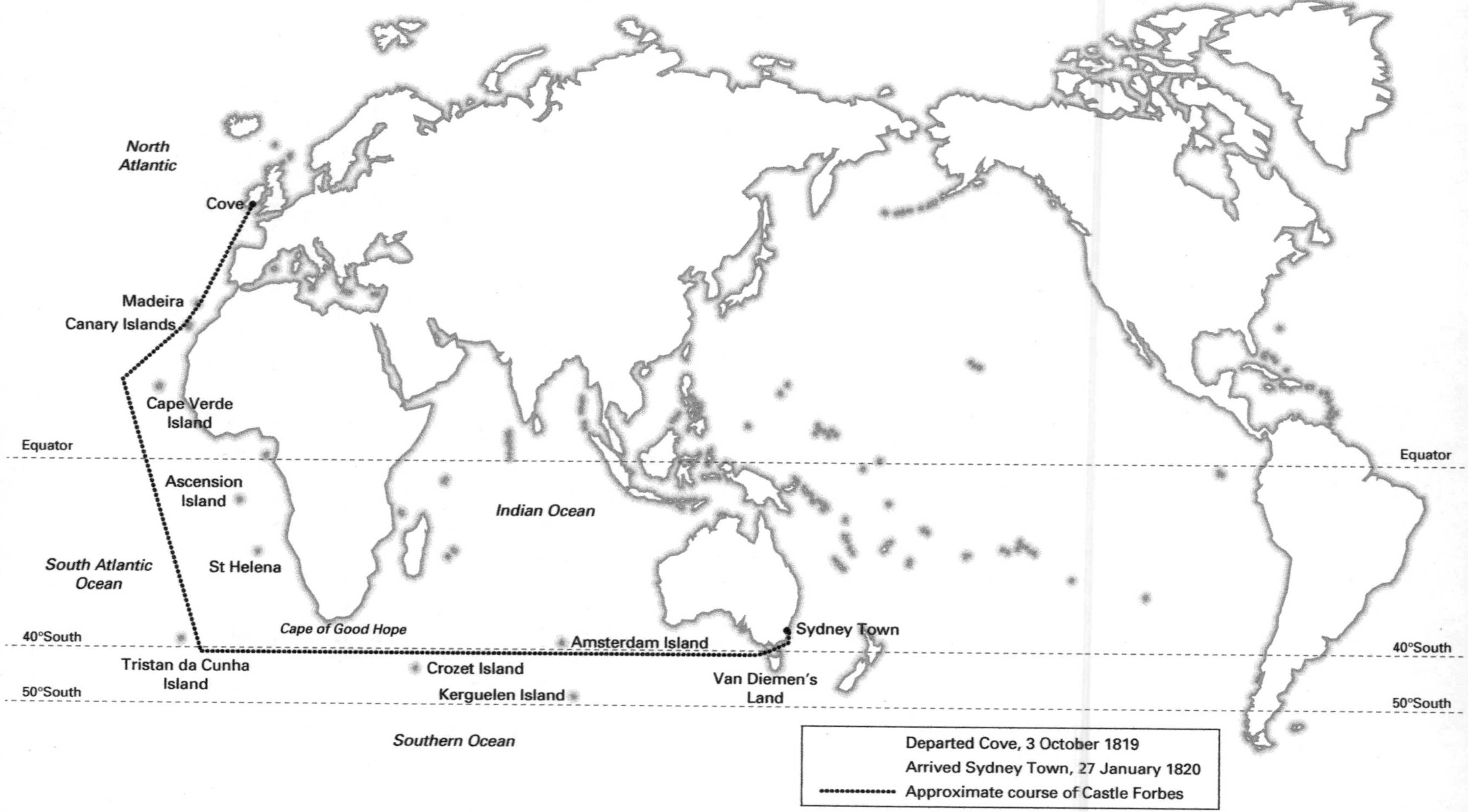

rying an exclusively human cargo: 140 Irish male convicts, out of Cove (today known by its Gaelic name, Cobh) in Cork Harbour on 3 October 1819, on a non-stop run to Sydney Town in the colony of New South Wales. She was already some three months into her journey.

As soon as they entered the great Southern Ocean well to the south of the Cape of Good Hope, Reid had set his course on 40°30' south latitude to stay about three to four degrees to the north of the mountainous Crozet Islands, which lay directly in his path. Together with icebergs, the islands could be a hazard for mariners, especially in fog. But by now the ship had left the Crozets far behind and was out in the vast emptiness of ocean that lay to the south-west of the isolated and largely unexplored western tip of the mainland of New Holland. Reid could afford to take his ship a little further south to pick up even stronger winds. But if they ran into trouble in these waters, there was absolutely no refuge to make for and certainly no one to rescue them. Even today, with satellite communications, the rescue of mariners in trouble in the Southern Ocean is still a difficult and dangerous task. Out in these vast seas humankind is bluntly reminded of its fragility in the face of the brute force of the natural world.

For the 'Roaring Forties' and 'Ferocious Fifties', as mariners have called these southern seas for several centuries, really do live up to their epithets. The weather is often abominable, and a calm or moderate sea can be suddenly replaced by a fierce storm or a savage squall. With no land mass to get in the way, except faraway South America's Patagonia and Tierra del Fuego, the winds and currents of the Southern Ocean are immensely powerful and remarkably consistent. We now know that the Antarctic circumpolar current connects the Indian, Atlantic and Pacific ocean basins and carries a vast volume of water around the polar continent. It is a major influence upon the temperature, rainfall and weather of the whole of the southern hemisphere, and is essential for the circulation pattern of all the world's oceans. Like the circumpolar current, the southern winds travel generally from west to east in a broad circle around the Antarctic continent. With no land mass to obstruct them, they pick up force and whip up enormous seas. Because of these prevailing winds, sailing through the Roaring Forties was the optimum way to go from England or Ireland to New South Wales for a sailing ship like the *Castle Forbes*. Occasionally such ships could travel up to 200 nautical miles (370 kilometres) in twenty-four hours.

But the flip side of a strong tail wind is rough weather. For sailors like Reid and his crew, trained and experienced in the weather patterns of the seas around the United Kingdom, the Mediterranean, Baltic or even the north Atlantic routes to the United States and Canada, the Southern Ocean was a new experience, and was terrifying. Once a ship had emerged from the South Atlantic Ocean, passed below the Cape of Good Hope and established itself on an easterly course somewhere between 35° and 45° south, it was often driven along carrying very little sail by gales, strong currents and mountainous seas that towered over the stern of the boat. They often averaged 8 knots per hour in these southern regions and occasionally reached speeds of 12 knots or more. For early nineteenth-century sailing ships this was extraordinarily fast. But this speed came with fierce winds, horrendous seas and frightening, dangerous storms. The *Castle Forbes* was sailing into one right now.

As the sky darkened and the rain became heavier, Reid was joined on the poop deck by the Surgeon-Superintendent of convicts, Dr James Scott, a naval reserve officer and an able, sensible, if somewhat autocratic 29-year-old Scotsman. Standing next to the helmsman, they discussed the situation. Fortunately, that morning the convicts had already been allowed on deck in groups for two-hour stints of fresh air and exercise. Scott had made sure that this occurred on almost every day of the journey, except when it was too rough. He reported to Reid that everything had been secured in the prison. The captain had already ordered a reduction in sail and that the ship should be battened down and prepared for the storm. It was now just a matter of waiting for the inevitable. The Lieutenant's Guard of twenty-six non-commissioned officers and soldiers, with their women and children, had retired to their quarters, except for those guarding the convicts. Only Reid, Scott, the officer of the watch and some of the other officers and seamen remained on deck.

The storm gathered strength as the afternoon wore on. Reid ordered all remaining canvas be taken down, except for a close-reefed foresail to assist in steering. Taking in sail was a tricky process for the sailors aloft in the rigging, especially as the wave heights increased and the ship began to roll with the heavy swell. The *Castle Forbes*'s sails were taken in successfully, but even with almost bare poles the ship was gathering speed as she ran before a following sea with winds out of the west-nor'-west. The seas grew bigger, with strong cross-swells. It became a herculean struggle for the helmsman as he fought to hold a heading straight before the weather, which fortunately for them was running pretty much in their direction.

Massive swells gradually built up behind the stern of the *Castle Forbes*; wave heights of 26 to 27 metres (85 to 90 feet) are common in Southern Ocean storms. At times the ship was almost surfing down, crashing into the bottom of the trough with an awful, jarring shudder. The vessel hardly had a chance to right itself before it began to climb up the next sloping wall of water. The sky darkened and rain poured down in torrents. With nightfall the situation became even more extreme. The gale kept up, intensified by squalls, with icy rain, sleet, thunder and lightning. Despite it being close to the southern midsummer, it was intensely cold. Storms like this can abate quickly or last for several days. Sometimes calm would return, only to be followed by violent, fresh gales, showers of hail or even snow.

The men working on the slippery deck faced grave danger of being washed overboard. Once a man was in the water he would have to be left behind, even if someone noticed that he was gone. The ship could not be turned around without the risk of broaching, so there was no possibility of rescue. Captain George Bayly, one of the most experienced nineteenth-century captains in the southern seas, reported that as a young seaman he nearly lost his life working the sails on a convict ship off south-western Australia in 1824, four years after the *Castle Forbes* made her first run to New South Wales. 'About 7 PM I was sent out to loose the jib [the triangular sail at the front of the boat]. The wind was on the starboard quarter, the vessel going about 8 knots and rolling heavily. While in the act of casting off the gasket [the rope used to secure the sail] she gave a tremendous roll to windward and rolled the sail upon me. I attempted to get hold of the boom, but missed my hold and fell back downwards. Providentially I fell on the martingale stay [a short, perpendicular spar at the front of the boat used to give stability to the jib boom] and succeeded in grasping it and getting on board again.' If he had fallen overboard he would have been run down by the boat. Bayly was lucky; many sailors were not.

If it was frightening for the sailors working on the slippery, pitching deck in this kind of weather, it was even worse for the convicts below decks and behind bars in the prison section of the *Castle Forbes*. They could do nothing, and even if they had been to sea before, they would never have experienced anything like this. Their fate was in the hands of the crew and dependent on the competence of the master. The prison deck was largely in darkness in stormy weather, even during daytime, because the air scuttles were shut to keep water out, and it was nearly impossible to keep a lantern burning. The convicts soon found their clothes and bedding wet through as the prison was flooded by the water which broke over the deck and poured down the main hatchway. Because the heads (latrines) were open to the sea, water washed backwards up through them into the convicts' living area. As the ship pitched violently, everything that was not screwed down or firmly tied was thrown all over the place. Tables, chairs, dishes, crockery, cutlery, kettles, saucepans, food of all sorts, buckets of human waste, furniture and loose objects went flying everywhere, and even convicts in their bunks could easily be thrown out if they did not hold on tight. Movement around the prison deck was very difficult. Bayly said that people could not walk upright but were 'slipping and sliding along the greasy deck; many not being able to walk went down on all fours like so many sloths or bears or whatever creeping animal you may be pleased to compare them to'.

It is hard to imagine what men with diarrhoea and dysentery did under these conditions – and Scott's medical log tells us quite a few were suffering from these illnesses on the *Castle Forbes*. Those who were seasick simply vomited where they lay. The movement and noise of the storm made sleep impossible; modern sailors in the Southern Ocean have compared the sound of mountainous waves that build up in a southern storm to that of a fast-approaching express train.

It was difficult to prepare anything to eat, especially hot food, under storm conditions, so if the tempest lasted a couple of days people would get hungry and weak. However, food would probably be the last thing on the minds of most, especially if they were suffering from seasickness. It is often forgotten in these days of refrigerators and frozen, processed foods that right into the late nineteenth century ships' decks often resembled stinking farmyards, with sheep, pigs, ducks, hens and sometimes even cattle carried for fresh food. On the *Castle Forbes* the terror of these animals in the storm can only be imagined. A particularly severe storm might wash most of them overboard, and the entire ship's company would then be reduced to salt meat and ship's biscuits for the rest of the voyage.

But the ferocity of this storm abated after about a day and a half, although the seas continued very high and the winds strong for several days. In thirty-six hours the *Castle Forbes*, under almost bare poles, had run 270 nautical miles (500 kilometres).

•

Storms only highlighted the problems that convicts faced, largely confined below decks in their prison. Here was a group of Irishmen snatched away from their homes, families and all that was familiar and dear to them, and transported to the ends of the earth across the most dangerous and rough seas in the world. The vast majority of them were never to see Ireland again. We know the names of every man on the *Castle Forbes* from the ship's indent, or record of transportees, and every detail of their medical history on the voyage, for Surgeon-Superintendent Scott's meticulous and careful Diary of Occurrences, including his medical record, has survived in its entirety.

All except one of the *Castle Forbes*'s convict passengers were born in Ireland, and all were tried there. Daniel Hogan was sixty-seven, Daniel O'Hegen was sixty-three, and Samuel Richardson, a boy of fourteen. James Robinson, the only non-Irishman on the ship – he had been born in Edinburgh – and John McColl were fifteen. Hogan, who was from County Cork, spent the entire voyage in the hospital, as did the Belfast-born O'Hegen. Scott reports that 'to maintain them in life gave more trouble than all the other patients'. Both were suffering from advanced forms of venereal disease. The thirteen boys under the age of seventeen were kept in a separate section of the ship's prison to protect them from sexual molestation by some of the older men. Most of the convicts were aged between nineteen and twenty-eight, and the majority had been sentenced to transportation for seven years; ten had received fourteen-year terms, and sixteen were lifers.

Almost half of the men had been 'labourers', which in the context of early nineteenth-century Ireland probably meant rural labourers. Otherwise there was the usual range of trades and jobs: weavers, indoor and outdoor servants, shoemakers, draymen, butchers, tailors, grooms, gardeners, stonemasons, whitesmiths and herders. There was also a grocer, a button maker, a hawker, a saddler and a clerk. Among the more unusual convicts were Andrew Donnelly, aged forty-two, from County Galway, who was a dancing master and fiddler, and Edward Fitzgerald from Dublin City, aged twenty, who doubled as both a theatrical performer and a clerk. William Leval, aged twenty, from County Derry, was listed as a jockey, and George Ryan from Dublin, aged thirty-eight, had been a soldier, sailor and labourer, while John Wilson, aged fifty-four, from County Wexford had been a gentleman's servant. Perhaps the two most useful men aboard, at least from the point of view of the Surgeon-Superintendent, were Patrick Hart from Sligo Town, aged twenty-four, a teacher, and Martin Edwards, aged twenty, from Dublin, who was a school assistant. Scott reports that three hours each day were set apart for school, and that Hart and his assistant managed to teach twenty men and boys, most of whom were illiterate, how to read and recite the Christian catechism.

The convict who is the focus of this story, Alexander Pearce, from County Monaghan, is not mentioned anywhere in the Diary, so we know that he neither misbehaved nor became sick on the voyage. In the ship's indent, Scott describes him simply as 'quiet'. By this he probably means that Pearce did not come to his attention in any way. The indent also tells us that Pearce was born in 1790. However, there is a discrepancy in other official records about his age on arrival in New Holland in 1820, and he might have been aged anywhere between twenty-seven and thirty. I have followed the indent and opted for thirty. His occupation is listed as 'labourer', and he was sentenced in County Armagh in 1819 to transportation to New South Wales for seven years. Much later, just before he was executed, Pearce told the Keeper of the Hobart Town Jail, John Bisdee, that he was convicted of stealing six pairs of shoes, which indicates he was something of a professional thief, and that this was most probably not his first offence. A person in desperate personal need of footwear only need steal one pair of shoes.

We know few details of Pearce's trial and criminal background, for all the Irish court files for the period between 1790 and 1835 were destroyed in April 1922 when the Public Record Office in Dublin's beautiful Four Courts building was badly burned during the Irish civil war. However, the courthouse in Armagh where he was tried is still there today on College Street, facing a park. It is a fine Georgian building, with a lovely Palladian entrance supported by four columns, completed in 1809 and recently restored. It stands behind a high, black steel fence, the product of Northern Ireland's ongoing troubles. No doubt Pearce would have missed the beauty of the formal architecture as he was led in through the prisoners' back entrance to face the judge who was to send him to the Antipodes.

As with so many ordinary people from the past, we know nothing about Pearce personally until he came to the notice of the authorities and was sentenced to transportation. His convict records consistently say he was born in County Monaghan, which today is in the Republic of Ireland but immediately to the south of the present border with Ulster and close to Armagh where he was tried. The town of Monaghan is only 27 kilometres (17 miles) from Armagh. It is an area of low, green rolling hills and small stands of trees, intensively farmed. However, Pearce himself confused the picture when he told John Bisdee that he was born in the neighbouring county of Fermanagh, which is now in Northern Ireland and just to the west of County Monaghan. County borders were probably not clear in Pearce's mind as he moved across the whole area of north-central Ireland seeking work.

Despite the truce of the last few years, violence is still endemic in this part of Ireland, and it goes back as far as the sixteenth century. Among the most potent contemporary symbols of this disturbance are the commemorative parades of pro-Unionist 'Apprentice Boys': formally attired, hard-faced 'Orangemen' in bowler hats and green, gold and orange stoles with furled umbrellas engage in provocative marches through poorer Catholic areas of Derry and Belfast to assert the 'Protestant ascendancy'. Although they have been re-routed nowadays, the parades still commemorate the successful defence of the city of Derry by a group of 'resolute apprentice boys' against a Catholic occupying army in December 1688, and the victory of the Protestant King William III over the Catholic King James II at the Battle of the Boyne in 1690.

We can assume that Pearce came from the lowest level of Irish Catholic rural society. The French Revolution had broken out in July 1789 about a year before he was born. Revolutionary ideas quickly began to permeate Ireland. Despite token attempts by the British government to conciliate the Catholics, Irish nationalists, both Protestant and Catholic, became increasingly anti-British. In response, the establishment-dominated Irish parliament passed a brutal *Insurrection Act* in 1796, and habeas corpus was suspended. Meanwhile, a yeomanry corps of conservative northern Protestants, under the pretext of defending the constitution and the establishment, revived an earlier campaign to push Catholics off their land and make the province of Ulster exclusively Protestant. Between 1796 and 1798 the British army, the militia and the Protestant yeomanry corps attempted to suppress rural agitation across the country. By this stage cruel reprisals were perpetrated on Catholics. The purpose of the exercise was to protect Protestant power and ascendancy. It was almost a foreshadowing of the post-World War I use of the notorious 'black and tans' by the British government to suppress the Irish, and of the uncontrolled violence of the First Parachute Regiment in January 1972 in the Bogside in Derry, when fourteen Catholic citizens were killed in a peaceful protest march. It has become an all-too-familiar pattern of British behaviour in Ireland.

In May 1798, when Alexander Pearce was probably eight years old, a long-delayed Irish nationalist insurrection broke out in the south-east in Kildare, Meath and Carlow. It quickly spread to the mountainous Wexford–Wicklow area. Through late May and June there were battles across county Wexford, but by early July the regular army had defeated the insurgents and a general amnesty was offered. Gradually calm returned to the country. Later outbreaks in Ulster were quickly dealt with by the government forces, and by the end of the year the insurrection was over. More than 30,000 people were dead.

Pearce was born into and passed his childhood in a volatile area in a dislocated society. He probably grew up as an orphan, or without a great deal of parental or adult supervision, and became a petty criminal early in life. He not only seems to have lacked sustained and loving intimacy with either parent, friends or extended family, but he also probably missed out on any type of moral, religious or social formation.

Pearce was born right in the middle of the population explosion that had begun in the eighteenth century and was first highlighted by Thomas Malthus's *Essay on Population* in 1798. In 1767 the population of Ireland was about two and a half million. By 1781 it was just over four million, in 1801 about five million, and by 1845, the year of the beginning of the terrible Potato

Famine, it had reached eight and a half million. In Ireland, with almost all land in the hands of Protestant landlords, this population increase led to ever-deepening poverty for the landless rural Catholic masses, the class from which Pearce came. This population increase also put immense pressure on both productive land and social structures, with the vast majority of Catholics living in grinding poverty.

At the 1819 Armagh Lent Assizes (an 'assize' was a travelling circuit court), Pearce was sentenced to transportation to New Holland. The name 'New Holland', given to Australia by Dutch explorers in the seventeenth century, was still generally used then. It was as far from England as you could possibly go, and was thus an ideal place for His Britannic Majesty's government to send – or 'transport' – convicted criminals. Transportation in the early nineteenth century was seen as a merciful alternative to the death penalty, which was then applied to a whole range of what are now considered minor crimes, such as petty theft. While there has always been something of a myth among Australian Catholics of Irish extraction that the majority of the 40,000 Irish convicts (made up of just on 29,500 males and over 9000 females) transported to Australia were either 'political prisoners' or 'pocket handkerchief thieves', driven to minor misdemeanours by poverty, starvation and an oppressive and bigoted Protestant British government, the reality is that most Irish convicts were like Pearce and the others on the *Castle Forbes*: petty criminals and thieves who already had one or more convictions. It was usually recidivists who were banished. Only a tiny proportion were 'political' in any sense.

Convicts sentenced to be transported to New Holland were usually returned to the local jail and held there while the keepers sent a list of the prisoners to the centre of British administration in Ireland at Dublin Castle. It was the responsibility of the Lord-Lieutenant of Ireland and his officials to deal with the details of the transport of prisoners from Britain's oldest colony, and to pay the cost of shipping them to New South Wales. After Pearce had spent several months in Armagh jail, approval from Dublin arrived, and probably some time in July 1819 he and about fourteen other convicts sentenced to transportation at the Armagh Lent Assizes trudged on foot under guard the 220 miles (354 kilometres) down the east coast of Ireland via Dublin to Cork.

Both men and women convicts often arrived in the southern city exhausted. They were briefly housed in Cork jail, an ugly, overcrowded, filthy, castle-like prison that had once been part of the city walls and gates. They were then moved to the nearby town of Cove on Great Island in Cork Harbour, the finest natural harbour in Ireland. It had been a British naval base since the late seventeenth century. In 1776 British troops were shipped out of this port to fight in the American War of Independence, and throughout the nineteenth century it was the primary port of departure for Irish emigrants going to the United States, Canada and Australia. It was also the last port of call for the *Titanic* before it struck an iceberg and sank in the mid-Atlantic in April 1912.

When he arrived in Cove, Pearce would have seen a town that straggled up a steep, wooded hill from the water's edge. A contemporary sketch shows nine two-masted ships lying at anchor offshore, served by smaller skiffs running back and forth between them and the shore. The convicts from Armagh would have boarded one of these skiffs and sailed out to the convict depot on Spike Island, which until 1822 housed both male and female convicts. Pearce was lucky in his timing because the depot was a lot more comfortable than the usual housing for convicts awaiting transportation – a hulk. At Spike Island he and his fellow convicts would have been stripped and washed, then issued with coarse grey jackets and breeches marked with the convict broad arrow. Their health would also have been checked. All up, Pearce spent about six months in the Irish penal system.

The *Castle Forbes* had meanwhile sailed from Deptford on the Thames on 18 July and arrived in Cork on 30 July 1819. Surgeon-Superintendent Scott had reported for duty on 7 July at the same time as a guard of four non-commissioned officers and twenty-two privates assembled from two regiments, the Thirty-Fourth and the Eighty-Ninth. This motley company were under the command of the none-too-competent Lieutenant Sutherland of the Thirtieth Regiment. Throughout the journey Sutherland had difficulty controlling his troops, who on a couple of occasions were close to mutiny. There was trouble with the guard right from the beginning: while the ship was waiting in Cork Harbour, a court-martial sentenced one soldier to the extraordinary total of 300 lashes and another to seventy-five 'for disobedience of orders and disorderly conduct'. The 'disorderly conduct' was to continue on the journey out to Sydney Town. Accompanying the soldiers were five wives, two of whom were pregnant, and four children, 'all in perfect health', as Scott commented. The same cannot be said for their menfolk, a couple of whom were suffering from venereal disease.

A man who had first-hand experience of what Irish convicts went through in the process of transportation was the young Cork priest John England, later to become the Bishop of Charlestown, South Carolina, and one of the most influential Catholic bishops in the nineteenth-century United States. England said that from November 1808 until May 1817 'I had the best opportunities of knowing the disposition and sentiments of the great bulk of convicts sent from Ireland to New South Wales, having been in constant attendance upon them in the gaol of the city of Cork . . . and in the transports at Cove'. The priest maintained that their greatest problem was the deep loss in leaving home and family forever, of being exiles who realised they would never be able to return. Most of these men had never been more than 50 miles from where they had been born.

England maintained that there was a sense of religious loss, as the only clergy in New Holland were Protestant. He used this as an argument for the need to provide Catholic clergy to minister to Irish convicts, and his efforts were rewarded when two Irish priests were appointed to New South Wales as official convict chaplains in 1820. Pearce was later to encounter and confess to one of them in Hobart Town, the Reverend Philip Conolly, as he prepared for his execution, and it was this priest who accompanied him to the scaffold.

The 140 *Castle Forbes* convicts were embarked on 16 September and underwent a superficial medical examination by Scott. From 16 to 27 September the surgeon himself was laid up in bed with what he called 'a bilious fever'. The men were left on board the ship for three weeks while its sailing date was delayed by the always slow-moving Dublin Castle bureaucrats. It was not until 3 October 1819 that the *Castle Forbes* actually got underway.

Before departure Scott issued a set of regulations for the convicts that he hoped they would 'cheerfully obey as they will not only be conducive to your comfort and the preservation of your health during the voyage, but by a close adherence to them a habit of regularity will be acquired; which in the new life you have just entered on will tend considerably to promote your future happiness and respectability'. While Pearce seems to have 'kept' all the rules, they did not promote in him either a 'habit of regularity' or 'happiness and respectability' after he reached Van Diemen's Land. The rules, however, do introduce us to some sense of what shipboard life was like for the convicts. Boredom could easily lead to trouble. The regulations were designed to keep the prisoners busy throughout the day. Perhaps the fiddler and dancing master, Andrew Donnelly, and the theatrical performer, Edward Fitzgerald, provided some entertainment on the long voyage?

The regulations decreed that Divine Service would always be

performed on Sundays, when circumstances permitted. This consisted of Scott reading from the Anglican Prayer Book, but especially in the latter part of the journey this was often cancelled due to bad weather or to wet, slippery decks. Prisoners were also to avoid blasphemy, rioting, disputing or gambling, as well as smoking and chewing tobacco below decks. The maintenance of cleanliness in the prison was all-important, and floors were swept and scrubbed out every day. Clothes were washed on Mondays and Fridays; prisoners were to wear clean clothes, which were to be kept in a proper state of repair, at the muster on deck on Sunday and Tuesday. Each man was given three shirts, two pairs of trousers, a pair of shoes, a Guernsey frock (a close-fitting woollen sweater) and a woollen cap. Prisoners could shave on Thursdays and Saturdays. Clothes and bedding issued to the convicts from the government stores were referred to as 'slops', following the usage of the British navy. The material was of poor quality and the clothes were threadbare by the time the prisoners reached Sydney Town, so they had to be refitted in the colony.

The convicts were divided into messes of six men for the purpose of keeping their area clean and distributing food. There was little problem on the *Castle Forbes* with the prisoners' behaviour, and very few punishments were meted out by the sensible Scott, who had complete control of the prisoners. Generally the food seems to have been adequate, and for the first couple of months while supplies lasted, their diet included bread, beef, pork, pea-meal, butter, rice, oatmeal and sugar. Throughout the journey sweetened lime juice was issued to ward off scurvy. However, the large number of digestive complaints in the last month or so of the voyage, including diarrhoea and dysentery, indicate that they had run out of fresh food and had fallen back on the ship's supplies of salt meat and pork. Even though this meat was kept in sealed containers, it was often badly adulterated. Ship's biscuits were sometimes so rotten they crawled with weevils and maggots. As the ship neared the New South Wales coast there was a serious outbreak of food poisoning from adulterated flour. Scott reports that 'thirteen of the guard and two of the ship's boys were attacked suddenly with violent vomiting and intense pain in the head and a burning sensation in the stomach extending to the bowels with constant thirst. Pulse about 140 in almost all of them, with the tongue very white and tremulous . . . I learned that they had all partaken of pudding which was made from the remains of a cask of flour. When eating it some of them remarked that the pudding had a singular taste'. Five days later several of them were still convalescing in the ship's hospital.

Fresh water was always a problem on non-stop voyages to New Holland. It was carried in sealed barrels, but was often putrid and undrinkable. Sensitive travellers found the water even too smelly for washing. Much of it was taken directly from the badly polluted Thames and had a particularly offensive smell and taste. So British ships often called at Madeira to dispose of their Thames water and to get fresh water from the Portuguese colony. Reid was taking a calculated risk in not calling anywhere on the journey, but it paid off because 116 days en route was very good progress for 1819–20.

The prison occupied most of the lower deck space in the centre of the ship. There were two rows of sleeping berths, one above the other, extending down each side. Each berth was six feet square and held four convicts, which gave each man a width of about 18 inches (46 centimetres) of sleeping space. The hospital was also housed on the prison deck, as was the special area reserved for the adolescent boys. The hatchway was the only exit from the prison to the upper deck and this was secured by an iron grate that was always guarded. Despite air scuttles and portholes, ventilation was an issue, especially as the ship approached the equator where the air was stiflingly hot, humid and oppressive. The men were allowed on deck every day in groups throughout the voyage in two lots of two-hour stints for exercise and fresh air. Even when the weather was bad, Scott always tried to give them at least two hours on deck.

Scott reported to the Admiralty that, throughout the journey, 'None of the prisoners were allowed to have their irons off, [except] those who contributed by their exertions to the benefit and convenience of the whole, or on account of sickness'. This is unlikely because the usual convention was that chains were only used until the ships were well clear of the Irish coast. However, when they were allowed on deck the convicts were usually chained together, with armed sentries posted on the poop deck. A convict mutiny was always a threat and there were occasional attempted revolts by prisoners. While in their bunks the men were sometimes ironed to ring-bolts attached to the end of each bunk. But as the voyage proceeded Scott seemed to have given the men increasing latitude, and in the last couple of weeks as the ship neared New Holland he allowed them to come on deck without irons at their leisure.

From Cork Harbour, Reid and his crew of three officers, a carpenter, sail-maker and cook, and twenty-five able and ordinary seamen and boys sailed the ship due south, skirting the western edge of the Bay of Biscay and Cape Finisterre, and then on down the Portuguese shore to the West African latitudes. After eleven days they had passed Funchal on Madeira, and then they were off the Canary Islands and sighted the peak of Tenerife. A few days out of Cork, Scott notes that many of the prisoners were a great deal affected by *Nausea Marina*. Acute seasickness was a constant accompaniment of shipboard life, especially early in the voyage, for people who had never been to sea before and could be completely incapacitating. Some people, like Charles Darwin, never got used to the movement of the ship throughout the long, three-year journey of the *Beagle*. In March 1835 he wrote: 'I continue to suffer so much from sea-sickness that nothing, not even geology itself, can make up for the misery and vexation of spirit'.

Headaches, fevers, boils, diarrhoea, dysentery, and constipation were also common complaints, and Scott dealt with them all. Purges such as sulphur magnesium and calomel (mercurous chloride), poultices, mercury and castor and olive oils often featured in his pharmacopoeia. He comments that 'men apply daily for dressings to slight boils and small sores'. With all the limitations of nineteenth-century medicine, and remedies that were often worse than the disease, this was still the best and most consistent medical treatment that these men were to receive in their lives. In some ways convicts were treated better than many steerage-class passengers who paid their own fares from Europe to North America and Australia two decades after the voyage of the *Castle Forbes*. At age twenty-nine, Scott was a kind, just and compassionate man, and also an able doctor, although in later life after he had settled in Van Diemen's Land he was to become somewhat eccentric.

The most serious illnesses that Scott dealt with were what he himself called the 'venereal cases'. In the course of the voyage seven soldiers and convicts reported to him with gonorrhoea and bubo (an inflamed lymph node in the groin), and the surgeon treated them with the conventional remedies of the time: courses of mercury or sulpha (a derivative of sulfanilamide) – or both. It is hard to tell if the medicines were of any use. Most of these men remained in the hospital for a couple of weeks and, as we saw, the two oldest of them, O'Hegen and Hogan, remained there throughout the voyage.

•

A month out of Cork the *Castle Forbes* was off the Gulf of Guinea in west Africa, just 8° north of the Equator. The weather was calm, with occasional rain. The convicts were already complaining about the heat. The mid-Atlantic near the Equator was the most difficult part of the journey, with a combination of intense heat, stifling humidity, equatorial storms, light and unpredictable winds, and long periods of being becalmed in what sailors accurately called the doldrums.

The *Castle Forbes* crossed the Equator on 13 November 1819 out in the mid-Atlantic north-west of Ascension Island. By 22 November they were due west of Napoleon's final prison, the island of St Helena. The ship made good time through the south Atlantic, passing Tristan da Cunha and Gough Island in early December, and by 8 December they had crossed the Greenwich meridian and had turned east. By 15 December they were 500 miles (805 kilometres) east-sou'-east of the Cape of Good Hope and were well out into the Southern Ocean. They were now on the northern edge of the Roaring Forties.

But there was trouble brewing – the military guard was near mutiny. There had already been conflict between Captain Reid, Dr Scott and Lieutenant Sutherland over their respective areas of authority. A major part of the problem was the failure of the government to delineate clearly their roles. There were also tensions resulting from people being thrown together in cramped quarters with minimal privacy for extended periods. Every little personal idiosyncrasy drove others mad, and tensions were often exacerbated by drunkenness.

However, it is also clear that the soldiers on the *Castle Forbes* had been troublesome right from the beginning, and that their commander, Lieutenant Sutherland, was incompetent. Scott said that on 16 December several of the guards lodged a complaint with their officer that their rum had been adulterated before it was made into grog, but 'no truth of the circumstances could be found on enquiry'.

There was also tension between the soldiers and the ship's crew. 'Some insulting language passed between the guard and the sailors; Lt. Sutherland authorised the corporals to wear their side-arms; excepting Corporal Wallace whom he said could not be trusted as he had threatened to use them on the sailors.'

Things got worse. Scott reported on 17 December that the soldiers were in an open state of mutiny. They acted with the greatest disrespect to their officers, left their posts when stationed as sentinels, and fought among themselves, with corporals challenging the privates and all of them acting in the most irritating manner to the sailors. This led to open conflict between Lieutenant Sutherland and Captain Reid. Things blew up again on 18 December, when Wallace abused the sailors without provocation. He also behaved in an insolent and disrespectful manner to Reid and Sutherland, and after he was put in handcuffs went forward and endeavoured to create more disturbance by jostling one of the sailors. He was confined to the hospital where he was put in irons.

There was trouble again with the soldiers over grog on 21 December, the day Wallace was released from the hospital. Despite Scott's protests, the soldiers were given their allowance of rum raw with neither lime juice nor sugar. The consequence was that privates Macquarie and O'Loughlin became intoxicated and 'were so insolent to their officers as to render it necessary to put them under the charge of a sentinel. Cunningham for the same was put into handcuffs for two hours'.

Right through the latter part of December and early January the *Castle Forbes* passed through stormy and cold weather, and it was probably this that quietened the soldiers down. No further complaints were heard from the guard for the rest of the trip. There is nothing like seasickness and diarrhoea to help you forget your other troubles! Scott reports that he let the prisoners come and go on deck in the stormy weather, possibly to escape from the smelly confines of the prison. On 8 January he reported: 'Weather more moderate. On account of so much motion yesterday the prisoners had no lemon juice, and the weather is unpleasant from cold and occasional rain, [and] with an increase of bowel complaints [I] refused to give them a double allowance of lemon juice'.

By 12 January they were about 250 miles (402 kilometres) due south of the western edge of the Great Australian Bight and the Recherche Archipelago. In an extraordinarily fast run, six days later they were just to the west of Bass Strait. The next day, 19 January 1820, at about noon, they first sighted 'the land of New South Wales about Cape Otway'. From the position given in the surgeon's log this was incorrect: they were actually a couple of degrees to the west of Cape Otway, and had possibly sighted Cape Nelson or Cape Bridgewater near the present-day town of Portland. By 22 January they were in the middle of Bass Strait, due south of Melbourne and Port Phillip Bay and just to the north-east of King Island. Again, with a remarkably fast run up the east coast of New South Wales, they entered the narrow heads of Port Jackson (now Sydney Harbour) five days later on 27 January, on a very hot midsummer day. They had arrived in New Holland.

In 1820 there were two colonies in New Holland. New South Wales was established in 1788, and theoretically took in the whole of the mainland of Australia, which effectively meant the east coast to the north, south and west of the town of Sydney. Van Diemen's Land, an island roughly the same size as Scotland, was first discovered and named by the great Dutch explorer Abel Janszoon Tasman in 1642. Settled from Sydney in September 1803, its tiny capital was Hobart Town. Since December 1855 the island has been known as Tasmania, and it lies about 140 miles (225 kilometres) immediately south of the south-east tip of the Australian mainland. The total 'number of souls' in Van Diemen's Land in the 1820 muster was 4901, of whom more than half (2666) were convicts, including 275 women. There were 3000 to 4000 Aborigines living in Van Diemen's Land at the time of European settlement.

If Pearce was on deck as they sailed up Port Jackson, he would have seen a land with a totally different feel and appearance from Ireland. The predominant colour of the landscape there is dark green, and the place is often wet, windy and cold with an overcast sky and soft rain. But in New South Wales the light is extraordinarily clear and in late January the temperature is often over 30° Celsius (the high-nineties Fahrenheit) with the heat intensified by humidity. Just inside the heads the south-eastern shore of the inner harbour is now part of an Australian naval base, but in 1820 it was open grassland, interspersed with eucalypt trees. Mobs of Eastern Grey kangaroos would have been sheltering in the shade, the big males sometimes standing up to 2 metres (6 feet) in height.

As the *Castle Forbes* passed Watson's Bay and the pilot's house, those on deck would have been able to see the flagstaff and the back of the South Head signal station, newly built by Governor Lachlan Macquarie. As they moved up the harbour the dry eucalypt forest came right down to the rocky, sandstone shoreline. In a small bay they would have seen the cottage of the Irish ex-convict, Sir Henry Brown Hayes, in the closed valley of Vaucluse. They would have also seen his exotic garden of tree ferns and flowers, and the raucous, squawking flocks of cockatoos and brightly coloured parrots he encouraged. The setting was surrounded by dense forest, although a large field to the south had been cleared. If they had climbed the hill behind the house they would have seen an extensive harbour, dotted with several small islands. And, if the day was clear with no smoke haze, away in the distance they might have glimpsed a rugged range of mountains with an odd blue appearance, now called the Blue Mountains.

As the ship came close to its anchorage, Eliza Point came into view. A little later in the year it was to be renamed Point Piper after that 'thoroughly good fellow', the generous and kind Captain John Piper whose waterfront mansion was then almost finished. The *Castle Forbes* dropped anchor off mid-harbour near Farm Cove, between what is now the Sydney Opera House on the south shore and the suburb of Kirribilli and Admiralty House, the Australian Governor-General's Sydney residence, on the north shore.

During their stay in Sydney, Scott allowed the prisoners on deck all day except for meal-times. They thus had a chance to see one of the most glorious harbours in the world. However, if they thought that Sydney Town was the end of their epic journey, they were mistaken. The only ones landed were the four sick men – the rest were destined for Van Diemen's Land. There, the Lieutenant-Governor, Colonel William Sorell, had requested additional convict labour for government work and for assignment to the small but increasing number of mainly middle-class English free settlers anxious to take up land and breed sheep and cattle in the new colony, which had been founded just sixteen years before. The 'Captain-General and Governor-in-Chief in and over the Territory of New South Wales and its Dependencies' (which included Van Diemen's Land), Major-General Lachlan Macquarie, therefore ordered that the *Castle Forbes* be rechartered from its owners, and that the Irish convicts on the ship be immediately redirected to Hobart Town. He also instructed that forty-four additional male convicts be sent to the southern colony, and they were transferred from the transport *Prince Regent*, which had arrived at Sydney Town from England on the same day as the *Castle Forbes*.

So, after a two-week sojourn in Sydney Harbour, the Irishmen were joined on 16 February by convicts from the *Prince Regent*. One distinguished passenger joined the ship: he was Edward Ford Bromley, Esquire, who had just been appointed Naval Officer at Hobart Town. Scott stayed on as the *Castle Forbes*'s

Surgeon-Superintendent, but the guards were replaced by a sergeant, a corporal and twelve privates of the 48th Northamptonshire Regiment of Foot, which was assigned to New Holland between 1817 and 1824.

That same day the ship slipped out of Port Jackson on the 1300-kilometre (800-mile) trip south down the east Australian and Tasmanian coasts, around Capes Pillar and Raoul, up Storm Bay and into the estuary of the Derwent River toward Hobart Town.

They arrived there on 28 February 1820. Again, it was a fast passage.

2
Convict No. 102

For much of January 1823, the Reverend Robert Knopwood, MA, parson of the Church of England and convict chaplain, was laid up in bed with a recurrent illness at his home, 'Cottage Green', in Battery Point, Hobart Town. Throughout the month the weather had been very hot and he was unable to do many of his duties as parson, chaplain and magistrate. He missed a number of important social occasions, including a dinner invitation to Government House from His Honor, the Lieutenant-Governor, Colonel William Sorell, and his lady, Mrs Sorell, more accurately described as Mrs Kent. In fact, when His Honor did see him he commented on how the reverend gentleman had 'shrunk and fallen away'.

'Bobby', as all the lower orders called Knopwood behind his back, seemed like a fixture in Hobart Town. He had arrived in February 1804 with the first Lieutenant-Governor of Van Diemen's Land, Colonel David Collins. He always exuded a parsonic *noblesse oblige* to those below him in the social pecking order, although it did not prevent him handing out some pretty severe floggings to convicts who appeared before him. But as more and more free settlers arrived, there were increasingly divided opinions about Knopwood and his parsonic talents. The smart convict conman Henry Savery said that he was basically a good fellow, an old-fashioned cleric with slightly high church tendencies, a remarkably placid countenance and easy and gentlemanly manners. Savery felt that his conversation was lively and agreeable. But others saw him as a lazy bon vivant who never missed a social occasion and who drank far too much. Some of his enemies characterised him as a drunken womaniser who failed to carry out his pastoral duties.

Illness forced Knopwood in late 1822 to hand in his resignation as the full-time local parson and convict chaplain, although he continued in a part-time pastoral capacity and as a sitting magistrate until 1828, ten years before his death at the age of seventy-three. He had many personal weaknesses, which were no doubt exaggerated in the vituperative atmosphere of the tiny colonial town, but there is no evidence to support the more extreme claims made about him, and he was certainly not a womaniser. He was a friendly clergyman who served faithfully for over thirty years in a prison camp and colonial outpost about as far from England as you could possibly go.

In early February 1823 he seemed to recover rather well and was able to welcome his ecclesiastical superior to Van Diemen's Land. This personage was the principal chaplain of the territory of New South Wales, the Reverend Samuel Marsden, the ox-faced, anti-Irish 'flogging parson', as he was popularly and justifiably known by the convicts and lower classes in Sydney Town. Accompanying Marsden was Knopwood's replacement as convict chaplain in Hobart Town and its surrounds, the strongly Evangelically inclined Reverend William Bedford, a former London stay-maker and prison visitor, whom the convicts quickly dubbed 'Holy Willie'. Henry Savery observed that Bedford possessed much affability of manner, that his lisp was 'by no means disagreeable', and that 'his well cased ribs bore evident marks that, whatever other doctrines he might preach, that of fasting was not one upon which he laid much stress, at least in its practice'.

On Sunday 16 February Knopwood performed the morning

and afternoon divine services at St David's church for, he was proud to note in his Diary, 'very full' congregations. In the early evening he dined with the surgeons, Drs Garrett and Spence, and later he smoked a pipe with Lieutenant Lewis. He went to bed reasonably early, but was soon in acute pain – it was his old problem, bladder stones. The pain was sometimes so bad that the surgeons had to use a bougie, a rod used as a kind of catheter, to relieve the pressure of urine in the bladder. Dr Garrett visited again and bled him, and also gave him a large quantity of laudanum, an alcoholic solution of morphine, which was used in the nineteenth century as a painkiller. Knopwood's Diary reports that he felt very ill and that at 4 a.m. 'a large stone came from me, which gave me relief'.

Yet, despite his medical problems, Knopwood had still been able to sit occasionally as a magistrate during January 1823. On Saturday 25 January, after having spent the morning at home resting, he was on the bench at 1 p.m. He was immediately faced with a problematic case. The convict brought before him was not up on one of the usual charges – drunk and disorderly, thieving, absconding, or insolence to an overseer, all of which could be easily and quickly dispatched with a sentence of twenty-five or fifty lashes. Convict No. 102, the Irish-born Alexander Pearce, was charged with escaping with seven others from the most secure prison in the colony, situated on Sarah Island in Macquarie Harbour, on the far west coast of the colony. When interviewed by the military who had captured him he talked incessantly about murder and cannibalism among the escapees during the trek across the unexplored wilderness east of Macquarie Harbour.

Pearce had been recaptured at Lower Marshes near the small settlement of Jericho early in the morning of 11 January 1823, right on the outside edge of white settlement, about 85 kilometres (53 miles) almost due north of Hobart Town. It was also exactly due east of the Macquarie Harbour convict settlement. Pearce had been on the loose for almost four months, and as the crow flies he had travelled at least 150 kilometres (93 miles) across territory that had never before been penetrated by Europeans and contained only a couple of known and named landmarks. What was significant was that he had escaped with seven other prisoners, only two of whom were accounted for. These two had abandoned the escape attempt and returned to Macquarie Harbour in a debilitated state twelve days after the group had first bolted. The Commandant at Macquarie Harbour, Lieutenant John Cuthbertson, had already informed Hobart Town about the return of the two men, Edward Brown and William Kennerly. What little that could be got out of them was that they had not been able to keep up with the rest of the group, and that they had decided to return and face the consequences of their attempted escape before they got lost and died in the bush. Unfortunately they died from exhaustion within a few days of arriving back at the penal settlement. As far as anyone in Hobart Town knew, they never said anything about murder and cannibalism.

Pearce's record was quite familiar to Knopwood. He had been in trouble with the magistrates several times before over the last eighteen months. The bench usually handed down summary justice to escaped convicts: what did the trick was a good flogging (fifty to 100 lashes), and a couple of months working in chains in the prison gang on public works during the day and confinement at night. If it was a second or third offence they were usually packed off to Sarah Island in Macquarie Harbour for the rest of their original sentence. The regime there had been established for troublesome recidivists like Convict No. 102.

Officially, escape from Macquarie Harbour was impossible. It was a long way from the 'settled districts' to the north of Hobart Town and the country in between was considered impenetrable.

But Pearce and his fellow escapees seemed to have made it through. So it was important to interview him formally to try to discover any weaknesses in the prison system to prevent more convicts attempting to emulate him and his seven companions. But it was not just a matter of working out how the men had managed to get all the way from Sarah Island to the edges of civilisation in the settled districts – they also needed to find out the route the men had followed and how they had managed to survive.

The investigation was complicated by the fact that Pearce claimed that when they ran out of rations and starvation set in, some of the other men had committed murder, and they had then all eaten parts of the butchered human carcasses. Because it seemed irrational for Pearce to implicate himself like this, no one could work out why he had spun them such a yarn. Both the prison authorities and Knopwood viewed No. 102 as a debased specimen of humanity, and an Irishman to boot, so no one believed his story. While in rare circumstances shipwrecked sailors might be driven to cannibalism by starvation, it was simply inconceivable to any official in Hobart Town that a European would ever stoop so low as to indulge in it. Sure, the black races, such as the local Aborigines, might sometimes be guilty of such barbarism, but never a white man, no matter how bad, nor how far down the penal ladder he had slipped. The assumption was that most, if not all, of Convict No. 102's five companions were still at large somewhere in the bush and he was covering for them by concocting a wild story about cannibalism and murder. It was a clever ruse to cover his mates' tracks.

To assist Magistrate Knopwood in his investigation on this hot Saturday afternoon, His Honor, the Lieutenant-Governor, had sent his trusted clerk, a pardoned convict and now apparently prosperous farmer named Thomas Wells, to take down the evidence and write it up in the official Bench of Magistrates Book.

As it turned out, Knopwood did not have to ask the prisoner many questions. Pearce seemed happy to tell the story in detail. But it was long, complicated and occasionally contradictory, and Knopwood became increasingly exhausted and bored in the stiflingly hot courtroom as the narrative – and the afternoon – wore on. Unlike Wells, he seemed not to notice the discrepancies in Convict No. 102's account. For instance, Pearce said that three men – Brown, Kennerly and Alexander Dalton – dropped behind and returned to Macquarie Harbour, whereas according to the report of Commandant Cuthbertson only two actually arrived, Brown and Kennerly, neither of whom explained what had happened to Dalton, nor even referred to him in any way. Also No. 102 made sure that the magistrate understood that he was not responsible for the murders. He made out that they had been committed principally by the sailor and de facto leader of the group, Robert Greenhill, assisted by his close mate, Matthew Travers. He did not say who killed Travers. He had to admit that he was responsible for the eventual killing of Greenhill, but stated strongly that it was entirely a matter of self-defence – which was probably true. Wells also noted that Pearce had been recaptured with two other escaped convicts turned highwaymen, William Davis and Ralph Churton, who were not part of the original party of escapees from Macquarie Harbour, but were sheep-stealers who had escaped earlier from a military guard on their way to Hobart Town. If the rest of his party was still alive, why had Pearce left them and taken up with Davis and Churton? As Wells listened he became convinced that the Irish convict was telling the truth. Murder and cannibalism had been committed in the wilderness.

When Pearce eventually concluded his narrative, Knopwood was in pain and felt exhausted and impatient. He was sure that even under oath, Convict No. 102 could not be trusted to tell the truth and that he was spinning an outrageous yarn to cover for his mates who were still at large in the bush. He was convinced that they would all be recaptured, as Davis, Churton and Pearce had been, and that they would all soon be back where they belonged – at Sarah Island. Anyway, even in the very unlikely event that the Irishman was telling the truth, and that there had been several murders and he was the only survivor, Knopwood argued to himself that there were no witnesses to any of the alleged crimes, and certainly no bodies, nor any possibility of recovering them. So, legally, as long as Pearce stuck to his story it would be hard – if not impossible – to commit him for trial. He had complete control of the story. Even if he was tried, it would be most unlikely that the Crown could obtain a conviction. As far as the Reverend Magistrate was concerned, there was nothing else to do but to send him back to his place of secondary punishment and let Commandant Cuthbertson deal with him. He simply sentenced Convict No. 102 to be returned to Sarah Island to continue to serve out his original sentence of seven years. Knopwood's pain was now so bad and he was in such a hurry to get home that he forgot to sentence Pearce to the customary 100 lashes handed out to an absconder.

However, as he took down the narrative details, the much more attentive and crafty Wells was impressed with the semi-literate convict's ability to recount what had happened. As he listened and watched and wrote the words, Wells was convinced that No. 102 was telling the truth. The tough little Irishman was a survivor and no fool, and he had thought through his account very carefully to cover himself as best he could. He may have heard that Brown and Kennerly had made it back to Macquarie Harbour, but he had no idea what they had confessed to Cuthbertson or even that they had died. So he probably felt that it was best to tell most of the truth about what had happened, but to embroider it in such a way as to protect himself. In this he had been successful with the none-too-attentive and sickly

Knopwood on that hot and oppressive Saturday afternoon.

The more Wells thought about it the more he realised that Pearce's was a great story and that it might be something he could sell to a newspaper or magazine in London, which would certainly pay well for it. He could already see the title: *White Cannibals in Van Diemen's Wilderness*. After all, he already had literary experience and had had his work published. Some years previously he had written a forty-page pamphlet, *Michael Howe, the last and the worst of the Bush Rangers of Van Diemen's Land*, which he had brought out in December 1818, and it had done reasonably well. Another convict story, especially one that involved cannibalism, would surely appeal. As Sorell's trusted clerk he could easily get hold of the Bench of Magistrates Book for January 1823 and write a narrative from it, using Convict No. 102's own words, which would give the story authenticity. Given public taste, he knew that he would have to inject a little moralising into it. He also felt that Pearce's blunt and brutal narrative would have to be softened in places, with their deeds given a slightly more civilised context by references to prayer, repentance and even ritual. But in itself the story was so good that he did not want to alter too many of the details and he was determined to use as much of Pearce's own vivid narrative as he possibly could.

Some days later, Wells realised that he needed to make sure that no one else could get the story out before him; he was after what today we would call an 'exclusive'. Confident that the sick and indolent Knopwood would not be interested, he worried there might be others who had heard about it and realised its literary possibilities. So he knew he needed to 'lose' the only written record of Pearce's story, the Bench of Magistrates Book for January 1823. As Sorell's clerk he had access to convict and court records, so after he had made two closely related versions of the story he proceeded to 'mislay' the Bench of Magistrates Book. It has never been found.

What Wells could not know was that within eight months Pearce would escape again from Macquarie Harbour and repeat his cannibalism, and then make a further detailed confession about the first escape to Commandant Cuthbertson at Sarah Island. So Wells's 'exclusive' had evaporated. But it really did not matter. A couple of months after Wells wrote Pearce's story, his protector, Sorell, was recalled to London, and by the end of 1823 Wells himself was bankrupted by unsuccessful speculation in the wool market. He had more on his plate than trying to sell the tale of an obscure convict cannibal to a faraway London newspaper.

Fortunately for us, two long-hand copies of Wells's account still survive. So we have two versions of the story of the escape and the terrible journey as told by Pearce: the first by Wells on the basis of the evidence to Knopwood; and the second the confession to Lieutenant Cuthbertson at Sarah Island.

•

Like every story, this one has a background and context and it makes no sense unless you know what happened before. So let's begin at the beginning. And where better to start than outside a hotel in Hobart Town on 25 November 1821?

The only way you could tell that the ordinary-looking, two-storey stone building was a hotel was from the sign above the door. It was situated in the centre of Collins Street, Hobart Town (or 'Hobarton', an affectation increasingly being used by the more respectable citizens of Van Diemen's Land), and it could easily have passed for a substantial private house. But the coloured drawing of a sailing ship on the sign hanging outside told you that this was the Ship Inn. Given that many of the lower classes and convicts were scarcely literate, pictographic signs on buildings were important. Throughout the nineteenth century hotels usually had colourful names like the Spotted Dog, the

Horse and Groom, the Dallas Arms, the Old Commodore, the Star and Garter, the Woolpack Inn, the Jolly Sailor, the Golden Lion, the Turf, the Half-Way House and the Cornish Mount, all of which were in business at one time or another in and around early Hobart Town.

The Ship Inn was a perfectly respectable, fully licensed establishment, and it doubled as the town's main coach terminus. It was one of the best of the almost twenty licensed premises in Hobart Town in 1821. The landlord and licensee was one Peter Copeland. Today there is still a Ship Hotel on the site at 73 Collins Street, Hobart, a descendant of Copeland's original premises. But convicts on the skids, like Alexander Pearce, did not need signs. If there was one thing that they knew, it was where all the pubs were, both the licensed ones and the sly-grog shops that existed outside the law and that often doubled as brothels, gambling dens and places where the unwary could be fleeced. Unlicensed premises survived because of the corruption of the constabulary. The police knew you could not skin a flint, so they always made sure that the sly-grog shops had turned a reasonable profit before moving in for their share of the takings in return for protection.

While the Ship Inn might have been a respectable establishment, most of the places where Pearce and his fellow convicts drank were pretty rough and ready, whether licensed or not. Usually the patrons gathered in a big front room with a large, open fireplace – the taproom. The small windows opening onto the street usually had no glass, only wooden shutters. Light was provided by oil lamps and the fire. Drinkers sat on wooden benches against the walls facing long, narrow tables. Chained to the end of each table was a large knife used for cutting the tobacco that both men and women stuffed into their pipes. Entering the hotel you were overwhelmed not only by the fumes from the fire and the pungent smell of tobacco smoke, but also by the noise as people sang and shouted and slammed down their thick glasses and tin beer-pots on the greasy tables. The grog was usually kept in the landlord's bedroom and only brought into the open taproom as needed. Rum was available in pint tumblers that patrons themselves poured into wine-glasses. It was usually drunk neat. Beer was more expensive and something of a luxury, and was served in tin quart pots.

Patrons usually ate cold meat and bread as they downed their liquor. A large pot containing a stew of meat, potatoes in their jackets and cabbage, all boiled together, hung over the fire from a pendant in the chimney. A meal cost one shilling. Patrons helped themselves from the pot. Those who had arranged to stay overnight often bedded down on straw-stuffed ticks, mattresses on the floor or tables in the taproom.

To the scandal of the more respectable citizens of Hobart Town, prostitutes often plied their trade in public houses, stolen goods were exchanged, the often intoxicated lower-class men and women mixed freely, and people danced in the middle of the floor to the sound of the hurdy-gurdy, fiddle, tambourine and hautboy, a kind of high-pitched oboe. It was always easy to work out where the sly-grog shops were: you could hear the incessant noise of music, drunken singing, raucous laughter, screaming, swearing and crying. You could also see the prostitutes hanging around the door looking for customers.

On the night of 25 November 1821 Pearce was at the Ship Inn drinking large amounts of Peter Copeland's cheapest Mauritius rum. Like most convicts, he preferred the dark flavour of Bengal rum but he could only afford the weaker Mauritius variety. The best things about rum were that it was cheaper than beer, it never went off, it warmed your innards quickly, it saved you having to drink the often polluted water, and its high alcohol content helped you forget reality. But, like many drunks, Pearce became more and more belligerent. He may have been the 'quiet' man on the *Castle Forbes*, but after a year and a half in Van Diemen's

Land, good behaviour was far behind him.

The nine o'clock curfew bell had already been rung and Convict No. 102 should have been back at his lodgings in the police watch-house. Earlier Copeland had warned him about his increasing drunkenness, and just after 9 p.m. the landlord physically threw him out. The constables who came to check that the hotel was closed arrested him as he lay in the mud outside. As they began dragging him back to the watch-house they noticed he had pocketed a wine-glass, the solid, thick, unbreakable type used by the patrons to drink their rum. No. 102 was charged with being drunk and disorderly, and also with stealing Copeland's property. The constables then deposited him in the watch-house to sleep off his debauchery.

The next morning, 26 November, Pearce had a terrible hangover – and worse, he was one of a number of prisoners to be brought before the sitting bench of magistrates for the day. The bench was made up of the Reverend Robert Knopwood, the convict chaplain, and Adolarius William Henry Humphrey, the Superintendent of Police, Chief Magistrate and the man charged with the licensing of bakers, butchers, carts and hotels. It was a bit rich for the Superintendent of Police to be sitting as a magistrate trying those charged by his own constabulary, but respectable men were in short supply in 1821 and the government had to make do as best it could. Humphrey was a particularly severe magistrate and was hated by the convicts.

No. 102 was soon before the bench. Looking at the prisoner the two magistrates saw a man a little under medium height peering over the edge of the dock. The records show that he was five foot three and a half inches tall, somewhat short even for a person of the early nineteenth century. His frame was thin, wiry and strong. Although he was about thirty-two years of age, he looked older. Dark-complexioned, his face was clean-shaven and pock-pitted – like many people of the time Pearce had had smallpox as a child. His eyes were blue-hazel and his brown hair was tousled in the style of the time, with sideburns reaching down below his ears. In other words, he looked like a perfectly ordinary early nineteenth-century man. There was nothing to distinguish him from the never-ending procession of convicts who traipsed through the Hobart Town courts, facing charges that ranged from minor misdemeanours such as absconding from work and insolence to overseers, to the major crimes of rape, murder and sheep-stealing, all three of which resulted in capital punishment.

As Pearce stood in the dock the charges were read. The evidence was obvious and not denied. Then his convict record was reviewed. It showed that this was the third time he had been before the courts since he arrived in Van Diemen's Land in late February 1820. On the first occasion he was accused of 'embezzling two turkeys and three ducks, the property of Messrs. Stynes and Troy'. Appearing before Chief Magistrate Humphrey on 18 May 1821, Pearce was sentenced to fifty lashes and to labour in the chain gang for fourteen days and to confinement at night. He was back before Humphrey again on 17 September 1821, this time accused of being drunk and disorderly and absent from his lodgings. The magistrate handed out twenty-five lashes. Without further ado the bench sentenced Pearce to another fifty lashes and discharged him from the service of Thomas Cane, a local constable, to whom he was currently assigned.

What had happened to the 'quiet' man from the *Castle Forbes* who had caused no trouble on the journey out? In order to answer this question we need to backtrack a little and examine how the world of convict settlements like Van Diemen's Land worked, and see how Pearce had fitted into that milieu.

The day after the arrival of the *Castle Forbes* in Hobart Town, Brevet-Major Thomas Bell of the 48th Regiment, the military commandant of Van Diemen's Land and Acting Engineer and

Inspector of Public Works, boarded the ship, mustered the convicts on deck, made a list of their names, ages, sentences, places of birth and trial, and their trades and callings, and noted for the Lieutenant-Governor the names of those mechanics who could be usefully employed by the government. Superintendent of Police Humphrey then took down a description of every man, noting height, hair and eye colour, and such personal details as 'pock-pitted' or 'lost two toes on left foot' or 'blue mark on upper lip' or descriptions of their tattoos – about 30 per cent of male and 10 per cent of female convicts had them. The prisoners were landed from the ship and marched up Macquarie Street and across George's Square by the Chief Constable and a party of petty constables to the jail on the corner of Murray and Macquarie streets, where their number was checked again. This was the first time that the *Castle Forbes* men had been on terra firma for more than 150 days.

There were many people about, walking or riding horses, or driving gigs, carts and other wheeled vehicles. It was late summer in the southern hemisphere, the streets were dusty and the heat dry and debilitating. Hobart Town in 1820 had a population of about 2700 and a scattering of official stone buildings and substantial houses, alongside private cottages of varying quality, huts, tents and hovels. They were all connected by unpaved streets and tracks that were muddy and often impassable after rain.

His Excellency, Governor Lachlan Macquarie, visited Hobart Town in April 1821 and, even allowing for the exaggeration inherent in descriptions by a superior visiting his dominions and admiring his underlings' achievements in order to enhance his own, he is lavish in his praise for the changes wrought since his first visit in 1811: 'The wretched huts and cottages, of which it [Hobart Town] then consisted, being now converted into regular substantial buildings, and the whole laid out in regular streets, several of the houses being two stories high, spacious and not deficient in architectural taste'. His Excellency was something of a statistician for he either went around himself, or sent an underling, to count the houses: all up there were 421. Clearly, by the beginning of the 1820s the settlement had begun the slow process of evolving from a prison camp to a town of free settlers, although the colony was still under the direct military control of His Honor, the Lieutenant-Governor. Because so much had to be imported from the home country, the cost of living was very high and rented accommodation was hard to come by and very expensive, as advertisements in the *Hobart Town Gazette and Van Diemen's Land Chronicle* constantly testified. Prices were higher than in the home country and even more than in London, which everyone agreed was a very expensive city.

The town lay on the western bank of the wide mouth of the Derwent River and sheltered directly below the 1270-metre (4100-foot) high Mount Wellington, then often called 'Table Mountain' because it resembled the similar massif near Cape Town in South Africa. The setting was spectacularly beautiful. Behind the town were the foothills of the steep mountain, its sides thickly timbered to two-thirds of the way up. In the narrow gullies, watered by cascades coming down from the melting snow, were many pockets of cool temperate rainforest. The top third of the mountain comprised organ-pipe-like cliffs and large areas of scree. Throughout winter Mount Wellington was usually covered in snow. A rocky mountainous plateau continued westward across the island from the peak of the mountain, which even today is not settled and is very rough country that is only crossed by walking tracks.

Despite the fact that Van Diemen's Land was a long way south, the weather in late summer was hot and dusty, the heat intense. Working out in the full blaze of the sun was utterly exhausting. Hobart Town and the Derwent estuary were surrounded by dry sclerophyll forest, woodland and native grassland that burned easily and regularly. Summer could be a season of scorching winds that quickly fanned wildfires that moved with ferocity and amazing speed. During February, the month that Pearce arrived, the vegetation would have been tinder dry, even though the summer of 1820–21 was relatively mild. These are the ideal conditions for bushfires and south-eastern Australia is the most dangerous place in the world for such conflagrations.

In 1820 Hobart Town was the southernmost settlement in the world. Even today, only Dunedin and Invercargill in New Zealand and Punta Arenas in Chile are further south. When Pearce arrived, the town was merely a European toe-hold on an isolated island of 6.62 million hectares (just on 16.3 million acres) that was largely unknown. Pearce was to be one of the first white men ever to pass through the worst of this wilderness and live to tell the tale.

At Hobart Town jail that morning in 1820, the convicts from the *Castle Forbes* selected for the public works were inspected by Lieutenant-Governor, Colonel William Sorell, who then addressed the gathering. At this stage Pearce and the others would have been assigned their convict numbers. The Irishman now became Convict No. 102.

Dressed in black and standing in the sun watching the arrival and muster of the convicts was a special visitor to Van Diemen's Land, John Thomas Bigge, Commissioner of Inquiry into all aspects of the government of New South Wales and its dependencies, and particularly into the cost-effectiveness of convict transportation as a means of discouraging crime. He had been appointed by His Majesty's Secretary of State for War and the Colonies, Earl Bathurst, in 1819, and had arrived in Hobart Town from Sydney just a few days before the *Castle Forbes*. Bigge was a snobbish high Tory of minor aristocratic lineage who never married. His reports give us considerable insight into the operations of the Australian colonies in 1820, but they were grossly unfair to Governor Macquarie in Sydney Town and played a major role in his recall. Bigge particularly objected to Macquarie's humanitarianism and willingness to re-admit emancipated convicts who had served their terms to mainstream society. The Commissioner, an academic lawyer, considered that this was incompatible with the purpose of criminal law.

No doubt for Pearce and his *Castle Forbes* companions, unaware of his importance, Bigge was just another pompous official inspecting them like cattle in the yard of the jail. They would have taken much more notice of Lieutenant-Governor Sorell in full colonel's uniform of black shako cap – a high round hat in the shape of a cylinder with a metal badge, and topped by a red-and-white pompom – bright red coat and short tails, a white sash across his chest, white breeches and long, black, knee-high boots. They knew that their fate and path to freedom lay ultimately in his hands, so they would have been more interested in him than the dark-clothed and sweating bureaucrat, Bigge.

Lieutenant-Governor Sorell was a likeable man and popular with most people in Hobart Town. He was a straightforward, blunt, decent soldier. More importantly, from the perspective of the British government and of his superior Governor Macquarie in Sydney Town, he was an unusually good administrator. Both Macquarie and His Majesty's Secretary of State and the Colonial Office bureaucrats in London had a high regard for him, even if his married life was, to put it mildly, confused. Early in his career he had married the daughter of a Lieutenant-General. It seems to have been a loveless match, even though they had seven children before they separated. His wife remained in London after he was appointed Adjutant-General at the Cape of Good Hope colony. Here he began a liaison with Mrs Kent, the wife of one of his officers, a Lieutenant. While the Colonial Office was aware of his marital status and de facto relationship, they still appointed him Lieutenant-Governor of Van Diemen's Land in 1816. Mrs Kent went with him, and was more or less accepted by most people in Hobart Town as his consort. Sorell had several children by her, and around town she was generally referred to as 'Mrs Sorell'. However, in 1817 Sorell was forced by the Colonial Office to pay the then enormous sum of £3000 as damages to Lieutenant Kent for 'criminal conversation' with Mrs Kent, as adultery was then charmingly called in British law. In 1819 the Secretary of State also forced the Lieutenant-Governor to pay £200 a year from his salary for the support of his first wife and seven children back in England.

In the two years before Pearce's arrival, Sorell had been subjected to a series of attacks from a local capitalist, Anthony Fenn Kemp, who had participated in the New South Wales Corps' mutiny against Governor William Bligh in Sydney Town in 1808. Kemp had subsequently moved his mercantile and farming interests to Van Diemen's Land. In November 1818 he complained bitterly to Earl Bathurst about Sorell's relationship with Mrs Kent, and he told Commissioner Bigge on 9 November 1819 that his complaint was that Sorell was 'in the habit every day of parading the garrison on horseback with the lady with whom he lives in adultery; that he introduces her to his table as Mrs Sorell; and that the magistrates and clergyman ... are in the habit of appearing with this person whose name is Kent in the public streets'. The real reason for Kemp's antagonism was that Sorell had put a limit to the merchant's grubby financial dealings, and had challenged his assumption that he could do what he liked in the pursuit of wealth. However, in the end it was the relationship with Mrs Kent that led to Sorell's eventual recall to London in May 1824.

Sorell administered a prison work camp rather than a jail. Convicts in New South Wales and Van Diemen's Land were not incarcerated in the contemporary sense. The penitentiary system was not established until a decade or more later, and then largely under the influence of an odd combination of Utilitarians and Evangelical Protestants who believed that the incarceration and isolation of prisoners would bring about repentance and amendment of life. In Hobart Town in 1820 convicts had much more freedom of movement than prisoners generally do today. Those working for the government usually had to find and pay for their own lodgings, so prisoners often had to be content with dreadful hovels, unless they could find a woman to move in with who already had a dwelling. But another problem was that women were very scarce. In 1826 Lieutenant-Governor George Arthur reported to London that there were 11,700 males and 3300 females in Van Diemen's Land, about 3.5 men to every woman. This was one reason for the widespread homosexuality in the convict system.

Convicts worked for the government from six until nine in the morning before an hour's break, and then again until three o'clock in the afternoon. They had the rest of the time for themselves. They also had most of Saturday and the whole of Sunday off, except for the church muster. This meant that they could work in their spare time to pay their rent and purchase what they needed. They drew their food rations and slops from the government stores on Wednesdays and Saturdays. Major Bell told Bigge that the system worked well for industrious men, who were able to make the most of it and work toward a ticket-of-leave. This allowed the prisoner complete freedom to work for himself, his only obligations being attendance at Sunday muster and not leaving his district without the permission of the Inspector of Public Works. Bell said that 'others, such as notorious thieves, London pick-pockets and housebreakers do not work [in] their after hours ... [Their free time is] ... principally spent in lounging about the streets, gambling and robbing at night'. When he was in town Pearce would have joined men like this. There is no evidence that he was in any way industrious.

Interestingly, from very early on the word 'convict' was avoided altogether in colonial speech, especially by convicts themselves, and the circumlocution 'government man' was preferred.

Convicts not chosen for government service would usually be assigned to free settlers, who were informed in advance when a new shipload arrived. Settlers were able to come into the jail and make a choice from the men available. It was something of a lottery from both points of view because a convict had no knowledge of the person he was going to serve, and the master had no idea how good a worker an individual convict might be. However, the imbalance of power was in favour of the master: as an assigned prisoner a convict could be reported to the courts on a range of charges from absconding to insolence and laziness. As a result the convict could be severely flogged by a magistrate who might be a friend or neighbour of the master. In exchange for his labour, the convict lived on the farm and was supposed to be given sufficient food, reasonable lodging, clothing and some free time.

Pearce was first billeted to a man named John Bellinger, who ran a farm of 500 sheep and a few cattle just north of Hobart Town on the west side of the Derwent, near what is today the suburb of Glenorchy. While Pearce apparently had no close personal ties to Ireland, he must have still hankered for the 'old country' with its familiar landscape. And even though the food was better in Van Diemen's Land and he was left much more to his own devices than he expected, he would still have been angry about what had happened to him. He found mates easily, but there is no evidence that he had any lasting friendships, so he must have felt very much on his own. From his perspective, life had always been a battle to survive, which could be won by those who could best manipulate the system. Yet, at the same time, his frustration often boiled over into impulsive acts such as getting into fights, stealing or bolting from his assignment. He also quickly learned that in Van Diemen's Land such actions led to the lash or the chain gang.

Also there were so few women that Pearce, like many other convicts, must have become sexually frustrated. Occasionally a captured Aboriginal lubra might be available, but there is no evidence that Convict No. 102 ever had enough money to pay a prostitute. Quite a few men found relief in either short- or long-term homosexual relationships. Sometimes, as the Catholic priest and Vicar-General of New South Wales, William Bernard Ullathorne, informed the 1838 Molesworth Parliamentary Select Committee on Transportation, both homosexuality and bestiality were practised in isolated rural areas. The surgeon John Barnes told the same Select Committee that bestiality was 'common' in the backblocks of Van Diemen's Land.

For Pearce, the most effective relief from loneliness came from grog, the more the better. As one traveller in Australia remarked, 'the great charm of life here is to be as drunk as often as possible'. Ullathorne says that he knew one small town with 1800 inhabitants that had fourteen fully operative public houses. There were hotels and sly-grog shops everywhere, often in bark huts just off the side of a main road.

Convict No. 102 seems to have stayed about nine months with Bellinger before being returned by his master to the government gang. Perhaps he was no longer needed, although one suspects he was lazy, surly, self-willed or drinking too much. He was then assigned to William Scattergood of New Norfolk, himself an ex-convict, but Pearce soon bolted from Scattergood's run (as sheep farms were called) and headed into the partially explored frontier country, which began about 32 kilometres (20 miles) to the north and north-west of New Norfolk. In an area within a 30-kilometre arc around the town, convicts laboured as shepherds on scattered runs that extended right out to the edge of white settlement and the beginning of Aboriginal land.

Probably Pearce was acting as a shepherd for Scattergood when he absconded. Most likely he could not stand the isolation and danger of the shepherd's life, and he was too far away from his mates and drinking companions.

•

The early 1820s economy of Van Diemen's Land was largely based on sheep, whose fine wool was exported to the industrial mills of England. On 30 November 1821 the statistically inclined Macquarie reported to London that there were 170,381 sheep in the southern colony, as well as 34,790 head of cattle, 4864 hogs (used locally for meat) and 550 horses. He did not give an account of the acreage already alienated, but there was constant pressure in both New South Wales and Van Diemen's Land to move further and further into Aboriginal territory. The expansion of European settlement was driven by the arrival of an increasing number of free settlers. Between 1818 and 1824 over 4000 arrived in Hobart Town, most of them being granted land by the government, and a convict servant. By 1830 there were a million sheep on the island, more than on the mainland of Australia. Thus there was constant pressure to expand the grazing areas and this quickly led to conflict with the Aborigines, who saw the newly introduced sheep and cattle literally as fair game.

This period saw constant conflict between blacks and whites. Shepherding close to the frontier was dangerous; the Aborigines did not hesitate to spear isolated settlers and shepherds, as well as their flocks. On their part the whites acted with appalling violence, especially toward Aboriginal women. Rape and abduction of Aboriginal women and unprovoked massacres were common. By the end of the decade there was open warfare between the Aboriginal owners of the land and white squatters. Eventually this would lead to the widespread destruction of traditional

Aboriginal life and to the decimation and large-scale removal of the Aboriginal people.

The porous borders of the settlement meant that it was easy for assigned convicts to slip away into the bush and form bandit groups of 'bushrangers', as these men were called from the early days of the colony. Having bolted from Scattergood's run, Pearce joined a group of four other escaped convicts. According to a Government Order of 10 February 1821, they had escaped from the county jail, a more serious offence than merely absconding from assignment. No doubt Pearce and his companions – James Letting, Thomas Lawton, Joseph Saunders and Thomas Atkinson – lived largely by stealing sheep from isolated flocks. If they had firearms – and they may well have done – they would have also been able to shoot 'boomers', as fully grown kangaroos were called, as well as indulging in the occasional hold-up of isolated travellers and raiding lonely farms. Men on the run grouped together like this in order to survive and gain some protection in numbers from attacks by the Aborigines.

These *banditti*, as bushrangers were also called, had reached epidemic proportions under Sorell's drunken and womanising predecessor, Lieutenant-Colonel Thomas Davey – 'Mad Tom' as the convicts and lower orders nicknamed him – who was Lieutenant-Governor from 1813 to 1817. Although Macquarie kept harping on Davey's 'dissipated and profligate' ways (he often slept with convict women), and the 'extraordinary degree of frivolity and low buffoonery in his manners' (it was said he often made rude faces at people on social occasions), he was popular with ordinary folk in Hobart Town because he was convivial, down-to-earth and often drank with them in public houses. But his administration was hamstrung by Macquarie's restrictive regulations, by a lack of resources from the home government and by the corruption of many of his officials.

From early 1815 to 1817 several gangs of convict bushrangers dominated the countryside. The best known group was led by Michael Howe, who called himself the 'Governor of the Ranges'. Davey tried to deal with the banditti by declaring martial law. When Sorell arrived in April 1817 he planned not only to capture the bushrangers with military force, but also to break the hold that they had on the poorer free colonists and ex-convicts who supported them. Within eighteen months the 'old man', as the white-headed 43-year-old Sorell was popularly called, had captured, tried and hung members of the Mike Howe gang. Howe himself was betrayed by a friend, and captured and killed by two bounty hunters in October 1818. Bushranging gangs were often riven by internal quarrels and tensions and informing on each other became common, especially if a reward was offered. However, the task of controlling bandits was ongoing; in the first part of 1821 ten out of twenty-six captured bushrangers were hung in Hobart Town. The others were sentenced to long prison terms. Order was very slowly restored to the settled districts, only for bushranging to erupt again with renewed ferocity with the Brady gang in 1824 to 1826.

The bushranging pattern was not forgotten by the convicts, and there was a constant flow of disgruntled prisoners absconding into the bush and forming groups like the one Pearce was in now. Pearce and his four companions were on the loose for about three months and probably moved around in about a 40-kilometre (25-mile) arc from the north-west of New Norfolk to the north-east of Hobart Town. Except for the river valleys, 43 per cent of the land surface at the time of European settlement was dry and wet sclerophyll woodland on extensive plateaux, dominated at the lower elevations by open eucalypt forests and by tall eucalypt forests at the higher, wetter levels. The area east to north-east of Hobart Town comprised already settled country.

This first period of absconding toughened Pearce up and taught him a little of how to survive in the Tasmanian bush. It also prepared him for the ruthless personal interactions that occurred between men who were living outside normal, ordered, civilised society and whose aim was focused on personal survival. He learned how to sort out who could be trusted and who could not, and about the loyalty and class solidarity of assigned convicts and small farmers, most of whom were ex-convicts. These people often lived largely outside the law themselves, and were regularly caught up in sheep-stealing and cattle-rustling, both capital offences. They were usually ready to provide help and information for convicts who had bolted. For these people class loyalty far outweighed obedience to government and authority.

There were several reasons why men like Pearce and his mates were not caught for months. First, the country itself: it was studded with wooded hills, mountains, narrow valleys and swathes of thick bush that provided hiding places everywhere. Even where the forest was open, it was easy to outrun and hide from a small force of pursuing soldiers. Large areas, some close to Hobart Town, were only semi-explored in 1821, and the population was spread fairly thinly. What habitation there was tended to follow the river valleys or the roads. This left expanses of open and closed woodland country where ex-convicts could hide for months on end from the prying eyes of authority. Even when they were recaptured it was often more by accident than design.

Secondly, the government was acutely short of trained personnel to police the colony. Constables were usually ex-convicts themselves, largely untrained, and their only pay was their keep. They were often unreliable. Sorell had very few troops at his disposal and would not have been in a position to deal with a serious revolt, and convict rebellion was always a lurking fear for the governments of New South Wales and Van Diemen's Land. When Pearce arrived in early 1820 the military contingent consisted of a commander, Brevet-Major Thomas Bell, four subalterns (officers below the rank of captain – that is, lieutenants) and ninety-two non-commissioned officers and privates. In the north around Port Dalrymple, George Town and Launceston, numbers varied but there were usually about 150 officers and men. According to the 1821 Muster the population of Hobart Town and the surrounding areas was 5542, and in the northern district there were 1643 people – a total of 7185. Of these 3827 were serving convicts, 1047 were either ex-convicts or had some form of pardon or ticket-of-leave, 1119 had come free to the colony, and 1192 were children. That means that a little over two thirds of the population were either convicts or ex-convicts.

Convicts were dispersed through assignment so they were more easily controlled, and the threat of the lash kept them on the back foot. The only concerted attempt to overthrow the government in Australia was the almost spontaneous rebellion in 1805 at Castle Hill in New South Wales, which mainly involved Irish convicts, and which was put down by the authorities with a viciousness born of a fear of convict revolt and a profound loathing for the Irish.

Pearce and his four mates might well have avoided recapture if they had not surrendered under an amnesty in late March 1821. We do not have a copy of this amnesty, but it no doubt resembled the one proclaimed nine months later in New South Wales by Macquarie's successor, Brigadier-General Sir Thomas Brisbane, on 15 December 1821. Brisbane's amnesty assured prisoners of the Crown and others who 'have absconded and are now at large within the woods in the interior of the colony' and who maintain themselves by pillage and rapine, that if they surrender before 31 January 1822 they will 'receive a full and sufficient pardon and go wholly free and unpunished', unless they had committed murder, or highway or house robbery with violence. It was a good deal, and Pearce and the others were probably now sick of living off the land and eating stolen sheep and boomers. They were ready for a few rums with their old mates. The *Hobart Town Gazette* of 5 May 1821 reports that they came out of the bush on Wednesday, 2 May and surrendered to Lieutenant John Cuthbertson of the 48th Regiment at the Coal River. Something must have happened at the time of the surrender or just before because the *Gazette* reported that one of the escapees, Atkinson, had had his hand blown off.

Sorell had a high opinion of Cuthbertson, who at that stage was in charge of a large gang of convicts working on the road to Coal River and Pitt Water, at a salary of five shillings per day. Thirteen months later Pearce would meet Cuthbertson again in very different circumstances.

The five of them were brought back to town in early May. But on 18 May Pearce was before Magistrate Humphrey, charged with 'embezzling two turkeys and three ducks, the property of Messrs Stynes and Troy', two ex-convicts who had a farm at Coal River. Whether this 'embezzling' happened before or just after their surrender we do not know. If Sorell's amnesty was worded in the same way as Brisbane's, one would have expected that a bit of petty-thieving would have been covered if it had occurred before the convicts' surrender. But given Pearce's personality, it might well have happened after they handed themselves over to Cuthbertson, while they were waiting to be taken back to Hobart Town.

Magistrate Humphrey sentenced Pearce to fifty lashes and to labouring the same hours as the jail gang for fourteen days, and to confinement in the watch-house at night. Sometime in July he was assigned to Constable Thomas Cane, but was still held in custody at night. He was back in court again on 7 July, this time not as an accused, but as a witness. He not only knew who had perpetrated a robbery, but also where the stolen goods were hidden. At the same time he had a perfect alibi: he had been locked up in the watch-house all night at the time of the robbery! The victim, a ticket-of-leave man named Hugh Morgan, approached Pearce and promised him a shirt, jacket and pair of trousers if he could get the property back. Pearce was able to recover some of the stolen goods for Morgan. Convict No. 102 did not miss an opportunity to dob in and use his mates when it suited his purposes. For Pearce there was to be no honour among thieves.

He managed to stay out of trouble until 17 September, when he was up before Humphrey again on charges of being drunk and disorderly and absent from his lodgings in the watch-house. This time the bench sentenced him to twenty-five lashes.

Three days later Pearce stole a wheelbarrow from the premises of one William Barrell, presumably to sell it in order to buy grog. This time Magistrate Humphrey sentenced him to fifty lashes and to six months' hard labour in the jail gang – in other words, working in irons for the government. Thus in six and a half months he had received 175 lashes, 100 of those within five days.

•

By the statistics of the convict period there was nothing extraordinary about this rate of punishment. Today most Australians would find flogging and most other kinds of physical discipline repugnant, even though we live in a world in which many governments systematically use torture as a means of maintaining their power. Physical and psychological torture are still widespread. The British military and navy used the lash to enforce discipline on soldiers and sailors until well into the late nineteenth century. The military lash was also used on convicts, and it was not until the 1930s that it was abolished in United Kingdom prisons as a way of administering the penal system.

From the seventeenth century local English magistrates had a lot of power over neighbourhood issues involving policing, law enforcement and punishment, and that system was reflected in early Australia. Police Superintendent Humphrey complained to Commissioner Bigge in March 1820 that single magistrates were limited to ordering fifty lashes and six months' imprisonment for each offence, and that two or more magistrates could not exceed 100 lashes and twelve months in the jail gang. However, this was clearly more honoured in the breach than the observance because two months later the Chief Constable of Van Diemen's Land informed Bigge that just the day before he had supervised five men receiving 200 lashes each, and two others 150 each. There is overwhelming evidence that throughout penal Australia, magistrates regularly exceeded the limits laid down by both the law and the governor's instructions.

The 100-lash limit was sixty-one more than courts in the United States could hand out to slaves at the same period. Americans felt themselves bound by the biblical thirty-nine lashes, derived from Saint Paul, who told the Corinthians (II Cor. 11:24) that 'Five times I have received from the Jews the forty lashes minus one; three times I was beaten with rods'. In the Book of Deuteronomy (25:3) Jewish judges were limited to inflicting forty lashes, because 'if more lashes than these are given, your neighbour will be degraded in your sight'. No such religious or human sensitivities operated in the convict system. In Australia men were flogged for what seem to us very minor offences. Laziness got you twenty-five lashes, as did insolence and swearing. Repeat offenders normally copped fifty no matter what the charge and, in places of secondary punishment like Macquarie Harbour, careless damage to tools or even items of clothing or slops also merited fifty. Flogging became so much part of convict life that a whole slang vocabulary grew up around it: a 'Botany Bay dozen' referred to twenty-five lashes, a 'bob' meant fifty lashes, a 'bull' seventy-five, and a 'canary' one hundred. The term 'red shirt' came to describe a flogged man's back.

So what actually happened when men were flogged? Pearce and the other convicts sentenced by the magistrates to corporal punishment would have been marched into the jail-yard the following morning. In Hobart Town the floggings were usually carried out under the supervision of the Chief Constable, Richard Pitt. Either the newly appointed Acting Colonial Surgeon, James Scott from the *Castle Forbes*, who had now settled in Van Diemen's Land, or more likely his assistant, Rowland R. Priest, would have been in attendance or close by; they could stop the flogging if they considered that the man being punished would be seriously injured. Pearce and his fellow prisoners would have been whipped either by a constable or a volunteer convict. Convict-floggers were considered by their fellow convicts the lowest of the low, class traitors of the very worst sort. Sometimes the flogger and the constable could be bribed to go easy on the victim, especially if there was no supervisor present, although it is unlikely that Pearce would have been able to find the money required.

Pearce would have been tied firmly to a triangular frame that was anchored to the ground, his hands secured together above his head, his feet attached to the base of the frame at ground level. He would have been stripped to the waist. Sometimes prisoners were stripped stark naked if they were to be whipped on the 'breech' (backside), as well as the back. Colonial magistrates had wide discretion, and this form of punishment could be ordered if the crime was considered particularly heinous, especially if the prisoner was convicted of buggery. The 'cats' (whips) were made of up to nine strands (usually there were three or four) of thick twine with knots, attached to a wooden handle. Most men began to bleed from the welts on their backs after three or four lashes. It took an average scourger about five or six minutes to hand out fifty lashes. Given that Pearce had been flogged just a few days previously, his wounds would have quickly reopened, the blood would have flowed down his back and trousers, and pieces of flesh would have been scattered around. It was an agonising process, and at the end of it he would have had difficulty standing or walking without assistance, and would have had to spend some days in hospital before he could start the second part of his sentence – work in the chain gang for six months.

It is a real temptation for us to want to ignore how degrading flogging was, and how the British legal system condoned such sadistic violence. Nevertheless, corporal punishment was central to the control of convicts in Australia. It helps to explain how such a small military force and a corrupt and inefficient police contingent were able to prevent serious revolt against the government. The imposition of such a draconian punishment on the convicts kept them always on the defensive. By using the lash, the authorities maintained the initiative, and by having it sanctioned by the courts, they maintained the legal high ground.

That is why flogging was maintained right up until the end of the system in the 1860s. Certainly, things had not changed a decade after Pearce's fifty lashes. The superintendent of the Hyde Park Convict Barracks in Sydney from 1833 to 1834, Ernest Augustus Slade, described some typical floggings to the 1837 British Parliamentary Select Committee on Transportation. Slade was an ex-soldier whose deadpan reportage to the members of the House of Commons gives a vivid sense of the reality of flogging. For instance, he says that a convict named William Graham who had been absent without leave was sentenced to twenty-five lashes. Slade reports that Graham's skin was lacerated at the thirteenth lash and that at the fifteenth 'the convict appeared to suffer great pain; but during the whole of the punishment he did not utter a word, nor groaned; but when cast loose the expression of his countenance indicated much suffering'. A man who copped his flogging without crying out was known by other prisoners as 'flash' or 'game'. This was the first time that Graham had been flogged. Calvin Simpson was sentenced to fifty lashes for stealing a pair of shoes. Slade says that 'blood flowed at the fourth; the convict cried out at the eighteenth and continued crying for a few succeeding lashes; his skin was considerably torn, and blood flowed during the whole of the punishment'. Simpson groaned and prayed while suffering his sentence, and Slade says that he was of the opinion that he was sufficiently punished at the twenty-fifth lash. Thomas Holdsworth had pilfered goods from his master, and the magistrate had sentenced him to fifty lashes. Slade's description paints a miserable scene: 'At the first lash the prisoner uttered piercing screams and continued screaming at each succeeding lash, and appeared to suffer greatly; the fifth lash brought blood, and the flesh was considerably lacerated at the conclusion of the punishment. This man says he was never flogged before, nor did there appear on his back any marks of former punishment. I am of the opinion that he was sufficiently punished at the twenty-fifth lash, for his bodily strength was nearly exhausted, as was manifested by his staggering gait when cut loose.'

Some of the citizens of Hobart Town expressed concern at the frequency of floggings handed out to convicts by magistrates. According to the semi-official *Hobart Town Gazette* of 22 April 1825, 'On Saturday, and also today, a scene was exhibited in the lumber-yard most dreadful to behold. The Commandant [then Lieutenant-Governor George Arthur, Sorell's successor] thinks that by a very severe mode of flogging, he will repress all disorders. He has got a very strong man to flog, who occupies about twenty minutes whilst inflicting fifty lashes. But to see the deplorable state of the men! Two I saw who were cut round into the throat, under the armpits, and on the belly and ribs of the right side! . . . Our worthy Pastor [the Reverend Robert Knopwood] declared in the church on Sunday that he could not rest the night before, owing to the dreadful cries of some of the sufferers . . . Nine were tortured on Saturday, four this day, and seven are ordered for tomorrow – for the most trifling crimes, such as being too late for muster, or absent from work.' One is tempted to be somewhat cynical about the unrest of the 'worthy pastor' of the Established Church, given that he himself doubled as a magistrate.

The Catholic priest William Ullathorne, who had wide experience of the Australian colonies in the 1830s, was opposed to flogging, for he maintained that it led to a person becoming deeply anti-social. He says that 'the man's soul is stung and a mortal poison, noxious to the human spirit, is imbibed from the knotted cords, that rankles long in his mental constitution'. Ullathorne, who was also opposed to transportation as a way of punishment and rehabilitation, saw the whole callous process as dehumanising and brutalising for all involved, including the convict, the flogger and the legal officers. He says that this struck him one day in 1834 when he visited the convict hospital in the town of Bathurst to the west of Sydney. He says he saw the triangle for flogging being erected in the hospital square in full view of all the sick men in their beds. 'On asking why it was put there, I was told that a lot of men were coming from the police court to be flogged, and that it was the most convenient place for the surgeon.'

•

By now the convict system was bringing out the worst in Pearce's personality. Looking back over his record we see an impulsive, angry, aggressive drunk who had learned nothing from experience, including his various arrests and floggings. He was happy to dob in his mates when it suited him. His brief stints on assignment probably indicate that he was an unreliable worker.

After his discharge from the hospital following the flogging, Pearce worked in the jail gang doing heavy work in chains on public projects. His six-month sentence would have concluded on 30 May 1822, but he had absconded again to the bush before then. He was to tell the jailer Bisdee before his execution: 'I forged several orders upon which I obtained property. On hearing the fraud was discovered, I was again induced to return to the woods', no doubt fearful that if he was found guilty he would receive a 'canary' – 100 lashes.

Pearce was presumably after easy money for grog. He attempted to forge a money order on Thomas Williams for the sum of £2 and uttering the same with intent to defraud one Richard William Fryett, a well-off merchant of Hobart Town and a pew holder in Saint David's church. There was no established currency in early Australia, so all transactions had to be carried out through either barter or private orders and promissory notes. It is hard to work out how Convict No. 102 could have forged a money order, given he could probably only read and write with difficulty at best. But he had seemingly been given a money order by Williams, an ex-convict constable, for £2 for some reaping that he had done for the merchant Fryett, and Pearce must have copied this and presented both to Fryett's wife, Ann. In her innocence Mrs Fryett must have paid up £4. Perhaps she, too, was illiterate? However, it would not have taken the merchant long to pick a forged note. News obviously travelled fast in the small town, and as soon as Pearce got wind of the fact that Fryett was looking for him, he absconded into the bush. This was sometime in late March 1822.

The *Hobart Town Gazette* of 18 May 1822 carried the following headline and official proclamation: 'Seventy Pounds Reward. Police Office Hobart Town 17 May 1822. Whereas Ralph Churton, William Davis, John William Bostok, Patrick Brown, Walter Archibald, John Harvey and Alexander Pearce, whose offences and descriptions are set forth underneath, have absconded from their usual places of residence, and are now at large in the woods. A reward of ten pounds each will be paid on their being lodged in H[is] M[ajesty's] jail in Hobart Town'. On 4 May a proclamation had been issued with only Davis and Churton's names, and then on 11 May another was issued with the names John William Bostock and Daniel Church added. The proclamation of 17 May adds the names Patrick Brown, Walter Archibald, John Harvey and Alexander Pearce, so these additional men must have absconded between 11 and 17 May and joined the others to form a gang in the bush. Daniel Church has disappeared from the list of abscondees; perhaps he had already been recaptured or had surrendered. Clearly they escaped at different times and gradually gathered together in the bush, and by late May were operating as a gang. Pearce was said to be charged with 'divers misdemeanours'. The proclamations contained a description of each of the escapees. Pearce confided to Bisdee that they were at large for three months – an exaggeration, as he was back before the courts again in early July, so he could only have been absent for ten weeks at most.

We know nothing of the details of this second period in the bush. Probably they supported themselves by raiding outlying farms and roughing it in the bush. The government was saved from having to pay the £10 reward offered for the capture of Pearce; he told Bisdee that he was nabbed by a party of the 48th Regiment, possibly in early July, and taken to Hobart Town. He was likely captured alone because the others were still on the loose after this date.

On 6 July Pearce was tried for absconding and for the forgery of the money order before a bench of magistrates made up of Knopwood and Humphrey, presided over by the Deputy Judge-Advocate, John Wylde, who was on circuit in Van Diemen's Land from Sydney. Pearce pleaded guilty to the absconding charge, but not guilty to the forgery. The case went to trial and Williams, called as a witness, testified that he and Pearce had been reaping hay together for Fryett and that he had given Convict No. 102 a money order for £2. But a second witness, Mrs Ann Fryett, claimed that Pearce had presented her with two orders, the second of which had been forged. The bench found him guilty.

At this stage the legal officers of Hobart Town had had enough of Pearce and he was sentenced to be transported to the penal colony of Macquarie Harbour on the west coast of Van Diemen's Land for the remainder of his original sentence. Ten days later he boarded the government brig *Duke of York* for the journey.

He was very lucky that he was not sentenced to receive 100 lashes as well.

3

Through Hell's Gates

Throughout his whole time in Van Diemen's Land His Honor, Lieutenant-Governor William Sorell, had an intractable problem with a small minority of convicts like Pearce who were regularly before the courts. He had no real jail, only the insecure and badly guarded watch-house in Hobart Town. Where could he hold recidivists? Was it possible to reform them? Should they be severely flogged for each offence to make an example of them to others? Was there something that they could do for society, the government, or even themselves in terms of hard labour? How could he usefully employ them and snatch them away from a dissolute life of regularly getting drunk on cheap rum, fighting and consorting with any woman – or man for that matter – convict, free or Aboriginal, who was drunk or hard up or stupid enough to be willing? And how could he prevent them from absconding, roaming the bush, causing conflict with the Aborigines and becoming highwaymen?

Until the end of 1820 the usual answer had been for the Hobart Town courts to send repeat offenders off to hard labour at the penal settlement at Newcastle, about 177 kilometres (110 miles) north of Sydney Town, which had been set up in 1801 precisely for the most recalcitrant convicts by the New South Wales Governor, Philip Gidley King. But Newcastle was a long way from Hobart Town, and it was very expensive to ship re-convicted men there. For other local offenders, like Pearce, who were regularly before the magistrates of Van Diemen's Land, it had no exemplary value. Newcastle was so far out of sight that it was completely out of mind.

But with the increasing number of convicts being shipped directly to Hobart Town from the home country, the problem of recalcitrant recidivism was getting worse. Sorell needed somewhere local to establish what were increasingly being called 'places of secondary punishment'. Here he could establish a harsh regime of very hard labour, often in chains, and he hoped that this would have an impact on the most incorrigible of the local criminal class. At the same time the place had to be so geographically isolated that escape was well-nigh impossible.

For several years Sorell had been urging Macquarie to get permission from London for him to open a penal establishment in Van Diemen's Land itself. Given the Sydney Governor's high regard for Sorell, he strongly supported the proposal, but his entreaties over several years to the home government in Whitehall had fallen on deaf ears and nothing had been done. So after discussion with Commissioner Bigge, who also approved the idea, Sorell wrote a long dispatch to the Under-Secretary of State for War and the Colonies, Henry Goulburn, at 16 Downing Street on 12 May 1820, saying that he was now pretty certain that he had identified the place they needed for a local 'place of secondary punishment': Macquarie Harbour on the west coast of Van Diemen's Land. There was good timber there for the convicts to work (Sorell described it as 'a species of cypress called the Huon Pine'), as well as superficial coal deposits. But the big advantage was that the place was so isolated that 'none but government vessels would frequent it . . . [and] the great tier of mountains which runs nearly north and south the whole length of the island, their base verging on the western coast, offers a barrier which renders escape by land, always very difficult, and for years probably impracticable'. Sorell was almost right. As we shall see, escape, while extremely arduous, was not impossible.

The Colonial Office continued to drag its bureaucratic feet, so Sorell and Macquarie decided to go ahead with the proposal off their own bat, although the New South Wales Governor's dispatch of 18 July 1821 to the Secretary of State for War and the Colonies, Earl Bathurst, shrewdly couched their decision in terms of seeking His Lordship's 'consideration and approbation'. From mid-1821 onwards preparations began in earnest in Hobart Town.

Both the colonies of New South Wales and Van Diemen's Land had originally begun as places of *primary* punishment to which His Britannic Majesty's government could transport the United Kingdom's criminals. Although this is often forgotten today, transportation was generally very successful in reforming those sentenced to it. Most male and female convicts made such a reasonable fist of their lives in the Australian colonies that they did not need to undergo any form of *secondary* punishment. The system was rough and ready, but it worked reasonably well, probably better than our incarceration of most offenders. If you omit the costs of shipping convicts to Australia, it was certainly a lot cheaper to operate. I believe that today we might learn a lot from the old system, where the underlying notion was that most people sentenced by the courts ought to serve their sentences working in and for the community. Incarceration would then only be used as an absolute last resort and usually only for the most violent and uncontrollable.

The change from a more open system of working in the community to an emphasis on the incarceration of prisoners occurred around the mid-1830s, due largely to the increasing influence of an unusual coalition of liberals, including the Utilitarian philosopher, Jeremy Bentham, and conservative Protestant Evangelical prison reformers, who felt that solitary imprisonment in completely separate cells created conditions in which the detainee could reflect on amendment of life in isolation and move gradually toward reformation. In Van Diemen's Land the classic example of this ideal was the Model Prison built in the 1840s at Port Arthur, along the lines of London's Pentonville Prison. Port Arthur had been established as a place of secondary punishment after Macquarie Harbour was closed down in 1831.

But earlier most convicts served out their terms either on assignment working for private individuals, or labouring on projects for the government. Once they negotiated all of the vagaries and inconsistencies of the system, with the men copping the occasional flogging and the women stints in the female factories, they eventually gained their tickets-of-leave, or a conditional or absolute pardon. Meanwhile they might have found someone to live with, eventually married and had children, and gone on to establish themselves as farmers, tradesmen, manual or itinerant workers, or even as professionals and merchants. They certainly ate better in Australia and enjoyed much better health than in the pollution of the English industrial cities or in the Welsh mining valleys. A small proportion of ex-convicts even emerged as successful *nouveaux riches*, setting a pattern often repeated in contemporary Australia. Many law-abiding Australian families these days can trace their origins back to a convict, and to have a convict ancestor is a point of honour.

Good, conservative military men that they were, Macquarie and Sorell were firm supporters of the old system. Macquarie was eventually replaced because he had fallen foul of the wealthy New South Wales 'bunyip aristocracy' of free settlers – they are a continuing force in Australian society – precisely because he had encouraged and protected those who had served their terms as convicts, been emancipated and wanted to play a role in the emerging society. In a statement in the *Sydney Gazette* of 27 January 1821, the emancipists declared themselves to constitute the emerging middle-class of the colony of New South Wales.

The history of Van Diemen's Land is somewhat different because there was always a much smaller group of emancipists, and Tasmanian society has always been more stratified and structured along the lines of those who came free and those who came as convicts. But despite all the limitations of life in the colonies, there is no doubt that emancipists were much better off in Australia in terms of wealth, health and opportunity than they would have been if they had remained in the mother country among the burgeoning under-class of the English cities, disposable workers in an increasingly industrialised country.

But our story is primarily about what happened to the 5 to 7 per cent of felons, like Pearce, who were not reformed by transportation and by their stint in the Antipodes. What were the authorities to do if convicts did not make the most of their opportunities in the new country? The answer then was to re-transport them to 'places of *secondary* punishment', where hard labour and severe discipline would at least keep them in their place in the pecking order, as well as give them the opportunity to learn more industrious habits. Convicts on the mainland would have been sent to Norfolk Island (established 1788), Newcastle (established 1801), Port Macquarie (established 1818) and, after 1824, to the steamy humidity of the infamous Moreton Bay settlement (now the city of Brisbane) where, as the balladic lament 'Moreton Bay' put it, 'excessive tyranny . . . each day prevails' under the flogging Commandant, Captain Patrick Logan, who, to the immense relief and joy of the convicts, was eventually murdered by a group of Aborigines while exploring the Brisbane River.

At Macquarie Harbour a similar regimen of secondary punishment was to prevail. Sorell's successor, Colonel George Arthur, a strong Evangelical himself and never a man to mince his words, spelt out bluntly in mid-June 1824 for the second

Commandant of the settlement, Lieutenant Samuel Wright, the purpose of penal establishments: 'Nothing I can imagine is more likely to lead to the moral improvement of the most abandoned characters in this Colony than a rigid course of discipline, strictly and systematically enforced . . . The constant, active, unremitting employment of every individual convict in very hard labour is the grand and main design of [these places of secondary punishment]'.

Sorell was more concise. He simply described Macquarie Harbour as 'a place of ultra-banishment and punishment of convicts'. But he also understood London's preoccupation with costs, so he emphasised the valuable products, like good ship-building timber and coal, that could be obtained there by convict labour, when he was writing to the Secretary of State and the bureaucrats of the Colonial Office.

The practical arrangements for the establishment of Macquarie Harbour penal settlement went on throughout the second half of 1821, while Pearce was sliding down the slippery slope of recidivism and accumulating court appearances on stealing, absconding and drunk and disorderly charges. With each new appearance before the bench, the magistrates could see that being sentenced to floggings and stints of working in chains in the jail gang was achieving nothing for Convict No. 102. He was fast becoming prime material for re-transportation to the newly established place of secondary punishment on Van Diemen's Land.

•

After Macquarie Harbour was discovered by Europeans in 1815, it had been visited several times and had been carefully observed and described by Captain James Kelly from the brig *Sophia*. He had personally given a detailed description to Commissioner Bigge.

Lieutenant Phillip Parker King of the Royal Navy spent two weeks there in January 1819. Early in the preparations for the penal settlement it was decided to establish the headquarters station at the southern end of the harbour on Sarah Island (sometimes also called Settlement Island), about 35 kilometres (22 miles) from the entrance at Hell's Gates, largely because the island seemed fertile enough to grow vegetables. It had been named after the wife of the owner of Captain Kelly's ship, Mrs Sarah Birch.

The entrance at Hell's Gates is at 42°11' south latitude, so it is directly in the path of the Roaring Forties. For thousands of miles to the west there is nothing but open sea and roaring winds that pick up enormous speed and moisture. The first land mass that they strike is the west coast of Tasmania. It is this constant westerly wind that determines not only the weather, but also much of the vegetation of Macquarie Harbour and the whole of the south-west. It is a land of strong winds, squalls, storms, rain, sleet, snow and a kind of saturating dampness that penetrates into the very core of your being, especially in winter. When Pearce arrived at Macquarie Harbour in July 1822 it was midwinter and wet, overcast conditions were constant. At this time of the year, the days are short: the sun rises at about seven and sets by five in the afternoon. Even when it is not raining, the sky is usually grey. At Sarah Island a misty and depressing drizzle can settle in for days or even weeks on end, the sun seeming to disappear completely from the world. While the coast is often damp, the steep, rocky inland mountain ranges are exposed to dry electrical storms.

On average the west coast of Tasmania gets about 2586 millimetres (about 102 inches) of rain per year. July, August and September are the wettest as well as the coldest months, and you can get snow down to 600 metres (1900 feet), which at higher elevations can build up to a depth of more than 10 metres (32 feet). It can sometimes blanket a rainforest completely. But if there is one constant about the weather of the area, it is that it is temperamental. The sun may come out on a mild morning, to be followed by rain or even snow in the afternoon. As people used to the weather in the south-west often say: 'Don't worry if it's pouring rain now; in ten minutes the sun will be out!'

Almost two centuries after Pearce's time the convict settlement at the southern end of Macquarie Harbour remains claustrophobic, especially in winter. Towering over the southern section is the 1144-metre (3700-foot) Mount Sorell, and in the distance, on the odd occasions when the weather lifts, you can see the 1446-metre (4744-foot) Frenchman's Cap, which is covered with snow all winter and sometimes even in summer. No one is certain who named this mountain, but probably some cynical wit at Sarah Island noticed that its glacier-formed summit resembled the 'cap of liberty', the conical headgear given to Roman slaves on emancipation and used as a republican symbol during the French Revolution. Its ironic name would not have been lost on better educated convicts born in those revolutionary years when the French king was overthrown and executed, and the equality of all people first proclaimed. Perhaps it was the same wit who named Liberty Point and Liberty Bay at the northern end of Macquarie Harbour.

The constraints of Sarah Island and convict life must have been particularly galling to Pearce and his fellow recidivists. While these men were seen by their contemporaries as unredeemable criminals, they were essentially social misfits and cranks, men usually from the lower ranks of society who were unwilling and unable to accept the social and class constraints of an increasingly rigidly structured British society. These were men who did not easily fit in anywhere. They had been born at a time when equality, democracy and the rights of man and the citizen were proclaimed by the American Revolution and the French Republic. They had grown up during the Revolutionary and

Napoleonic Wars, and had come to manhood in a time of profound social unrest in Britain and Ireland. This unrest was as much economic and social as it was political. The machine age was beginning, population pressures were increasing, and landless and dispossessed small farmers were being forced by economic circumstances into the ugliness of the burgeoning industrial cities. Many people were understandably Luddite: they tried to destroy the machines and the new social structures that had abolished the way of life that their families had followed for centuries. In the words of the poet William Blake, England's 'mountains green' and 'pleasant pastures' were increasingly being replaced by 'those dark satanic mills'.

Many of the men who ended up at Sarah Island were the by-product of industrialisation. And much of their protest against the constraints of prison life was really the expression of their unwillingness to accept the social, political and economic process in which they were caught.

In the early years of the Macquarie Harbour settlement, in order to try to break their spirit, most of the prisoners were used in what amounted to slave labour in logging operations at various places on the mainland, primarily around Kelly's Basin, which was a narrow bay about 8 kilometres (5 miles) almost directly east of Sarah Island. They also worked up the Gordon River at the southern end of the harbour.

In both places the predominant vegetation is cool temperate rainforest, which nowadays is very rare anywhere in the world, making up only about 5 per cent of all remaining rainforests on earth. In the northern hemisphere cool temperate rainforests are found only in isolated pockets around the rim of the Pacific Ocean, such as in the United States's Pacific Northwest, and Canada's coastal British Columbia. There are also small pockets in south-eastern China. But the last strongholds are in the southern hemisphere – in far southern Chile, in a few areas in New

Zealand, and in southern Australia. These are some of the rarest and most important forests in the world.

But even in Australia they are under threat. Probably one of the largest continuous cool temperate rainforests anywhere in the world was in Gippsland in south-eastern Victoria, especially in the Strzelecki Ranges. These low, rolling hills were covered until the beginning of the twentieth century with rainforest containing some of the tallest trees in the world: the great mountain ash with the wonderful botanical name *Eucalyptus regnans* (reigning eucalypt), which often grow more than 50 metres (162 feet) in height, and which are known to have reached 100 metres (325 feet). Only a minuscule portion of this magnificent and massive virgin rainforest now survives: in total about 2500 hectares (about 6000 acres), mainly in a couple of tiny national parks, out of an original 500,000 hectares (1.2 million acres). After the final destruction of the rainforests in central Gippsland early in the twentieth century, the most extensive remaining examples in the world of these now very rare forests occur on the Errinundra plateau and surrounding areas in far-eastern Victoria, and in western Tasmania. It is for this reason that a considerable proportion of the south-west of Tasmania was declared a World Heritage Area in 1982, in the face of last-ditch legal manoeuvring by the state government. Even today large tracts of rainforest and other environmentally valuable forests remain outside the protected areas, and some of them are still being logged for export woodchips to Asia.

The other determining element in the formation of the south-west is the geological history of the landscape, which largely took on its present shape through the recurrent ice ages of the mid- to late-Pleistocene period (from about 30,000 to 9000 years ago). You only have to look at a map of the south-west to see that the mountain ranges run either almost due north-south, or north-west by south-east, thus creating a protective barrier between the land affected by the extreme weather patterns of the Southern Ocean and the flatter, dryer uplands and midland plains of central, north-eastern and south-eastern Tasmania. The mountains of the south-west are made up of a series of ranges and peaks that vary in height from 600 to 1600 metres (1950 to 5200 feet) above sea level. Flowing down from and in between these mountains are three short but spectacular river systems, rushing through narrow, deep valleys, that carry up to twenty times more water than that carried by the much longer, slower-moving mainland rivers of south-eastern Australia. In the northern half of the west coast are the Arthur and the Pieman systems; in the southern part of the south-west is the Gordon–Franklin system, which is central to the story of Pearce and his fellow escapees.

The Gordon is the most important river in western Tasmania. It rises near the centre of the island and drains a vast area of both the central-west and south-west. After flowing through treacherous rapids and the Gordon Gorge, it is now trapped in a vast hydro-electric dam called Lake Gordon, completed in November 1974. Just to the south of this pondage is another dam that impounds Lake Pedder. Only a tiny 60 megawatts of power are produced by this vast impoundment, which has drowned a whole series of valleys. Below the Gordon dam wall a series of other streams flow into the river, including the Franklin, and these all eventually drain into Macquarie Harbour just south of Sarah Island. In 1979 another proposal was put forward to dam the Gordon just below its confluence with the Franklin. Again a whole pristine river system would have been drowned. A three and a half year campaign was waged against this proposal worldwide and eventually, by the narrowest of margins, the High Court of Australia overruled the Tasmanian government's determination to destroy the Gordon below its confluence with the Franklin.

The most important recent factor in the shaping of the south-western mountains has been glaciation and the freezing and thawing of water. A series of ice ages began about 730,000 years ago and lasted until just 9000 years ago. Sea levels fell as water was absorbed into the ice-sheets, and rose during the warmer intervals. Australia was then connected to Papua New Guinea, and the southern Australian coast reached about 100 kilometres (60 miles) further south into the Great Australian Bight than it does now. There was also a land bridge between the mainland and Tasmania. The glaciers that formed around the mountains of Tasmania tore away at them, creating massive cliffs, deep hollows, moraines and large areas of scree, such as those on Mount Wellington above Hobart Town. Frenchman's Cap, the mountain that so dominates our escape story, was shaped by the ice and snow of the last ice age.

The last ice age from about 25,000 to 9000 years ago created most of the geological features of the mountains of the south-west. During this cold, dry period the landscape looked something like the contemporary Arctic tundra, with rainforests just surviving along the river valleys and in the wetter areas. We know that Aboriginal people were present in the south-west during at least part of this ice age, the southernmost human beings in the world at the time. With a rise in the earth's temperatures and sea levels, the rainforests began to expand again from their river valleys and reoccupy the south-west in response to a wetter climate. At the same time the coastal valleys such as Macquarie Harbour and Bathurst Harbour were flooded by rising sea levels. It was at this time that the isthmus leading to the Australian mainland was drowned, creating Bass Strait. Van Diemen's Land was now an island.

The first detailed descriptions of Macquarie Harbour were provided by three men. The first was the experienced sealer and whaler Captain James Kelly, born of uncertain paternity in the town of Parramatta, just to the west of Sydney, in November 1791. The second was Lieutenant Phillip Parker King, born at

Norfolk Island in 1791, the son of Governor King. King junior mapped Macquarie Harbour in December to January 1819–20. The third was the Deputy Surveyor-General of Van Diemen's Land, George Evans, who accompanied the first settlement at Sarah Island.

Kelly told Commissioner Bigge in May 1820 that he had been to the harbour seven times, and that the entrance was very tricky and narrow, requiring the wind to be from exactly a northerly direction for a ship to negotiate its way through safely. The vessel also needed to be of shallow draft. Getting into any harbour was difficult for sailing ships because they were so dependent on wind direction and velocity, and in adverse weather many harbour entrances were almost impossible to negotiate. This was particularly so at Macquarie Harbour. Evans advised that if the wind was contrary, especially if it was an easterly, a ship would simply have to lie outside the entrance in a roadstead: a safe place to ride at anchor. There was one situated on the ocean side to the south-west of the Macquarie Harbour entrance – Edwards Bay, which was protected to some extent by Trumpeter Rock to the north-west and Olsen Reef to the south-west. Here a ship could anchor safely until the wind came around to a northerly. Nevertheless, anchoring could still be a tall order as there was not a lot of shelter from the winds and massive swells that rolled in from the west. Sometimes vessels had to wait for days, even weeks, to negotiate the entrance, which was about 80 yards (72 metres) wide.

For the captain, helmsman and pilot, steering a ship through the entrance could be a hair-raising experience, especially if the sea was up to any extent, and impossible when a really big sea was running. It must have been even worse for the passengers, who were sometimes ordered below deck for passage into the harbour. There was an outer sandbar with only 8 to 9 feet clearance (2.5 metres) at high tide, and Kelly warned that the tides in the area were often unpredictable. After passing the outer bar, there was a narrow channel between shoals and rocks, and mariners often had to contend with a very strong undertow out of the harbour. Beyond the channel there was a shifting inner bar, again with only about an 8-foot clearance at high tide. Even today, after a lot of dredging has been done in the entrance and a massive breakwater built on the south-west side, the channel is still very narrow and deceptive and requires extremely careful navigation. It was not for nothing that right from the beginning the entrance was called 'Hell's Gates'. Often in the early days of the penal settlement, ships would have to unload their cargo to lighten themselves before negotiating the entrance, and then reload once they had got through.

About 35 kilometres (22 miles) sou'-sou'-east from the entrance is Sarah Island, the location chosen for the settlement. Just across from Sarah Island is tiny Grummet Island, which is about 385 metres (400 yards) in circumference. It soon became a place for the punishment of those for whom even secondary punishment was insufficient. It also housed the convict hospital.

•

As preparations proceeded in Hobart Town for the formation of the penal settlement, one of the most important decisions facing Sorell was the appointment of a commandant. The man chosen was Lieutenant John Cuthbertson of the 48th Regiment of Foot, an Irish-born career soldier of thirty-five, who had been granted a lieutenancy in 1808. He had been praised for bravery at the Battle of Talavera (27–8 July 1809) near Toledo in Spain during the British campaign against the Napoleonic occupation of the Iberian peninsula. It was the two battalions of the 48th that saved the day at Talavera and decided the battle. In a moment of great danger, the English Commander, Sir Arthur Wellesley (afterwards Duke of Wellington, victor at Waterloo, and Prime Minister from 1828–30), ordered the 48th to advance against the French line, which they did with admirable discipline and steadiness. It was their moment of glory. The regiment continued fighting in the Peninsular Campaign in Spain and suffered heavy casualties. They had a stint in Ireland after the end of the Napoleonic Wars in 1815, and then a battalion of the regiment was sent to New South Wales from Cork in 1817. A detachment of about 250 officers and men – out of a total of 800 in Australia – were sent to Van Diemen's Land with their wives and families.

Among them was the unmarried Lieutenant Cuthbertson. By mid-1818 he was serving in various capacities, especially in the supervision of convict road gangs. Sorell had a high opinion of him, and his experience with convicts seemed to make him a natural choice as the first Commandant at Macquarie Harbour. His pay for this hardship posting was reasonably good for the time: seven shillings and sixpence per day. When he established the Sarah Island settlement Sorell was adamant that heavy work was to be the centrepiece of the reform process. He told Cuthbertson to make sure that every convict was involved in 'constant, active, unremitting employment ... in very hard labour'. Cuthbertson and his successors took their instructions seriously and eventually made Sarah Island the only penal settlement in the Australian colonies that covered its costs and turned a profit for the government. The prison's lumber production became very lucrative and was the most important form of labour in the first years of the settlement.

Cuthbertson's power over the convicts was almost absolute. As a magistrate and justice of the peace he could sentence recalcitrant prisoners who broke any of the numerous regulations to solitary confinement never exceeding fourteen days, or up to 100 lashes with the particularly nasty cat-o'-nine-tails used on Sarah Island. Cuthbertson was seen by the convicts as a sadistic bully; the punishments handed out by him, and his successor, Lieutenant Samuel Wright of the 3rd Regiment, which replaced the 48th in 1823, seem to support the view that they both had sadistic tendencies. Many convicts at Sarah Island saw commandants like Cuthbertson and Wright as 'inhuman tyrants', with one relatively literate prisoner making an unflattering comparison with the Roman Emperor Nero.

But the problems facing these soldiers in the very isolated places of secondary punishment like Macquarie Harbour were enormous. By August–September 1822 there were about 170 convicts on the island, and Cuthbertson only had a 'Lieutenant's Guard' of seventeen non-commissioned officers and soldiers to support him. Usually four of these men were at the pilot's station at the harbour's entrance at Hell's Gates, and he had already lost two soldiers in a wild-goose chase after eight convicts who bolted from the settlement in early March 1822. That left only eleven men on the island itself, where the possibility of a convict revolt would always have been at the back of the Commandant's mind.

This never eventuated. A small number of guards can control much larger numbers of prisoners if the regime is geared to keep those incarcerated constantly on the defensive. This was achieved at Macquarie Harbour through the use of exhausting work and detailed regulations which were enforced with the threat and imposition of brutal punishment. They were to grind down the will to resist. So, rather than saying that Cuthbertson was a sadistic bully, perhaps it would be more accurate to say that he was a somewhat brutalised soldier who had some glory at Talavera and who now had to live and work in a very dangerous environment in which he had the power to take whatever steps he thought necessary to fulfil his instructions and to keep the situation under control. There was also a sense in which the careers of most of the civil and military officers at Sarah Island had reached the bottom of the bucket; you certainly would not accept a posting in such a place if you could avoid it. These were men with nowhere else to go.

•

Without ceremony, Kelly's 90-ton, two-masted brig *Sophia* and the government brig *Prince Leopold*, of similar tonnage, slipped out of Hobart Town on 11 December 1821 for Sarah Island, with 111 people aboard who were to be the pioneers of the penal settlement. Among them were Commandant John Cuthbertson, Deputy Surveyor-General George Evans, the Assistant Surgeon, James Spence, the Harbour-Master and pilot, James Lucas, a constable to supervise the convicts, seventeen non-commissioned officers and soldiers of the 48th, with four soldiers' wives and eleven children. To help with construction Sorell sent eleven convict artificers and mechanics of good character, eleven other convicts of useful avocations and eight untrained female convicts to work in the hospital and to do domestic work. The rest of the human cargo was made up of forty-four male convicts under sentence to Macquarie Harbour who were of 'bad character and incorrigible conduct', as His Honor described them for Under-Secretary Goulburn in Downing Street. They were to work the coal and timber resources of the Macquarie Harbour area.

It was not an easy passage to the west coast for the two brigs. As soon as they emerged from the protection of land and turned south-west, they hit the full force of the Southern Ocean. They became separated in a storm on 17 December and, after a difficult eighteen-day voyage tacking north up the west coast, the *Sophia* arrived off the entrance to Macquarie Harbour on the second-last day of 1821. After unloading her stores she passed through Hell's Gates, reloaded her cargo and headed down the harbour to Sarah Island, where she arrived on 3 January 1822.

The *Sophia* stayed three weeks at Macquarie Harbour and, after loading a cargo of Huon pine and negotiating Hell's Gates again, she arrived back in Hobart Town with reports from Cuthbertson and Evans, having managed a four-day passage, on 7 February 1822.

The *Prince Leopold*, meanwhile, had run into terrible weather. She lost a seaman overboard, her main boom was carried away, her mainsail was split, one of her boats was dashed to pieces on the deck, and the bulwark was stove in by the sheer force of the sea. She had been blown right up the west coast and had to wait so long to negotiate the entrance she ran low on food and had to sail up to Bass Strait and turn east to the settlement at Port Dalrymple to be resupplied. As a result she did not arrive at Sarah Island until late February. The delay caused a severe problem for Cuthbertson because the *Prince Leopold* had the trained carpenters on board, so presumably the contingent on the *Sophia* lived either on the boat while it remained, or in tents or rough temporary shelters for the first seven weeks. This was the first of many long voyages for ships heading up the stormy west coast for Hell's Gates and Sarah Island. There are few places to shelter: Port Davey, with its extensive bays, inlets and islands, was one possibility; and Spero Bay under Point Hibbs, about 50 kilometres (30 miles) south of Hell's Gates, was the other. Both are still used by local fishermen to shelter from storms.

Cuthbertson told Sorell in his first report that Sarah Island was about a mile in circumference (1.5 kilometres) and about a quarter of a mile (about 500 metres) from the western shoreline of the harbour. The island, which was about 600 metres long by about 150 metres wide, was originally thickly wooded, but during the twelve years in which it was occupied by the penal settlement all drawings and pictures show it to have been cleared completely. Even though the soil was poor and gravelly, the Commandant was confident that they would be able to grow vegetables there, which was true to a limited extent. As the settlement developed, soil and compost were brought from the mainland to try to encourage the growth of the gardens. They had some success, but there were never enough vegetables to feed everyone. Nowadays the trees and rainforest are coming back on the island and it is starting to resemble what it probably originally looked like. Cuthbertson says that they had trouble in the first couple of weeks unloading the stores because of rain squalls and rough weather. However, they eventually got everything ashore safely, and they managed to erect a store-house. In those first three weeks the convicts cut down and prepared enough Huon pine to send the *Sophia* back to Hobart Town fully loaded. Clearly, the Commandant was taking the 'very hard labour' aspect of his orders seriously.

Deputy Surveyor-General Evans, meanwhile, had been exploring the shores of the harbour, probably with Kelly, and estimating its commercial potential. On the eastern side of the island there was good anchorage protected from the severity of the prevailing west and north-westerly winds which, the Deputy Surveyor warned, could stir up a considerable sea, even in the far southern end of the harbour. Evans proposed that Sarah Island be made a headquarters camp, and suggested that the work gangs of convicts be billeted on the western shore of the harbour where water was available. This might have been a good idea, but Cuthbertson, fearing escape attempts, decided to establish everything on the island itself, including the convicts' dormitory. Thomas James Lemprière, who lived at Macquarie Harbour from 1826 as Commissariat Officer, basically agreed with Evans; he never understood why Sarah Island had been chosen, given that there was no water there and, after all the trees had been removed, no wood for fires. All supplies had to be transported. Evans also realised that considerable work would have to be carried out to clear enough land to plant grain to supply the settlement and, while they tried many times to grow wheat, this was never successful. Evans reported that the whole harbour area was destitute of pasture, so bringing in cattle and sheep was out of the question.

The Gordon River flowed into the south-eastern end of the harbour and Evans sailed 32 kilometres (20 miles) up to the first rapid. He walked about another 5 kilometres (3 miles), probably as far as the confluence with the Franklin River. He matter-of-factly described the country as 'closely covered with heavy timber and almost impenetrable vines and brushwood'. He perceived no commercial value in the place and he certainly made no comment about its natural beauty. Nowadays, with more sensitivity to the splendour of the environment, the Gordon is recognised as one of the wonders of the world and is an integral part of the World Heritage Area that covers so much of south-western Tasmania.

Evans also penetrated 24 kilometres (15 miles) up the King River to where 'it winds between a range of hills of great height, impenetrably covered'. This river flows into the northern end of Macquarie Harbour, just to the south of where the present-day town of Strahan is situated. The King also did not seem to him to be a particularly promising proposition in commercial terms.

The Deputy Surveyor was, however, pleased to inform His Honor back in Hobart Town of two important issues. First, Huon pine grew in great abundance on the eastern shore of the harbour and it could be obtained without too much difficulty by gangs of convicts. It grew, Evans told Sorell, on the banks of streams or wherever there was sufficient water. Other good timber was available too. He also commented that, even more importantly, Macquarie Harbour was surrounded by rugged, closely wooded and impenetrable country, so that escape from the settlement was next to impossible. Evans was certain that convicts sent here could not possibly have any communication with the eastern side of the island, let alone reach the settled districts, which was exactly what was intended.

Throughout the first half of 1822 Cuthbertson's little settlement grew apace. Sixty-seven more convicts were sent before the end of March, among them William Haines, who stole an iron pot and two gallons of wine from his master, for which he received 100 lashes and Macquarie Harbour for the rest of his original sentence. William McFarlane, George Nisbitt and William Thompson stole a boat to escape from the colony. They were sentenced to 100 lashes each and Macquarie Harbour for the duration of their original sentences. Walter Simpson was sent for forging and uttering an order for £3 10 s; he received fifty lashes and Macquarie Harbour for the rest of his original sentence. Stephen Orlando, who stole a silver watch, copped fifty lashes and Macquarie Harbour for three years. Joseph Thomas and Joseph Ollery, who stole and received promissory notes to the value of £20, received fifty lashes and three years each at Macquarie Harbour. Benjamin Gibbs and Richard Johnstone, who stole two sheep, got two years; Jacob Waterhouse stole a grubbing hoe, hemp and other articles from a lumber yard – 'the property of His Majesty', as the charge put it – and was sentenced to 100 lashes and Macquarie Harbour for two years. For a bit of variety a convict named J. Vicars was sentenced to Macquarie Harbour for seven years for setting fire to his overseer's hut; John Gillespie received two years for false accusation, and Joseph Stockley and John Newton were sent there in chains for absconding into the woods.

Commandant Cuthbertson was having large numbers of prisoners foisted on him long before he could get buildings up to house them or grow sufficient food to feed them. Back in Hobart Town, however, the government was putting the best gloss on the situation. According to an optimistic report in the *Hobart Town Gazette* of 16 July 1822 that largely reflected the government line, the settlement continued to make good progress: houses for the Commandant and Assistant Surgeon had been completed, as had the barracks, the store, the hospital and a building large enough to lodge the convicts. The *Gazette* assured its readers that by the next summer the settlement would be well supplied with vegetables, that coal was easily obtainable (it soon proved to be of very poor quality and of little use) and that the timber 'though growing mostly on marshy ground answers every expectation . . . and [affords the] most valuable product for human labour'. Timber-getting and boat-building were to be the real successes of the penal settlement.

A sour note is struck when the *Gazette* admits that in early March eight convicts had bolted into the bush, and that the two soldiers, three armed convicts and two kangaroo dogs who had gone in pursuit of them had not been heard of for three months. All thirteen escapees and pursuers were presumed dead. The *Gazette* commented that their melancholy fate had come about either from having ventured too far into the mountains where they had got lost, or that they had been killed by the Aboriginal people of the area. The newspaper speculated that it was most likely that the soldiers and trusted convicts had got lost and had perished from hunger, 'a fate which [also] most likely attended the gang of runaway convicts of which they were in pursuit'.

Although the *Gazette* did not mention this, the constant cold and wet conditions meant that in Pearce's time at Sarah Island rheumatism was widespread among convicts and officers alike. There was always a surgeon stationed at the settlement, and the ramshackle 'hospital' on nearby Grummet Island was staffed by untrained convict women, who sometimes also provided sexual favours to soldiers and convicts. The *Gazette* does mention that scurvy and dysentery had already broken out; they became endemic in the early years, largely due to the inadequate and often infected food.

•

So, despite the official optimism about the future of the Macquarie Harbour penal settlement, when Alexander Pearce was marched with other convicts in leg irons aboard the government brig the *Duke of York* under the command of Captain Chase in Hobart Town in mid-July 1822 to serve out the rest of his sentence, he was heading for a very grim place. The *Duke of York* was none other than the former brig *Sophia*, sold to the government after the death of its owner, Thomas William Birch, and renamed after the second son of George III. It set sail for Sarah Island with Convict No. 102 on board on one of its regular runs on 16 or 17 July 1822, midwinter in the southern hemisphere. The ship was used precisely because it was small with a shallow draft, drawing less than eight feet when loaded, and so it was able to negotiate Hell's Gates reasonably well. There was no special accommodation set aside for convicts on the *Duke of York*, so Pearce and his companions had to doss down as best they could in the hold on top of the cargo, or on the rock used as ship's ballast, with the stinking bilge water lapping around them. Besides Pearce there were Alexander Dalton, Thomas Murray, Dennis Redmond, Aaron Chevel, Benjamin Jackson and another unidentified convict.

On this particular trip the *Duke of York* sailed down the Derwent estuary, through Storm Bay and then turned west-sou'-west out into the Southern Ocean. For the next 160 kilometres (100 miles) south of the Tasmanian mainland they sailed directly into the Roaring Forties. Once the *Duke of York* had reached the South West Cape of Van Diemen's Land and began to tack to the north up the western coast of the island, the brig ran into another set of contrary winds that in winter are deflected south-east onto the west coast of Tasmania from the Australian mainland. Pearce and his mates were lucky. They were on a reasonably fast trip, for the *Duke of York* was back in Hobart Town in late August, which means that it reached Sarah Island in late July or early August. On the two-week voyage Pearce struck up a friendship with Alexander Dalton, an ex-soldier who had been transported after a trial in Gibraltar in 1818 and was also an Irishman.

On arrival at the settlement, before they were taken ashore, Pearce and his companions were thoroughly searched. The guards were looking especially for tobacco. As part of the punishment regimen all prisoners at Sarah Island were denied tobacco completely, which for nineteenth-century lower-class men and women was a serious deprivation. Given the men's addiction to smoking, a smuggling operation was soon in place, with the military being the main conduits and middle-men. Rum was occasionally provided as an antidote for rheumatism, but no other intoxicating drink was allowed. The convicts' original clothing was taken, as were any foodstuffs. They were then issued with their prison uniform: a pair of dark yellow pants made out of a light canvas material, shirts, a short half-yellow, half-black coarse woollen coat, leather boots, a neckcloth, a cap, a hammock or mattress and blankets. The outfit led to convicts being nicknamed 'canaries'. All items of clothing had the prison broad arrowhead symbol stencilled on them, plus the individual felon's number. New uniforms were issued every six months, but at Macquarie Harbour men hung onto their old clothes and often wore them underneath their new uniforms to keep warm.

There were already about 170 prisoners at Macquarie Harbour when Pearce and his companions arrived. Much of the rainforest on the island had already been cleared and quite a number of timber buildings erected, including residences for the officials, a barracks for the soldiers and the penitentiary or convict dormitory. In such a cold, wet climate, adequate food was essential to avoid scurvy and in theory each prisoner was supposed to receive ten pounds of bread and seven pounds of salt beef or salt pork per week, plus a daily ration of four ounces of skilly, a thin gruel or porridge-like soup made from oatmeal or wheat, flavoured with meat. Vegetables were supplied when available. Sometimes in the early days of the settlement the convicts were expected to do very heavy work on virtually starvation rations. In winter when the arrival of supply ships from Hobart Town was erratic due to the weather, rations were scantier and scurvy prevalent. James Spence, the Assistant Surgeon, reported to Hobart Town eight months after Pearce's arrival that 'At the formation of the settlement the prisoners were very much exposed to the inclemency of the weather, which was generally rainy, and being deficient of bed and body clothing, Dysentery and Rheumatism were very prevalent, but since the barracks have been formed these diseases are very much less frequent'.

To supplement their diet, which was little different from that of the convicts, the soldiers and officers hunted the local wildlife, especially the black swans, which are native to Australia. It is estimated that about 200,000 of them lived on the harbour prior to 1821. The swans' numbers were drastically reduced by 1833 when the penal settlement was finally closed, due to shooting and to the collection of their greenish-white eggs; a clutch could contain between four and ten. Nowadays you still do not see many black swans at Macquarie Harbour. The soldiers also hunted kangaroo, wombat and even echidna, the egg-laying spiny anteater that is a first cousin to the platypus, to get fresh meat. None of this was available to the convicts, who were denied fresh meat unless they were in hospital.

The prison regimen at Sarah Island was unremitting. Men were often forced to work in irons and shackles. An endemic part of life was the lash, which was used freely and brutally for even the slightest infraction of the regulations. As a magistrate the Commandant could order up to 100 lashes and he often did so with the vicious cat-o'-nine-tails. Between 1822 and 1826 a total of 835 convicts received 32,723 lashes, or about thirty-nine for every man there in a five-year period. Each lash was meticulously noted and the records sent to the Principal Superintendent in the Convict Department in Hobart Town. By way of comparison, between March 1815 and November 1817 in New South Wales, the Parramatta Bench of Magistrates handed out 11,321 lashes to just 200 offenders, an average of fifty-six lashes per offender. These figures were far in excess of anything happening in the United Kingdom at the time which, with a much larger population, only had an average of 234 court-ordered floggings per year in the whole period of 1811 to 1827.

Every morning, except Christmas Day and the King's Birthday (then always celebrated on 23 April), Pearce and the other convicts rose when the bell rang at around six in the roughly built wooden penitentiary, or prisoners' dormitory. This was a hotchpotch of buildings divided into sections, which was eventually replaced in the middle of the decade by a stone building, the remnants of which still survive. But around the beginning of the twentieth century it seems that someone from nearby Queenstown tried to blow it up, feeling that all vestiges of convictism in Tasmania should be eliminated, so that the local population could rid themselves of the so-called 'stain' inherited from their early history. In a vivid demonstration of changing attitudes, Sarah Island is now to be preserved for future generations as both a historical site and as part of the World Heritage Area.

The men in the dormitory slept, as convicts in government service usually did at this period, in hammocks strung from wooden frames, or if these were not available, they simply kipped down on the floor as best they could. Hammocks were a very effective way of housing large numbers of men in a small space, while still maintaining some level of basic cleanliness. As Pearce and the other men slowly arose in the morning there would have still been some residual heat coming from the stone fireplaces in the penitentiary. This was probably the only time of the day when their clothes were reasonably dry and their bodies warm. Men could go to the privies, which were just across from the penitentiary, and were built out over a low cliff face with the high tide acting as a natural flushing mechanism. Pearce would then have dressed in his basic prison uniform.

As the weak midwinter sun was rising, the men assembled on a basic parade ground, and the convict muster began when Lieutenant Cuthbertson arrived with his small contingent of troops. They were dressed in bright red coats with narrow white stripes and silver buttons, white crossed shoulder belts, epaulettes, dark grey pants and knee-length black boots. Their colourful uniforms and black, cylindrical, peaked shako caps with regimental badges, each one crowned with a red-and-white woollen pompon, would have looked bizarrely out of place against the background of cool temperate rainforest, surrounded by a grey, miserable southern sky that threatened rain. Since this was the 48th Regiment, whose proudest moment was back in 1809 in the Iberian peninsula fighting against Napoleon, their badge had one word emblazoned on it to remind them of their day of glory – 'Talavera'.

At the muster the convicts were counted, and then Cuthbertson made announcements and assigned the work gangs to their duties in either logging operations or mining the superficial and useless coal. Better behaved prisoners on 'billets' (lighter duties) were sent either to work in the gardens on Sarah Island or to serve as tradesmen and overseers. But the unskilled majority laboured in the gangs over on the mainland around Kelly's Basin or up the Gordon River. Once assigned, those working off the island were marched the short distance down to the jetty, and before getting into their boats they were searched for food that could supplement their diet, or be used in an attempted escape. The men then rowed themselves away from the jetty and out onto Macquarie Harbour. Throughout winter it was damp and cold in the early morning, and the sea could often be turbulent, especially when there was a big swell running or the wind was a westerly or sou'-westerly.

The convicts quickly came to hate the dark brown, tannin-stained water, which they thought looked like discoloured piss. In a rough sea it often whipped up into an ugly froth. The stale urine colour was the result of the thick peat deposits through which the fresh water percolated before joining the rivers and creeks that flowed into the harbour. As is usual where fresh and sea water mix, the harbour's surface water was fresh, whereas the deeper water was salt. Despite its colour the water was perfectly pure, and serious pollution did not come to Macquarie Harbour until the early twentieth century when the Mount Lyell Mining Company of Queenstown began dumping its toxic waste there via the King River. As the convicts rowed their whaleboats across to Kelly's Basin, the large black swans took off slowly and awkwardly into the cold, misty air, white under-wing-tips and bright red beaks a striking contrast to their jet-black bodies.

•

When he arrived at Sarah Island Pearce had quickly marked himself as a man who could not adjust to prison life and for whom penal discipline was an almost impossible burden. For him escape was the only option. It was quite clear from his previous three ill-planned and impulsive attempts at bolting into the bush that it did not matter where he went, or with whom. He also did not care what the consequences of running away might be, as long as he was free from detention. Sarah Island had been established precisely for men like him, its operating premise being that if the Pearces of this world were isolated completely in a dank, jungle wilderness and subjected to rules and regulations, unremitting supervision and very hard work, they would eventually knuckle under and submit. Having been broken, they could then be trained to abandon their ungodly, criminal ways and become obedient prisoners who would be transformed into productive and law-abiding subjects of the Crown.

Pearce was assigned to a work gang in which escape was very much the topic of conversation. This gang of eight men worked around Kelly's Basin in logging operations. Together they felled, prepared and lashed together logs of Huon pine, celery-top pine, blackwood and myrtle, which were rafted to the island where they were processed and loaded on the *Duke of York* and other ships for transportation to Hobart Town. The most prized of these trees was Huon pine, a yellowish timber that was – and still is – highly regarded for ship-building. Found only in Tasmania, the trees are extremely slow-growing, needing heavy rainfall for them to prosper. At 30 metres (95 feet) high, a mature tree could have been a sapling when Socrates flourished in Athens 2500 years ago. Even after it has been chopped down the wood has an amazing ability to survive, so that timber from a tree in Pearce's time can still be used today. Its longevity is derived from a special oil it produces, which retards the growth of destructive fungi.

The convicts not only felled the trees and prepared the logs for flotation across the harbour by stripping them of their branches and bark, but at day's end they had to assemble and tow the large rafts of logs back to the island's saw pits. Working in freezing water up to their chests, they lashed the logs together in lateral groups to construct the rafts. If there was any swell at all running, towing these huge rafts behind them as they rowed across the harbour became a dangerous as well as an exhausting job. A drawing from about 1831 by Lemprière depicts three of these boats towing fifty logs, bound together in five groups

Thomas James Lemprière, *Philips Island (from the eastern shore of Macquarie Harbour)*, ca 1828. Grey ink wash on paper. The whale boat is the kind used for getting logging crews across to the mainland for logging operations. (Courtesy Allport Library and Museum of Fine Arts, State Library of Tasmania.)

of ten each to make up one enormous raft. The smaller lead boat has six oarsmen and the two larger boats behind have eight apiece. The boats are attached to each other by ropes and look like diesel locomotives hauling an extremely heavy freight-train. The water is dead calm, which would have been essential for such an operation.

Back at Sarah Island the logs were landed and milled into sawn timber. The major difficulty facing the government was in getting the prepared timber from Sarah Island to Hobart Town in heavily laden ships which had to navigate the narrow entrance, treacherous rip and sandbar at Hell's Gates, as well as the perilous seas between Macquarie Harbour and the colony's capital. The authorities soon realised that it would be much more efficient to use the timber to construct ships on the island itself, and as a result a ship-building industry was established in 1824. It grew rapidly after the arrival in 1828 of the Scottish-born and Boston-trained shipwright, David Hoy, under whom the shipyard

Thomas James Lemprière, *Grummet Island Off Sarah Island*, ca 1828, Grey ink wash on paper. Note the two whale boats towing a large raft of logs from Kelly's Basin to Sarah Island. (Courtesy Allport Library and Museum of Fine Arts, State Library of Tasmania.)

became by far the most productive in Australia. Before its closure in 1833 Hoy had designed and built ninety-six ships and boats. Largely as a result of his efforts, Macquarie Harbour became an industrial site where the prisoners were able to gain some autonomy and ability to use the system because their labour was needed for boat-building.

•

Given the hardship at Sarah Island in the early days of the settlement and his own obstreperous nature, Pearce was lucky to find himself in a work gang determined to escape. The most influential man in his group was an Englishman named Robert Greenhill, who also seemed to find the constraints of convict existence unbearable. He had been sentenced to transportation for fourteen years for 'larceny from a person' at the Middlesex Assizes in the session commencing 28 June 1820. He had been born in 1790 and his occupation is listed in the Newgate Jail records as 'mariner'. He had stolen a coat. The person from whom he had filched it and who had had him charged was none other than his wife, Judith Greenhill! Perhaps he had been away at sea for too long and Judith had taken up with someone else. Or perhaps he was a violent drunk who was obnoxious to live with when he was on shore leave. Perhaps she was just sick of him. Whatever the cause, there was obviously no love lost between the two. Greenhill arrived in Van Diemen's Land, aged thirty-one, on the *Lady Ridley* on 27 June 1821.

Greenhill's closest mate was Matthew Travers (sometimes called 'Trevors' or 'Travis'), a 27-year-old Irish labourer from County Dublin, who had been given a life sentence for the crime of stealing at the County Kildare Sessions in July 1816. He had arrived in Van Diemen's Land on the ship *Pilot* in late 1817. Greenhill and Travers had met in the colony and struck up a friendship, apparently when they were working as convict shepherds in the back country beyond the settlement of New Norfolk, north-west of Hobart Town in the Derwent valley. In the early 1820s this isolated and dangerous area was only just being settled by Europeans, and the frontier between white settlement and Aboriginal land was about 55 kilometres (35 miles) beyond New Norfolk. The Aborigines of the Big River tribe, who traditionally occupied this region, strongly resented European incursions into their land, and they actively resisted white settlement. Convict shepherds such as Greenhill and Travers were especially vulnerable to Aboriginal reprisal raids with spears and clubs. So men tended to look out for one another and especially for their good mates.

Until he met Greenhill, Travers had been a well-behaved convict and had even rented some land on which he ran about 150 sheep of his own. However, despite his good record, and no doubt influenced by Greenhill, Travers began to chafe against the constrictions of convict life. In September 1821 he 'concealed himself on board the ship *Grace* with intent to escape from the colony'. He was caught, lost his leave pass and received twenty-five lashes. He was twice more before the magistrates in December: first for missing the church muster, and secondly for neglect of duty, for which he received another twenty-five lashes from Magistrate Humphrey. Then on 30 March 1821 Travers and Greenhill, together with three other prisoners, Richard Hurlstone, John Wilkinsen and William Walker, attempted to escape from Van Diemen's Land by 'absconding from the public works and feloniously stealing and carrying away a schooner' moored on the Derwent River near Hobart Town, owned by none other than Sorell's and Mrs Kent's nemesis, Anthony Fenn Kemp. While many convicts bolted into the bush in escape attempts, it was more unusual to try to flee by stealing a boat. Indeed, the attempted hijacking of a boat was a serious offence, for it amounted to an act of piracy.

Greenhill, Travers and Hurlstone were caught and sentenced to 150 lashes each and incarceration in a place of secondary punishment – Sarah Island. On the night after they were caught trying to steal the schooner, they again attempted to escape. They were quickly recaptured but only received 25 lashes because, as the *Hobart Town Gazette* put it, 'They appeared very sorry for their offence'. An excess of mercy toward the convict population was not the usual characteristic of Hobart Town magistrates, including the Reverend Robert Knopwood, who was on the bench at the time. Perhaps it was because the men were already up for 150 lashes? Whatever happened is not clear, but the second part of their sentence stood, and they were shipped to Sarah Island in early May 1822 on the *Duke of York*. Walker and Wilkinsen were not caught until early October. They were tried before Knopwood and received the same sentence of 150 lashes and transportation to Macquarie Harbour. But by then both Greenhill and Travers were dead.

Besides Pearce, Greenhill and Travers, the work gang also included No. 102's new mate, Alexander Dalton, the pock-pitted, 25-year-old Irish ex-soldier from Kilkenny who had served in Gibraltar and who had been transported from there to Van Diemen's Land. After working on assignment in the colony, he had been up on charges of being drunk and disorderly, assaulting and kicking his overseer (for which he received fifty lashes), and neglect of duty (twenty-five lashes). On 6 July 1822 he perjured himself when giving evidence on behalf of a convict mate, for which offence he was sentenced to 100 lashes and transportation to Sarah Island for the rest of his original sentence.

The 22-year-old English farm labourer, Thomas Bodenham, was the only one in the work gang who had any record of violence. He had been before the bench ten times during his first three years in Van Diemen's Land. The charges included stealing and receiving stolen goods, neglect of duty, being drunk and disorderly, and missing church muster. On 2 May 1822 he was charged with 'Assaulting and beating William Reason on the King's Highway [between Hobart Town and Launceston] and putting him in bodily fear and stealing from his person £4-3-6 and a pocket book with several notes of hand in it'. The attack earned him the penalty of working out four years of his seven-year sentence at Sarah Island.

Also in the work gang was William Kennerly, who occasionally used the alias 'Bill Cornelius'. He would be the first among them to bruit the notion of cannibalism in the days ahead. Probably of Irish origin, he had received a seven-year sentence at Middlesex. After serving some time near George Town in the north of Van Diemen's Land, he was sentenced to Sarah Island for 'absconding from the public works gang . . . and remaining absent until apprehended'. John Mather, a 24-year-old bread baker by trade, was a fair-headed and ruddy-faced Scotsman from Dumfries who had received fifty lashes for misconduct and abusing his overseer, and twenty-five more for being absent from his lodgings. He had been sent to Sarah Island for forging an order for £15.

The oldest man among them, probably in his late fifties, went by the nickname of 'Little Brown', no doubt an ironic reference to his height. In official documentation he was known as both 'William' and 'Edward' Brown. There is good evidence that Brown might have at one time been an assigned convict servant for the Reverend Knopwood. Certainly, an Edward Brown, one of the parson's convicts, was given twenty-five lashes and sent to Macquarie Harbour for five years for 'stealing two shirts, the property of his master'. In any event, Little Brown was an 'old lag', a long-term convict who had had the life beaten out of him by the system. It is apparent that he went along with the others in the work gang not really knowing what he was getting himself into, and in the end he simply did not have the stamina to keep up with them.

Greenhill was intelligent and a natural leader and he soon quietly suggested to the men in his work gang that despite what their jailers said, escape from Macquarie Harbour was possible. In fact, within two months of the establishment of the penal colony in January 1822, eight convicts had already escaped into the bush: John Green and Joseph Saunders absconded on 4 March 1822, to be followed six days later by Patrick Cheevors, Henry and Philip Flanagan, Patrick Hickey, Matthew McKivion and John Martin. They were all 'supposed to have perished in the woods', either through becoming lost or being killed by the local Aborigines. On 17 March Cuthbertson sent two of his soldiers, Reynolds and Parker, along with three trusted convicts, George Groves, William Smith and John Walker, as well as kangaroo dogs, in pursuit, but they also disappeared. An argument had broken out among them soon after they had landed on the mainland, but no sign was ever seen of any of them again. The cold banality of the official explanation ominously notes that 'they were all armed'. The total disappearance in the bush of convicts and soldiers within two months of the foundation of Sarah Island seemed to support Sorell's view that a successful escape in a southerly or easterly direction toward the settled parts of Van Diemen's Land was impossible, and that it would lead to disaster and death for the escapees, either from starvation or from the action of hostile Aborigines. But Greenhill reassured his mates that this was merely propaganda, arguing that the previous escapees had disappeared completely because they had already reached the settled districts and had not been recaptured. He suggested that they might even have escaped from Van Diemen's Land altogether.

Whether the previous escape had been successful or not was irrelevant now to Pearce, Greenhill and the others because they were not going to try the overland route at all, but planned instead to seize a whaleboat while they worked over on the mainland at Kelly's Basin, and sail it out through Hell's Gates to freedom. Presumably they were going to attempt this ambitious plan under the cover of darkness to avoid detection by the pilot and the four soldiers stationed at the harbour entrance. Once out in the Southern Ocean they would sail to any port in the world that would put them beyond the reach of British justice.

A rural labourer like Pearce might never have travelled much further than 35 kilometres (20 miles) from where he was born, except if he were unlucky enough to be transported to Van Diemen's Land. Hence he would have only had the vaguest idea of the exact locations of foreign countries, as would most of his fellow convicts, the majority of whom were transported on ships which either made non-stop trips to Sydney and Hobart Town, or at the most stopped at one port, usually Rio de Janeiro. As a sailor Greenhill, however, would not have been so geographically naïve and may well have had a destination in mind for the whaleboat escape. He would almost certainly have known about Batavia (now Jakarta) in the Dutch East Indies, a journey of about 8850 kilometres (5500 miles) nor'-nor'-west of Van Diemen's Land, as well as ports in southern China, or even Japan. And then there was the vast Pacific Ocean and its many islands.

While it may seem inconceivable to us today that men would undertake a long and precarious journey in such a small boat, we need to remember how desperate they were and that they knew that escape by sea was not impossible. For instance, in 1819 a party of convicts boarded and stole the 40-foot brig *Young Lachlan* from Hobart Town, and sailed her to Java, where they destroyed the ship and disappeared. The *Governor Sorell* was seized in 1820 and the *Sea Flower* in 1822. Even a ship as large as the *Castle Forbes* was briefly taken over after it had dropped its convicts and sailed south down to the Huon River to pick up a timber consignment for India. The spot is now known as *Castle Forbes Bay*. And two years after the Pearce escape, in June 1824, thirteen convicts led by one Matthew Brady grabbed the whaleboat *Blue-Eyed Maid* in Macquarie Harbour and sailed her to the Derwent, where they abandoned the boat and turned to bushranging. The brig *Cyprus* was seized in Macquarie Harbour in the late 1820s and sailed to Polynesia, and in January 1834 ten convicts from Macquarie Harbour seized a 121-ton brig, the *Frederick*, and sailed her to Chile. So Greenhill's idea was plausible. The hardest task would be to get the whaleboat out of Macquarie Harbour without it being spotted.

Greenhill, Pearce and the others were forced to put their escape plan into action prematurely on the morning of Friday, 20 September 1822. They had just found out that James Lucas, the pilot at Hell's Gates, was coming down the harbour that very day with a boatload of whale oil that, as a lucrative sideline, he sold to the officers at Sarah Island. Pearce and the others needed supplies for their journey, and they intended to steal Lucas's provisions while he was at the island, and then slip out through Hell's Gates in the dark to avoid being seen by the soldiers stationed at the harbour entrance. Very probably they learned of Lucas's movements from John Douglas, an intelligent and literate convict who acted as clerk to both the Commissariat and the Commandant, and who was not averse to helping prisoners. Later Douglas was to provide information about excessive and illegal punishment of convicts at Sarah Island to members of parliament in London.

Pearce's work gang was to be guarded that day by only one overseer, Constable Logan, and they reckoned that they would easily be able to overpower him. The one hitch was that a couple of days before, Greenhill had been assigned to another work gang collecting coal from the superficial excavations on the mainland, just inland from the appropriately named Coal Head. This was 14 kilometres (9 miles) north of Kelly's Basin where the rest of the group were working in the logging operations. Now they faced a dilemma, for Greenhill's navigational skills were essential if they were to sail their way to freedom. Quickly they devised a new strategy: the seven of them would overpower Constable Logan at Kelly's Basin, row north around the coast of the harbour to Coal Head in the boat in which they had come over to the mainland, commandeer another larger whaleboat that was anchored nearby and pick up Greenhill. Then they would destroy their own boat, row up to Hell's Gates, where they would raid Lucas's store and escape under cover of darkness through Hell's Gates out into the Southern Ocean. Given the distances involved this would have taken them all day and it would have been dark by the time they got to the harbour entrance.

Setting a northward course they would sail up the west coast of Van Diemen's Land and head east through Bass Strait and out into the Pacific Ocean, or wherever fate took them. Pearce says that they also discussed Hobart Town as a possible destination, probably because it was a place they knew and it was relatively close, although there was a considerable risk that they would be recognised. They probably hoped they could steal a bigger boat there; after all, Greenhill and Travers had been sent to Macquarie

Harbour precisely for attempting to steal Kemp's schooner.

The weather at dawn that Friday morning was what one would expect in early spring – overcast and cold. The morning muster began just as a weak sun was beginning to cast some light from behind Mount Sorell. Pearce and the others stood together only half-listening to the instructions being announced by the Commandant, for they were worried about picking up Greenhill. They would now have to land near the mines, find him and get him aboard before they could discreetly row north up the harbour. Their landing at Coal Head was going to add enormously to the risk that they would be caught. If they were captured the flogging that would follow would be severe – 100 lashes – and they would also probably serve time in solitary and several months working in leg-irons and chains.

After the muster, the usual search occurred before they boarded their boat to row across to Kelly's Basin. As they rowed, Constable Logan sat comfortably in the stern smoking his pipe. Pearce and the other prisoners hated men like Logan, seeing them as class traitors who had ingratiated themselves with the authorities either through good behaviour or by impressing Brevet-Major Thomas Bell, Inspector of Public Works. Overseers like Logan were not paid, but were better treated than ordinary prisoners. They were usually unarmed and their real power lay in their ability to report a man for insubordination, laziness, neglect of work, swearing or even losing an item from slops. A report from Logan to Cuthbertson would almost certainly lead to a flogging, which might even be followed by a stint in solitary confinement or a month or more of working in leg irons. Using prisoners to guard prisoners was effective; it was inexpensive and therefore appealed to the convict administration in Hobart Town and the Colonial Office bureaucrats in Downing Street.

Although rain in early spring was common, there was none that morning, though it was very overcast. When they got to their workplace, the men laboured in a kind of misty half-light. It was this way much of the time and the convicts often longed to see and feel the sun. The area around Kelly's Basin is generally flat, but it is hard to reconstruct today exactly what the forest would have been like in 1822. In the late 1890s the town of Pillinger was established on Kelly's Basin as a port for shipping out the copper produced by North Mount Lyell Company. In the late 1890s a 60-kilometre (36-mile) railway line was pushed through to the port by the company from the mine site just east of Queenstown. During the period of Pillinger's prosperity about 1000 people lived in the area. Much of the rainforest was cleared inland from the Basin; it is only now returning to its pristine state and the torn-up but excellently graded former railway track is used for bushwalking.

However, in Pearce's time we can assume that the forest was a mixed one in which various types of beech trees as well as extensive stands of Huon pine grew, all of which are now gone. At present stands of wet sclerophyll or eucalypt forest are found on both the northern and southern shores of the Basin, although there is some scrub, and around the former port the rainforest is recovering. From the shoreline to about 5 kilometres (3 miles) inland the landscape is fairly flat. Here the rainforest is relatively open, although near the shallow gullies and swiftly flowing creeks there is a very thick understorey dominated by flowering shrubs, myrtle and leatherwood. So the escape party would have had some experience of rainforests and been familiar with working in waterlogged conditions. But none of this could have possibly prepared them for the difficulties that lay ahead.

Despite the sweat induced by the back-breaking work of felling, stripping, cutting, pruning and preparing the Huon pine logs for flotation back to the island, they still found it dreadfully cold work. But they were also excited.

Liberty was beckoning, and they looked forward to it nervously.

4

The Transit of Hell

Constable Logan didn't stand a chance, even if he had tried to resist. At seven to one, the odds against the unarmed overseer were too great. They jumped him during their break for breakfast when his guard was down and he was enjoying his cup of sweet tea. Pearce is vague about exactly what happened next, but it is likely that they tied Logan to a tree in the forest after stripping him of everything they could use, including his clothes. The temptation to wreak some form of revenge on him must have been great, especially given that several of them had probably suffered floggings or punishment because of his reports to the Commandant. But there is no record that they did so, and he was alive and well a year later, and still acting as an overseer in the very gang to which Pearce was assigned after his return to Macquarie Harbour.

The men had arrived at Kelly's Basin just after dawn and had worked until it was time for their first meal of the day around 9 a.m. It consisted of a serving of bread and skilly, their only meal for the day until they returned to Sarah Island in the evening. Given that they were doing very heavy work, this diet was completely inadequate. To prevent prisoners from hoarding their bread rations for escape attempts, ergot, a fungal disease of rye, was added to the dough in the baking process to make it go stale and then rotten quickly. We now know that ergot has hallucinogenic qualities and there is a possibility that an accumulation of this fungus in their systems may have affected Pearce and the others later on during their ordeal when they came to contemplate the act of cannibalism.

With Logan taken care of, the escape began in earnest and the men returned to their whaleboat tied up at the jetty. About 6 metres (20 feet) in length with places for six oarsmen, the boat was double-ended, very seaworthy and designed for quick turning and use in rough weather. It had no rudder and the steersman guided it with an oar trailing aft. This was the moment when the whole plan could fall apart. They had to make their way out of Kelly's Basin and turn north across the open entrance to Farm Cove, the next bay, and then on up to Coal Head, a distance of about 11 kilometres (about 6 miles). They still would have been just visible from Sarah Island, except for the brief time when they were behind Philips Island, but it would have been difficult to see something so low in the water and the whaleboat would have been hard to pick out against the shoreline. But they could be spotted by any sharp-eyed overseer or soldier. In their favour was all the activity associated with logging and coal-gathering around the harbour, so convicts, soldiers or anyone else seeing them might well have presumed that they were on official business.

Up at the coal works Bob Greenhill would have been on the lookout for them. Pearce says, 'as soon as ... [he] perceived the boat approaching ... he was in perfect readiness to go with us'. Here there was a bigger whaleboat with a lugsail on a short mast, and while one man remained with the boats, Pearce, Greenhill and the others, armed with axes, went to the miners' hut, smashed down the door and took 'therefrom all the provisions we could find', which amounted to about ten pounds of flour, six pounds of beef and an axe. This was to be their entire food supply for the next week until they turned to the consumption of human flesh. Pearce reports that they also poured water over the wood pyres that had been prepared to signal escapes to prevent the overseers lighting them and sending smoke-signals to the military lookout on Sarah Island to let them know that a convict break-out had occurred. By then it would have been just after midday.

Although Pearce is not clear as to the order in which things happened next, luck was not on their side. It seems that, first, they swamped the smaller boat so it could not be used to pursue them. Then, having loaded their meagre supplies, the men took to the larger whaleboat. Their intention was to row north up the harbour, which would have taken the whole afternoon and early evening, raid Lucas's store and then slip out under the cover of night through Hell's Gates. But they had only gone about 500 metres (a third of a mile) when they thought they saw a light astern, and Pearce said, 'We observed the miners making fires all along the beach'. They had not drenched the signal pyres sufficiently, and the overseers and convicts from the mines had been able to ignite them quickly. Perhaps it was just by chance that someone had seen the boat. In any event, they knew that once the break-out signal had been sighted at Sarah Island, the Commandant would send boats in pursuit and would alert the troops at Hell's Gates via the semaphore signalling system. The whole escape plan was unravelling.

The escapees had to quickly make a basic decision: should they continue by sea, hoping to out-row any pursuers, or alter their plan and head inland by foot? They chose the bush.

They beached the whaleboat just north of Coal Head, probably at a point where a small creek flowed down to the beach, and Pearce reports that 'a consultation took place between us respecting the manner in which we should dispose of the boat and sails. Upon which we decided to cut her to pieces and to secret [sic] the sails near the place where we was'. He also says that it was Greenhill, supported by Travers, who suggested destroying the boat. The ex-mariner was already beginning to assume leadership of the group. It is not clear why they went to the trouble of cutting up the boat, but it certainly committed them to an overland escape route. By now it was early afternoon and their only course, short of surrendering, was to head into the bush along the creek, every man carrying an equal share of the luggage.

The overland route would lead them in an easterly direction toward the sparsely populated 'settled districts' in the centre of the island. Greenhill and Travers, as well as Pearce, had already lived in the back country to the north-west of Hobart Town and New Norfolk. However, they would have had only the most general notion of where Macquarie Harbour was in relation to the rest of the island. Terry Reid, Senior Ranger for the Tasmanian Parks and Wildlife Service in Queenstown, who was born on the west coast, says that it is easy to make mistakes in navigation in the type of terrain the escapees were now entering. 'We use maps and sometimes fly over the country in a helicopter or fixed-wing aircraft in order to pick out a route. Greenhill would have had to do it by trial and error, often in misty, miserable weather'. Reid points out that if the chosen route is impenetrable, modern walkers can always back out and try another approach. But the escapees did not have this luxury. Fear of pursuit meant that they had to keep going no matter what the landscape was like, although the upside was that any soldiers following them would have faced the same difficulties.

Greenhill correctly sensed that they had to head pretty much due east and, despite all the vicissitudes of the journey and the difficulty of the country through which they travelled, he maintained a steady easterly course for more than forty days, until he was killed by Pearce. It was an extraordinary feat of navigation by dead-reckoning, using the sun and stars without the benefit of a compass. The others were totally dependent on him; clearly

Greenhill was drawing on his life at sea and his experience of foreign places. Without him the others would have been completely lost.

Their immediate task, however, was to get as far from Macquarie Harbour as they could, in as short a time as possible before Cuthbertson sent troops in pursuit. By going directly inland they precluded the possibility of the soldiers catching up with them by boat. But by choosing such a route they faced an even more formidable reality: the implacability of the natural world, and the indifferent otherness of the Tasmanian bush.

The place on the coast where they abandoned the boat was gently sloping, lightly timbered rainforest without a lot of understorey. It also gave them good cover. After about 3 kilometres (1.8 miles) moving inland they came to open country, but were hidden by the coastal forest from Sarah Island. In this area they would have crossed the creek-sized upper reaches of the Braddon River. They had set out on an east-north-easterly course toward the 1144-metre (3753-foot) Mount Sorell, and Pearce reports that they were at its base by about three o'clock in the afternoon. They had probably followed the creek up to the base of the southern side of the mountain. He says that on ascending Mount Sorell 'we could very distinctly perceive Macquarie Harbour and the Island which is inhabited by the officers and military. We secreted ourselves as much as we possibly could behind the brushiest parts of the mountain we could find, lest the Commandant by the assistance of his telescope perceive us. The principal part of the mountain being so barren and we being so many in number, we travelled on in this cautious manner until we arrived at the summit of the mountain'.

This matter-of-fact account glosses over the enormous difficulty they would have had climbing Mount Sorell. Terry Reid says that it would be possible to climb to the ridge-line in an afternoon, especially given that most of the escapees were young,

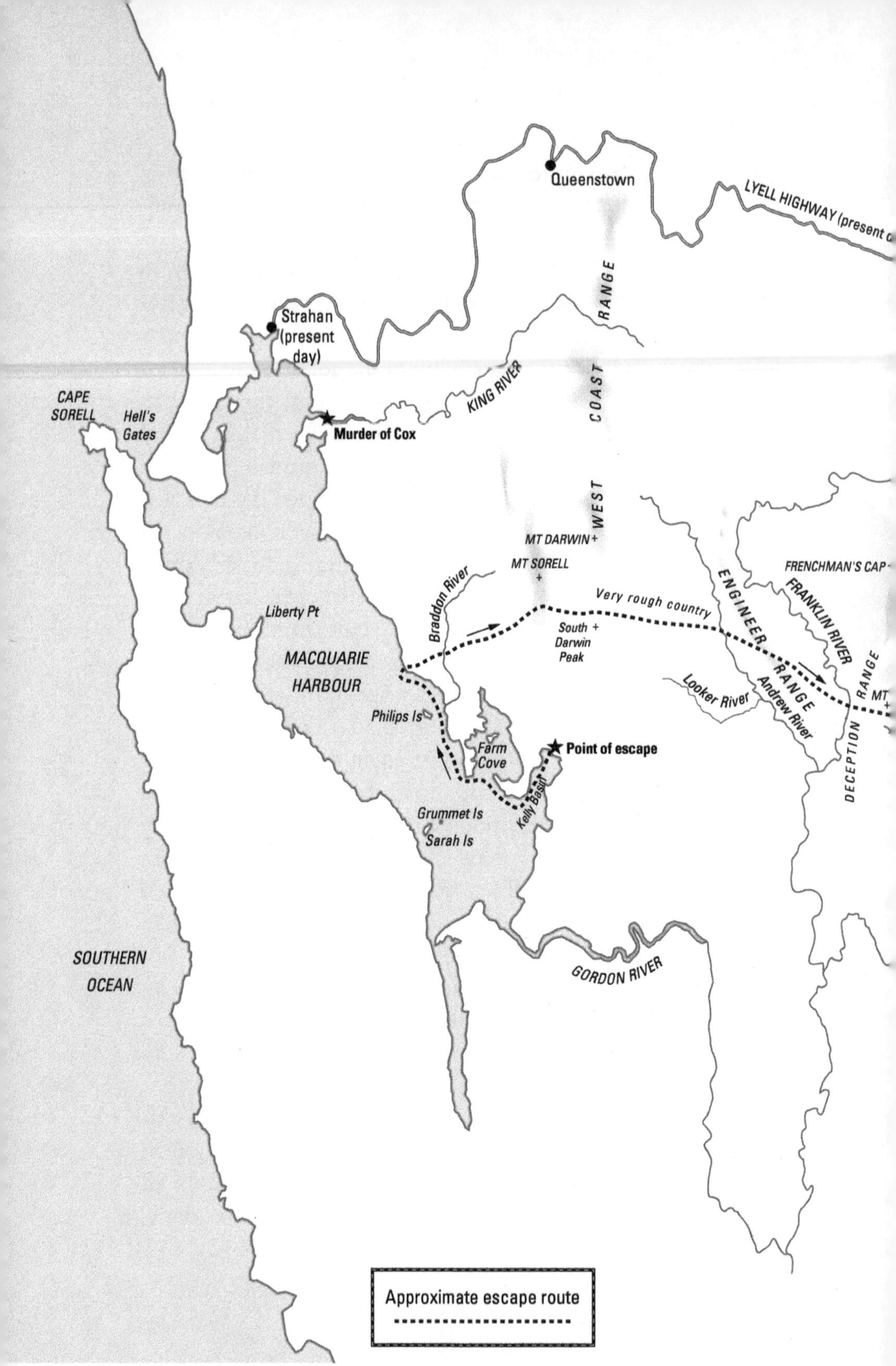

Macquarie Harbour area.

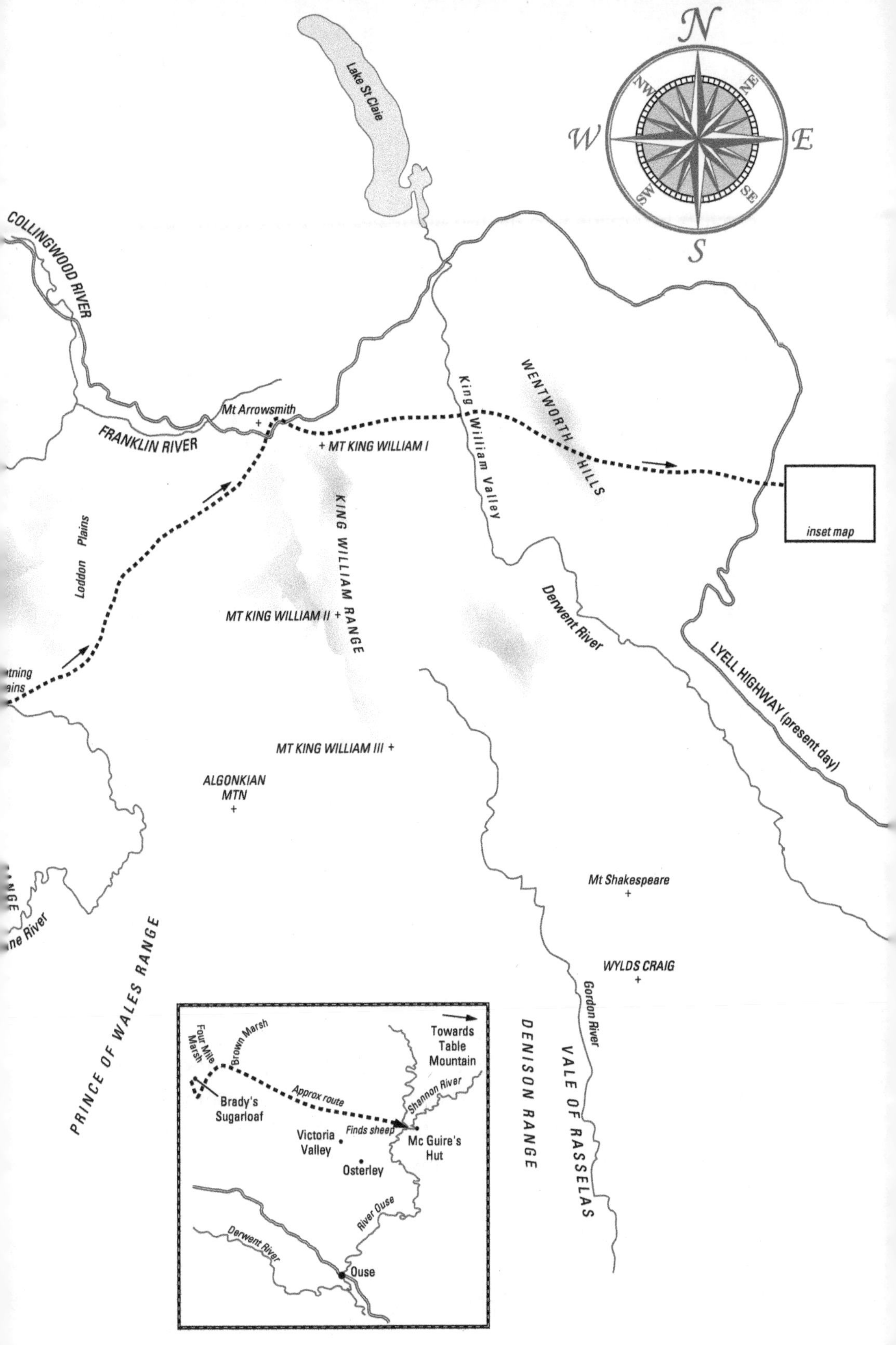
N
NW
NE
W
E
SW
SE
S
Lake St Claie
COLLINGWOOD RIVER
FRANKLIN RIVER
Mt Arrowsmith
MT KING WILLIAM I
King William Valley
WENTWORTH HILLS
inset map
Loddon Plains
KING WILLIAM RANGE
MT KING WILLIAM II
Derwent River
LYELL HIGHWAY (present day)
MT KING WILLIAM III
ALGONKIAN MTN
Mt Shakespeare
WYLDS CRAIG
Gordon River
PRINCE OF WALES RANGE
DENISON RANGE
VALE OF RASSELAS
Four Mile Marsh
Brown Marsh
Towards Table Mountain
Approx route
Shannon River
Brady's Sugarloaf
Finds sheep
Victoria Valley
Mc Guire's Hut
Osterley
River Ouse
Derwent River
Ouse

wiry and strong, and this was their first day out. But he also points out that the climb is a very arduous one. Certainly, other convicts had made it to the top of the nearby 1033-metre (3389-feet) high Mount Darwin. Later explorers found convict shackles there, so someone had got that far with their ankle-locking devices still on; the climb must have been horrendously difficult and painful. They either knocked them off with a stone and went on until they were irretrievably lost, or else they perished there, where the carrion-eating Tasmanian devils would have disposed of the bodies. It is not recorded if any bones were left.

By nightfall the Pearce party was at the top of Mount Sorell or, more likely, the lower ridge-line to the south of the peak. But they knew that all the way up the steep rock-face they would be exposed because there would be a clear line of sight from Sarah Island 8 kilometres away (5 miles), and the afternoon sun would have provided a spotlight for the Commandant peering through his telescope at the escaping convicts. Unless he was totally incompetent – and nothing indicates that he was – it is most likely that Cuthbertson would have noticed the eight men on the bare and exposed western elevation of Mount Sorell.

The escapees fully expected that the Commandant would send soldiers after them. Yet Cuthbertson's hands were tied to some extent. Seven months before he had already lost two soldiers and three reliable convicts whom he'd sent on a wild-goose chase after a group of six escaping prisoners. With only a very small military contingent under his command – about sixteen men – it is most likely that he would have decided to allow this second party of fleeing convicts to make their way without pursuit. Either the escapees would soon return from the inhospitable bush, their tails between their legs, to face their punishment, or else nature would do his work for him and, like the previous groups of escapees, Pearce and his companions would be listed in the official records as 'Supposed to have perished in the woods'. So why waste energy and resources in any attempt to recapture them? For the moment Cuthbertson would have eight fewer mouths to feed, although there would soon be more convicts on their way from Hobart Town to take their places. Even so the men on the run did everything they could to elude 'the vigilant search we were confident would be made after [us]'.

They had climbed up to at least the ridge-line from sea level in about three hours under difficult conditions. Once at the top they set up camp for the night, 'after making', Pearce says, 'the necessary fires for securing ourselves from the inclemency of the weather and regaling ourselves with a little of our provisions after the fatigues of the day's journey'. Perhaps they gave three muted cheers for freedom and no doubt they felt that they had 'beaten the bastards' back at Sarah Island. But it had started to rain and their clothes were little or no protection from a dampness that would slowly begin to permeate their very beings. It was desperately cold during the night on the exposed mountain. Vigilance was their watchword: 'We considered it requisite that one of us should watch while the others slept'.

'Early the next morning we arose after arranging matters respecting our luggage. [We] kept to the tops of the mountains for our travelling' whenever possible to avoid any pursuing troops. In other words, they were following the ridge-lines, which experienced bushwalkers in this area agree was probably the best way to go. Pearce tells us that 'we made toward the east, keeping off Gordon's River for fear of the soldiers'. Since at this point they were about 17 kilometres (10½ miles) due north of the Gordon River, they had little to fear from the military. But they did not know this.

With the exception of Mount Sorell, Frenchman's Cap and the Gordon River, none of the geographical features of the landscape had been named in 1822, and Pearce's narratives of the journey are vague on exact locations. From the information given in the Pearce accounts, a reasonably accurate estimate can be made most of the time to within about 15 kilometres (just over 9 miles) of their actual route.

As soon as they descended the eastern side of Mount Sorell that morning, they would have been in the narrow valley of the Clark River, which at that point was more of a creek. After fording it and getting through some rainforest of medium density, they would have had to climb steeply to the Darwin Plateau, the ridge-line between Mount Darwin and the South Darwin Peak. Like Mount Sorell, the Darwin Range is a steep, rocky, exposed escarpment about 650 metres (2130 feet) high on a direct north to south alignment, and descending from it would have involved in places hand-over-hand rock-climbs. This type of terrain quickly sapped their strength, especially now that they were no longer driven by the adrenalin of escape. Probably no European had ever been through this area before them, and it was only intermittently visited by the Aborigines – the landscape around Macquarie Harbour and the mountains to the east constituted the border between the territories of the North-West and South-West tribes, and there is debate as to how often the Aborigines visited.

To the east of the Darwin Range they descended into what Pearce calls 'very rough country'. That is an understatement: they were now heading east–south-east, and although the tops of the mountain ridges are bare, down at the lower levels the escapees had begun to penetrate a wide swathe of implicate rainforest, the scientific name for the thickest, most tangled, inaccessible type of country. But it is not just a matter of getting through. Describing this area, Terry Reid says, 'Down in the valleys you have scrub, and also you have to cross drainage creeks and then the Andrew River. The Andrew is in a very deep valley. The whole area is well vegetated, with very fast-flowing streams, and in September there is a lot of water around.'

Reid correctly uses the word 'scrub' to describe the forests that the eight escapees were now entering. The predominant and most obvious species are the various types of beech trees: botanical name *Nothofagus*, the remnant vegetation from Gondwana, the original southern super-continent that centred on the South Pole and began to break up and drift northward about 160 million years ago. So Pearce, Greenhill and their six companions were now entering what had been the natural home of the dinosaurs until the great extinction of the reptiles at the end of the Cretaceous period, some 65 million years ago.

These cool temperate beech forests long outlasted the dinosaurs and were the predominant vegetation in Australia until the major changes in climate that occurred between five million years ago and fairly recently. During the recurrent ice ages the atmosphere became drier and the *Nothofagus* rainforest species slowly disappeared from most areas on the mainland, and the acacias and eucalypts gradually took over across the Australian landscape. They still dominate it. Modern research has shown that especially over the last 750,000 years, the rainforests have expanded and contracted after the major fluctuations in climate brought about by the ice ages. Since the arrival of humankind in Australia, probably as long ago as 60,000 years, the deliberate lighting of fires by Aboriginal people to flush out game and maintain grassy areas has also favoured the eucalypts and acacias over all other species, because these plants need fire for their germination.

It is only in far eastern Victoria and south-western Tasmania that remnant Gondwana vegetation has survived. These forests are quite different from the tropical rainforests of northern Australia and the equatorial regions. That is why they are historically and biologically so important.

But Pearce and his seven companions would have had a very different view of this landscape. The area that they were traversing was dominated by myrtle beech. As far as they were concerned it was an alien landscape full of almost impenetrable scrub through which they would have had to cut a path to make their way. At ground level the beech forest is a twilight world – cool, damp and still. In a mature rainforest these trees form a dense canopy that can vary in height from 7 to 36 metres (20 to 120 feet) above the ground. The ground is littered with rotten fallen trees and branches. There are great festoons of vines and mosses, as well as large and small fern-trees, one of the few species that can grow in this closed atmosphere.

Climbing over fallen trees and pushing their way past branches and vines, the escapees often fell, cutting themselves and putting a terrible strain on their bodies. Occasionally they would have seen an isolated remnant mountain ash, or even a small stand of them, that poked out of the forest-cover like a thin, leafy spire on a cathedral – a sure sign that the rainforest had reclaimed an area that it had surrendered to the eucalypt forests several hundreds of years before, following a wildfire. Besides myrtle beech, Pearce and the others would have also seen southern sassafras, celery-top pine, leatherwood and an occasional stand of Huon pine. In the higher mountain valleys and gullies the predominant species they would have encountered were deciduous beech, celery-top pine, King Billy pine and pencil pine.

But the escapees were too busy and too exhausted to give a darn about the various species of beech and pine, most of which had not been named, let alone catalogued, at that time. They were about two to three days out of Macquarie Harbour when they passed to the north of the Darwin Crater, where a meteorite hit the earth 750,000 years ago, a major source of glass-like silicate, much valued by the Aborigines and widely traded throughout Tasmania. Although they did not know it and nothing in the landscape had been named at that time, they were actually pushing on toward the Andrew River and the Engineer Range, some of the toughest country in the world. Even today there is no walking track, let alone a road that follows their course. Only the best equipped and most experienced twenty-first-century bushwalkers would attempt to follow in the Pearce party's footsteps, and then only using accurate and detailed survey maps, compasses and probably a Global Positioning System (GPS).

But as the convicts cut their way toward the Andrew River, they soon realised that they were not just facing dense, implicate rainforest, difficult creek crossings, steep mountains and deep valleys. They were also beginning to experience some of the nastiest vegetation in the world. Interspersed with the beech trees and often growing around and through them, especially where fire had disturbed the rainforest, was the notorious horizontal scrub with the odd botanical name of *Anodopetalum biglandulosum*. This type of scrub literally becomes horizontal rather than vertical, after growing 2 to 5 metres (6 and 15 feet). The main stem grows vertically until it is forced to lean over under its own weight, and it then spreads out, forming a thick tangle of horizontal branches. The whole process is repeated over and over as further stems grow upwards and then bend over under their own weight. The denseness of 'horizontal', as it is called in the south-west, creates a near inaccessibility; there is simply no way you can move through it or stand upright in it. You are constantly thrown off balance. It tears at the front of your legs and chest and you can easily fall over and break a limb. There is no way of boring a path through without an axe and much exertion. Even trying to hack a path is often unsuccessful. You can attempt to crawl beneath it, but here you find uneven ground and a clammy, slippery, slimy, wet surface with fallen logs, mosses and debris. As you crawl along, the stems grab at your clothes and skin. It is soul-destroying, and no matter what you do, you quickly tire and become disoriented. So the best you can do is to chop your way through, especially if you can't go around it. This is what our escapees would have tried to do.

One way of dealing with the horizontal scrub is to walk on top of it. This is possible in some places because it is so dense, although it can be very risky and you can fall through and hurt yourself badly. There is a story told in the south-west of a massive D-8 bulldozer, whose driver felt the vehicle gently rocking from side to side as he drove it along, just as though it was riding on a sponge. Fearing that the dozer would roll over, he jumped down and was amazed to find that he had driven it onto horizontal scrub so strong that it supported the heavy machine. Henry Hellyer, a surveyor for the Van Diemen's Land Company, reported in March 1827, five years after the Pearce party, that he tried to move across the top of the horizontal: 'We were obliged to be walking upon these never-dry, slippery branches, covered with moss, as much as twenty feet [six metres] above the ground, which, being in many instances rotten, occasioned us many awkward falls, and tore our clothes to rags. We were not able to force our way on five hundred yards in an hour in some of these horrid scrubs'.

Adding to the inaccessibility of the horizontal are stands of tea-tree that grow to 3 or 4 metres in height (10 to 13 feet), and paperbark trees that can grow up to 9 metres (30 feet). They are often accompanied by silver banksia, a shrub that can also grow to up to 9 metres with a conspicuous honeycomb-like flower. The ground is often sodden underneath these shrubs and trees, with a mixed undergrowth of ferns and mosses. But even more frustrating for Pearce and the other escapees would have been the bauera – pronounced 'bow-ra' – a thick understorey shrub. It looks a little like tea-tree and has a rather lovely flower and soft leaves. But it grows in dense clumps, sometimes occurring around and through the horizontal. One of Tasmania's most experienced bushwalkers, and a campaigner for the Wilderness

Society, Geoff Law, describes bauera as 'a yielding sort of vegetation that absorbs all the efforts you throw at it, and you just end up in a complete tangle. It grows up to 2 to 3 metres [7 to 10 feet] tall. You can push through and down on it, you can try to crush it, and the more you push and crush, the more it falls back in on you. It is like trying to fight with a trampoline!'

Perhaps the most vicious form of vegetation in the southwest is cutting grass. Its name says it all: it cuts any exposed skin it comes in contact with and leaves a nasty wound that usually becomes infected and festering. It grows in tussocks 2 to 3 metres high (9 feet) and often becomes intertwined with other clumps of cutting grass, or attaches to branches and fallen logs. It makes any movement forward almost impossible. The combination of bauera, horizontal and cutting grass, together with sassafras and leatherwood, can tear your clothing to pieces and sap your energy and patience – a completely morale-destroying situation. If it does that for well-fed, fully equipped, modern bushwalkers, you can imagine the effect on a group of poorly equipped, poorly dressed escapees.

After some time battling through this kind of bush, even if you are on a path, you tend to slip into a kind of psychological automatic pilot. You become so tired in body that your mind withdraws and you revert to a semi-conscious state. It is precisely when you are in this state that you can miss your footing and fall over. Going downhill is sometimes worse than going up because you put so much strain on your knees and leg muscles. Certainly you can pick up pace on the downward slope, but if your mind and eyes are not closely focused on where you are walking and where you put your feet, the mud and slippery ground and rocks can give way and lead to serious falls. For the convicts this lack of attention would have been exacerbated by hunger, yet the Pearce party could have survived in this type of bush as long as they did only by withdrawing mentally.

By about day four into the escape there was trouble brewing. Even as they crossed the Darwin Range, Little Brown, the oldest man in the group, was becoming a problem: he could not keep up with the others. Pearce says that even on the second day he was 'suffering more by the fatigues of the journey than the others' and that he 'could not keep pace with us, and was frequently at a considerable distance behind us which compelled us to stop for him'. Little Brown had been in the convict system for a long time. His spirit was already broken, and probably his desire to reach freedom was largely gone. He was 'the worst walker of any', Pearce says, 'which detained us much'. He had really gone along with the others because he was part of the group and he did what they decided. But by now their patience was growing thin, and while they 'compassionated [with] his sufferings', he was told bluntly that despite all his 'remonstrances . . . it was our determination to leave him if he did not endeavour to keep pace with us'. They were adamant that 'We would not lose so good an opportunity of gaining our liberty through him'. However, to try to help him they shared out among them his 'burthen', which can't have been much. But by now the realities of nature were impinging on them all. Pearce says in an understatement: 'The ground over which we travelled [had been] dreadfully rough and bushy', and this slowed them down considerably.

The second night out they ate some more of their provisions. They used a portion of the flour to cook damper, the bush bread made from mixing flour and water, which was then baked on the coals of the fire. It was not particularly nourishing, but it filled their empty bellies.

Things were even worse the next day. Pearce says that they 'arose at the very dawn of day the third morning and proceeded on the journey through thick woods of brush in a very melancholy state'. They were now in the implicate rainforest to the west of the Andrew River, still difficult country.

The rain that had begun to pour down on the first night did not let up. 'It kept on a constant rain', Pearce reports, 'which greatly added to make us far [more] miserable than we was'. Such weather is typical for south-western Tasmania, where the deluge can last for up to a week or ten days. Even in summer the rain often turns to sleet and sometimes even to thick snow. It is bone-chillingly cold, particularly at night. When the rain stops, frosts or fogs are common. Pearce confirms this when he says that 'the weather still continuing to be very wet and foggy made it very disagreeable travelling', and that the rain made them 'far [more] miserable . . . and [it] was also excessively cold particularly at nights, and not having sufficient nourishment and being exposed so much to the night dews greatly impaired our constitutions'. Also their clothing and footwear, which would have been of poor quality and pretty rough and ready to start with, would now have become torn and frayed and would have offered them little or no protection.

•

By the fourth day of the escape they would have already climbed over Mount Sorell, crossed the Darwin Range, and penetrated the valley of the Andrew River 4 to 5 kilometres (2½ to 3 miles) north of its junction with the Franklin River. Immediately in front of them lay the Engineer Range, and beyond that the south-flowing Franklin, where water levels would have been high with the rain and the melting snow of late winter. As they moved toward the valley the Pearce party passed through forests of myrtle, King Billy pine and Huon pine, and cutting grass and bauera with dense tea-tree and horizontal scrub. As they got close to the river itself they found themselves in a tall eucalypt forest. The Andrew was in full September flood, but they must have found a fairly easy crossing-place because two of the party could not swim. It was probably a couple of kilometres (a mile or so) north of the Looker River's junction with the Andrew.

Immediately they confronted a steep line of mountains on a more or less north–south axis – the Engineer Range. Although they did not know it, beyond that was the Deception Range, lying on the same axis across their route. While these mountain chains are not particularly high – on average they are about 700 metres (2290 feet) – they are extremely steep and treacherous, comprised of ice- and glacier-eroded Cambrian rock, with a number of sheer cliff faces and drops down to the Franklin River. Terry Reid says that the Engineer Range is not as hard to climb as Mount Sorell, although its difficulty would have depended on the direction in which they approached the ascent. He says that the fact that a couple of them were already exhausted shows that they were perhaps trying to cover too much ground each day. The one prominent point in the whole area that had already been named was Frenchman's Cap; Greenhill would have used this as a reference point. Reid feels sure that they would have been trying to get to the east of Frenchman's Cap as fast as they could. Then they would have felt safe from pursuit because they were well beyond the area that could be seen or reached from Sarah Island.

The party had now covered about 23 kilometres (14 miles) as the crow flies from the eastern shoreline of Macquarie Harbour. Pearce says that food was running low and there was 'not the least prospect of procuring any more for there was not a single reptile in that part of the country where we was'. Aboriginal people would have known where to look for 'bush tucker', and there were wallabies around, such as the red-necked wallaby and the Tasmanian pademelon (pronounced 'paddy-melon'), as well as wombats, ring-tailed and brush-tailed possums, and some species of birds. But the wallabies are shy, fast-moving and good at camouflage, and the possums are nocturnal and tree-dwelling. Without experience of the bush and lacking both the knowledge and wherewithal, Pearce and the others would have had no chance of catching them. There would not have been any birds' eggs at that time of the year. Some people have suggested that they could have chased and caught wombats by hand, but both Terry Reid and Geoff Law point out that this could only have been said by those who have never tried to catch these seemingly awkward, but tough, burrowing marsupials. Wombats have a real turn of speed when necessary, they are bulky and strong, and when chased they make a bee-line straight back to the safety of their burrows, or they disappear into the scrub or forest. There were also some edible plants, but these were unknown to the escapees. As well there would have been the carnivorous marsupials: the now extinct thylacine (the Tasmanian 'tiger'), the carrion-eating Tasmanian devil, the cat-like spotted-tailed quoll and the smaller eastern quoll. The quolls are nocturnal, and thylacine cautious and well concealed, and the devils are too fast-moving.

The crisis that was brewing among them found its first expression on the fourth night out. They had begun to ascend the Engineer Range, but got caught halfway up when darkness fell, having underestimated how arduous the climb would be in their exhausted state. Pearce describes the range as a 'high barren hill. On ascending it we could not perceive a single tree, nothing but small sticks of decayed bush'. This tallies with the appearance of the Engineer Range now, a rather narrow ridge whose sides are covered with scrub. The men had to hack their way up the slope, which rises to a series of peaks almost 600 metres (1960 feet) in height. Pearce reports that they had great trouble getting a fire going that night to protect themselves from the cold air and the nocturnal dews. The scrub was probably green, wet and not very combustible.

That night profound doubt began to set in. 'Some of them

began to see their folly', Pearce says, 'and wished themselves [back] at Macquarie Harbour, although it was a place where they undoubtedly had to encounter numerous difficulties'. The Knopwood narrative says that they felt that 'they had plunged themselves into greater miseries and hardships than ever could be experienced at that place [Sarah Island]', and that they had 'not the least prospect of ever arriving at any place from whence they might expect to find relief'. It is doubtful whether these are Pearce's actual words; they sound more like a sanctimonious editorial gloss by Thomas Wells or whoever was the final compiler of the Knopwood manuscript. No doubt that night Greenhill had to use all his leadership skills to keep them focused on the fact that they had come this far and that freedom was still within their grasp.

The men's relationships were now becoming very strained, with some of them feeling that they had reached the end of their tether. Most probably it was Brown and Kennerly who complained most, with some support from Dalton. They seem to have already formed a group on their own, probably because they were the oldest and therefore the slowest walkers, unable to keep up with the younger group that was setting the pace. The more motivated men – Greenhill, Travers, Pearce, Bodenham and Mather – were much stronger physically and they seemed to be more able to summon up the psychological resources to keep going.

'On the fifth day', Pearce says, 'the weather still continuing to be very wet, the rain falling in torrents, made us very uncomfortable which enabled us to make but very little progress'. They were still either climbing the western face or beginning to descend the equally steep eastern face of the Engineer Range and were particularly exposed. Reflecting on their experience from his own knowledge of the bush, Terry Reid says that they would have been suffering from considerable mental stress. 'These days we've got good clothing and all the necessities, including food and a fuel stove so we can light a fire. We've also got an understanding in the back of our mind that we can make it through the bush. They wouldn't have had any of that. Take that level of stress and add it to their physical condition, the lack of food, not knowing exactly where they are, the fear of being pursued.' All of this would have brought about a rapid deterioration in physical and psychological attitudes. Reid says that at times you have to get down on your hands and knees to crawl through the scrub and bauera, or you have to jump against it.

As soon as they found some good shelter on level ground on the fifth day, Pearce says they stopped 'and remained in a very dejected state until the sixth evening'. Obviously, they were so exhausted that they turned this into a rest day. The flour from which they made bush damper and the salted beef they had stolen from Macquarie Harbour were totally inadequate. The damper would have given them some carbohydrates and the meat some protein, but not nearly enough. The escapees were using an enormous amount of energy on their trek and, because of their poor diet at Sarah Island, they probably had little in the way of reserve calories to begin with. For very active people a rule of thumb for daily calorie needs is to multiply body weight by twenty. Estimating the average body weight of the men at 130 pounds (59 kilos) and multiplying by 20, we get a daily requirement of 2600 calories. Pearce and the others were getting nothing like that at Macquarie Harbour, and obviously without some form of nourishment they were in grave danger of dying from starvation.

Exhaustion was one enemy, cold was another. Given the conditions they were in, it would have been a challenge for them to keep warm. Impending or mild hypothermia must have been a risk. Even today, bushwalking in Tasmania can sometimes produce fatalities through exposure and hypothermia if hikers are not properly equipped and aware of the dangers. The rain is so persistent that eventually it penetrates even the best quality Gore-Tex outerwear. Once your underclothes are wet through, the cold seeps right in.

Chilled to the inner core by a cold that is intensified by wet and windy conditions, a person with hypothermia experiences a gradual physical and mental collapse. It is an insidious process and the victim is usually the last to realise what is happening. Normal physiological functioning requires a core body temperature in excess of 37° Celsius (98.6° Fahrenheit). Once the temperature drops so low that the body loses heat faster than it produces it, intense shivering begins, the body's way of trying to create warmth through a rapid succession of contractions and relaxations of the muscles. If the exposure continues, the person gradually loses the ability to maintain vital functions. As cold reaches the brain, physical coordination declines and the person begins to fall and slip often, speech becomes slurred and judgement impeded. The first signs of hypothermia are tiredness and a reluctance to keep moving, followed by shivering and exhaustion. In advanced cases coma and death can follow quickly. It is surprising that some of the escapees were not already suffering from hypothermia. Possibly the weather was warmer than usual for September, and probably the conditions they had already experienced at Macquarie Harbour had extended their bodies' tolerance to intense cold.

Making a sheltered camp with a fire on the sixth day also probably halted the advancing effects of hypothermia, but the eight were exhausted and hungry. Their rest day seemed to do them little good psychologically, however, because that evening 'We were all disputing who should get wood for the fire. Some brought it and made fires for themselves. Kennerly made some tinder this night and put it by as he had some intention of returning to the [Sarah Island] settlement'. This also seems to be the night when Kennerly suddenly said, in what may have been a sick joke, that 'he was so hungry he could eat a piece of a man'. It was the first mention of cannibalism.

They were now ravenously hungry, not having eaten for a couple of days since their meagre rations ran out. Without sustenance they would die and, as we have seen, their knowledge of bush skills was negligible. Although it is hard to tell from Pearce's account, Kennerly's comment was most likely incidental. And indeed he did not participate in the subsequent cannibalism. But they all heard it and it articulated what the ex-mariner, Bob Greenhill, had been thinking. He was already asking himself if the time had not arrived to initiate 'the custom of the sea'. Greenhill was a strong-minded man, and probably something of a bully, and it was he who was to carry out most of the killings. His intimate friend, Matthew Travers, supported him and together they usually cowed the others into submission. Pearce, although short in stature, was as strong physically as Greenhill and Travers, or maybe even stronger, but he couldn't navigate and he didn't have the psychological stability to be a leader.

As Pearce reports it, they were about seven days into their desperate journey when they began to talk seriously about cannibalism. They had spent a couple of days negotiating the escarpment of the Engineer Range and were probably somewhere in the scrub and rainforest country near its south-eastern base, moving eastward toward the Franklin River. Pearce says that on 'the seventh morning the elements had a promising appearance', and as they set out, 'four of us happened to be in front of the others'. The four were Pearce, Greenhill, Travers and Mather. Bodenham must have dropped back with the older men. As they struggled through the bush they began to discuss Kennerly's comment. Pearce says, most likely quite truthfully, that it was 'Greenhill [who] . . . first . . . introduced the subject of killing one of their companions and eating him'. He suggested that eating a man was perhaps the only option they had left. Greenhill said, according to Pearce, 'that he had seen the like done before, and that it tasted very much like pork'.

Mather replied that 'It would be murder to do it.'

Greenhill retorted, 'I'll warrant you, I will eat the first part myself, but you all must lend a hand that we all may be guilty of the crime.'

The unspeakable had been articulated.

•

It is significant that it was the ex-mariner who initiated this discussion, for it was not unknown for shipwrecked sailors to resort to cannibalism. The term 'the custom of the sea', originating in the seventeenth century, referred to the practice of drawing lots in situations of starvation to see who would be sacrificed to save others. Just a year and ten months before the Pearce party escaped from Macquarie Harbour, the Nantucket-based whale ship Essex had been attacked and sunk by a massive and boisterous sperm whale in the middle of the Pacific Ocean, just over 3220 kilometres (2000 miles) almost due west of the Galapagos Islands. The twenty-one officers and crew took to the boats, and after ninety days two whaleboats containing eight survivors were picked up near the coast of Chile. In one boat two emaciated men sat sucking the marrow from the bones of their dead comrades as the rescue ship came alongside. The survivors had drawn lots to see who would be killed, and they did not hesitate to eat the bodies of the dead.

Later there would be the story of the yacht *Mignonette*, which sank off the coast of West Africa in 1884 after being hit by a 12-metre (40-foot) rogue wave in a storm. It left the four English crewmen adrift in the mid-Atlantic in a small dinghy for over two weeks. They were all starving and the captain announced that they would have recourse to the time-honoured custom. One of the four, a cabin-boy, was already delirious and close to death.

Eventually they decided that the captain would kill him and they would all eat him. Three days later they were rescued, but when they got back to England they were charged with murder. The English legal establishment was determined to stamp out this type of customary law, and in a test case the captain was put on trial and condemned to the mandatory death sentence, although this was commuted to six months' imprisonment 'without hard labour'. The English Chief Justice, John Duke Coleridge, ruled in convoluted legalese that 'the temptation to the act which existed here was not what the law has ever called necessity . . . The absolute divorce of law from morality would be of fatal consequence; and such a divorce would follow if the temptation to murder in this case were to be held by law an absolute defence of it'. It is safe to assume that Lord Chief Justice Coleridge had never been lost at sea in an open boat without food or water.

But cannibalism was not confined to shipwrecks. The most famous case of it in United States history is that of the George Donner party, a group of ten unrelated families and sixteen other individuals, eighty-seven people in total, headed for California, who were trapped in the high Sierra Nevada, south-west of Reno, by the early snow of the winter of 1846–47. About half of the survivors resorted to cannibalism, although there was no direct killing of anyone for the purpose of eating them. They simply ate the bodies of those who had died. Cannibalism is thus something that even 'normal' people will resort to in extreme situations. What was particularly interesting in the Donner case was that the women had much better survival rates than the men. The reasons for this are twofold: first, women are generally smaller and so they need less food to support their basic metabolism. Second, women have a higher proportion of body fat and a lower basal metabolism than men, giving them better heat insulation against cold. Using less energy than men because of smaller body weight, these fat reserves sustain them longer against hunger.

While survival cannibalism can be distinguished from ritual cannibalism, as found, for instance, in pre-European Mesoamerica, the distinction should not be pushed too far. Dr Tom Waite of Adelaide University argued that cannibalism was very common in nature and also among humans, especially hunter-gatherers, for whom it was a common practice, 'albeit disguised by various religious or cultural justifications . . . A study in 1974 of pay-back warfare and cannibalism among small isolated groups of Papua New Guineans showed that it contributed 10 per cent of the protein to the diet of people living where game was in chronically short supply'.

•

There is no strict parallel between these cases and the behaviour of our escapees. By the standards of other situations, they resorted to cannibalism very quickly. There was also seemingly a lot less compunction about it, perhaps because starvation affected them speedily. Pearce also talked constantly about the cold and especially its effects at night. The body temperature of a starving person drops considerably and they have poor circulation, leading to a dangerous interaction between hunger and the threat of hypothermia. Other symptoms of starvation are similar to hypothermia: a tendency to fall over and to trip resulting from a loss of a sense of balance, an inability to walk in a straight line, and a proneness to bump into other people or surrounding objects, leading to bruises, cuts and abrasions. Blackouts and fainting are other characteristic symptoms. Starving people experience severe emotional and psychological effects as well, becoming apathetic, dull, depressed and discouraged, and lacking in empathy for the needs and sufferings of others, having become increasingly focused on their personal need for food. Irritability and a tendency to explode with frustration and anger also characterise very hungry people.

Pearce, Greenhill, Travers and Mather had a brief discussion about the rights and wrongs of cannibalism. Pearce says bluntly: 'We then consulted who should fall'. According to his account, it was Greenhill who took the lead in nominating the victim: he said it should be Dalton.

Why Dalton? Because, Greenhill argued, 'He had volunteered to be a flogger'. Whether Dalton had volunteered for this duty or not we don't know, but the others clearly believed it was true, so he was quickly chosen as the first victim.

Pearce vividly describes what happened very early the next morning, well before dawn, on their eighth day out from Macquarie Harbour, in a rainforest somewhere near the western bank of the Franklin River: 'When we stopped at night, Dalton, Brown and Kennerly had a fire by themselves and a little break-wind. About three o'clock in the morning, Dalton was asleep. Greenhill got up, took an axe and struck him on the head with it, which killed him as he never spoke afterwards. Travers took a knife, cut his throat with it, and bled him. We then dragged the body to a distance, cut off his clothes, tore his insides out and cut off his head. Then Mather, Travers and Greenhill put his heart and liver on the fire to broil, but took them off and cut them before they were right hot. They asked the rest would they have any, but we would not eat any that night. Next morning the body was cut up and divided into equal parts, which we took and proceeded on our journey a little after sun rise'.

There is so much detail in this account that it is unlikely to have been a fabrication. With Travers, Mather, Bodenham and Pearce looking on, Greenhill killed Dalton, as he had said he would. Brown and Kennerly were probably asleep at the time like Dalton, and were too surprised to do anything to defend the Irish ex-soldier. They were also now outnumbered five to two. Pearce cooperated in the killing of his mate without any compunction.

Travers bled and butchered the body with a professional hand, no doubt drawing on his background of slaughtering and butchering sheep in the back country of New Norfolk. It was Mather, Travers and Greenhill who were the first to overcome their repulsion about eating human flesh. They offered to share pieces with the others, who refused. The next morning Bodenham and Pearce also overcame the taboo against cannibalism, but it was too much for the older men, Kennerly and Brown, for Dalton had become something of a mate, sharing a fire with them. They must have realised that one or the other of them would be the next victim, and they decided to flee. There was nowhere to go except back to Macquarie Harbour.

The next morning, after the uncooked portions of Dalton's body had been cut up and divided, the party prepared to set out. Pearce says that 'About this time there was a man appointed to go in front every day, who had nothing to carry, but was to clear the road for the others'. His role was to chop a way through the scrub. No doubt strengthened by the protein derived from human flesh, the five stronger men set out on the next stage of the journey with some gusto. Pearce says that 'Kennerly and Brown said they would carry the tin pots and a little tomahawk, which were given them. We had not got more than a quarter of a mile . . . till they were missing. We stopped and "cooeed" and got no answer; nor could we see anything of them'.

The two older men had quickly retreated in the opposite direction and had begun the journey back to Macquarie Harbour. Although they had no food except their portions of Dalton's flesh, they made it all the way back to Sarah Island, arriving there on 12 October, twenty-two days after the initial escape and about thirteen days after fleeing the scene of Dalton's murder and dismemberment. The official report says they 'were in a state of the greatest exhaustion', but neither suitable food for starving men nor adequate medical care would have been available for them at

Sarah Island. Brown died on 15 October, and Kennerly on 19 October 1822. It seems certain that they had mentioned neither the murder of Dalton nor the cannibalism to Cuthbertson. They were no doubt fearful of the legal consequences for themselves if they confessed to being present at a murder and a cannibalistic feast, even if they did not take part.

The others were at first very worried that the two bolters would give information that would lead to soldiers being sent in pursuit of them, and they were fearful that their information about the murder and cannibalism would hang them all. Their concern was exacerbated by the knowledge that they were close to a large river and they feared that Cuthbertson might send soldiers in a boat in pursuit. Pearce says that they decided not to give chase to Brown and Kennerly for they reckoned the two would not make it back to Macquarie Harbour and would die on the way. Why waste the energy?

So they pushed on. They were now about 28 kilometres (17 miles) north of the confluence of the Franklin and Gordon rivers and, although they thought it was the Gordon, immediately ahead of them was the Franklin, which at that stage had not been named. Crossing it proved to be very difficult as there were few places to ford the river, its banks 'being so rough and steep', as Pearce correctly puts it. Both Terry Reid and Geoff Law agree that they probably approached the Franklin somewhere close to the northern end of the Great Ravine, a series of cliffs, gorges and rapids into which the river flows near the southern end of the Engineer Range. Reid says that the Franklin 'is very narrow, very sheer on both sides. You can get yourself down onto the banks of the river via the little creeks'. Law concurs, saying that, 'Trying to get down to the river, let alone cross it, would have been horrific. Given September, the river would have been very high. The rocks on the sides of the gorges are very slippery.'

Rising on the western side of the King William Range in

central Tasmania, the Franklin runs for much of this part of its length through deep gorges and over dangerous rapids and shallow waterfalls. In early spring it is usually running high and very fast. Nowadays it is one of the premier rafting rivers in the world.

James Erskine Calder, who traversed this area in 1841, describes the Franklin as 'a beautiful stream, of considerable width, depth and rapidity. Its banks are mostly high, and often perpendicular, overhung with handsome myrtles, and many fine pines; the branches of the latter, like those of the willow, often drooping to its surface in a manner which much contributes to the beauty of the stream'. It is still like this but, as the Pearce party soon found out, the beauty was deceptive. First, how were they to get down to the river? And secondly, how were they to get across?

The rain had started again and it was only 'with great trouble [that they] effected a passage to the river' through the tangled maze of rainforest and scrub that surrounded it. After much searching, probably in the area somewhere south of what is now called the Sideslip and probably inside the northern end of the Great Ravine, they eventually found a possible crossing point. It was the evening of the eleventh day out from Macquarie Harbour. Pearce takes up the story: 'Early the next morning they arose and consulted among themselves respecting the manner in which they could be able to cross the river with safety as two of them could not swim'. The non-swimmers were Travers and Bodenham. To try to get them over they cut down two large trees, hoping to use them as a bridge across the swiftly flowing river. But the current was so strong and fast that it swept the trees away immediately. After some further exploration they found a place 'where a rock projected from the other side to the middle of the river'. The three swimmers dived in and swam across to the rock, towing behind them 'a wattle pole of some 30 or 40 feet in length', which they then used to pull the two non-swimmers across. It must have been a hair-raising experience for them all, but especially for Travers and Bodenham. In these slower, broader parts of the river the water looks black and seemingly bottomless. Plunging into the raging river required rare bravery and, whatever else they lacked, these men certainly had courage.

Reid thinks that they must have found a spot in the northern part of the Great Ravine where the river widens out and settles down sufficiently for them to have found calmer water. It would have been impossible to cross in the narrower parts of the river where it is 4 to 7 metres (12 to 18 feet) wide and raging. The Franklin is generally about 15 metres (about 50 feet) across – not crossable either for the non-swimmers unless they had a very long pole or, as Pearce says, there were rocks sticking right out into the middle to foreshorten the distance. But even with all this in their favour, Reid warns that 'The current is very strong. Once you've been caught by the current you're going to get swept away into the rapids and never be seen again. We [the Tasmanian Parks and Wildlife Service] would not recommend that anyone would contemplate going down the river at that time [of the year]'. The Franklin carries a vast volume of water, especially in September, which averages twenty days of rain, to be added to by the melting snows coming down from the mountains.

Once across they made a fire and remained all night. At this stage Mather must have been acutely constipated because Pearce says that 'Mather took a purging and begged that we remain a little longer', presumably waiting for his bowels to move. The most common purgative in the early nineteenth century was calomel (mercurous chloride), but it is unlikely that convicts would have access to this unless it had been given to them by the Sarah Island surgeon, James Spence. We can only speculate that Mather might have had it because he had had previous problems with constipation. Perhaps he had saved it, purposely smuggled it over from Sarah Island for the escape and brought it with him. Their state of near-starvation would have affected all of their bodily functions. So they rested on the east bank of the Franklin for another day and night.

Ahead of them was what Pearce calls 'very mountainous country'. The Deception Range, as it was to be named two decades later by Calder, is a southern spur of the snow-covered Frenchman's Cap massif, which they could see to the north of them on the occasions when the sky cleared. Calder explains: 'I called these hills collectively Deception Range, from the frequency with which I was foiled, or deceived in my attempts to lead the path across them. This locality presents no other view but that of a sterile wilderness, and scenes of frightful desolation'. From the 600-metre (1960-foot) ridge the escapees could see back to Macquarie Harbour and estimate how far they had already come: in a direct line it was about 28 kilometres (about 18 miles), but they had probably walked a lot further. When they looked east they saw barren ground, mainly buttongrass plains, for miles ahead of them. This is what Calder was later to name the Lightning Plains because he got caught there in the open one night during a terrible electrical storm.

The ascent of the Deception Range was no less arduous. There were only a few places where they could ascend, and they probably did so somewhere near Mount Lyne (880 metres/2860 feet). At times the grade was so steep that it would have been a near vertical rock-climb. There are 500-metre (1640-foot) cliffs on this range. They would have been trying again to get high and keep to the ridge-lines using Frenchman's Cap as their reference point. Their aim would have been to avoid constantly having to drop down and climb out of valleys and gullies full of rainforest and impassable vegetation. Along the ridge-lines of both the Engineer and Deception ranges, and around the higher mountains above 1000 metres (3500 feet), you come upon the south-west's extraordinary alpine vegetation, another survival from Gondwana. Rain, hail, high winds, ice, poor soil and deep snow make life difficult for all but the hardiest plants. There are tough shrubs and herbs that survive in these conditions, some of them with rather beautiful flowers. Perhaps the most unusual is the pandani tree, a kind of giant grass-tree which tends to be found in the wetter areas. It can grow to a height of 12 metres (almost 40 feet). It is also found in a stunted form in alpine herbfields. The nastiest vegetation at the higher levels is scoparia, a flowering coniferous shrub. It has sharp leaves that tears at clothing. There is also the stunted deciduous beech which, as Terry Reid says, 'is not called tangle-foot for nothing'. There is no water on the ridge-lines so you have to descend through the gorges to the creeks for water. But you can't see what you are getting into as the country keeps dropping away, and as it get steeper the vegetation gets thicker. Geoff Law says, 'You keep wondering what's coming next. You fool yourself that it's not going to get any steeper, but inside you know that it is.'

Physically the escapees would have now been in very poor shape. Besides starvation, they would have been suffering from cuts, scratches, bruises, sprains and abrasions, many of them quite serious, from frequently falling over. In the type of country they had traversed you regularly slip and slide and fall over, both backwards and forwards, many times every day. Many of these wounds would have become infected, especially those caused by cutting grass. Often on slippery ground they would have fallen over in filthy slime which covers your clothes and hands and any exposed surface and just sticks there. They would also have been bitten by insects and had their blood sucked by leeches that get under clothing and attach themselves to the body. The men had been working in cold water for a long period before their escape, and on the trek they would have been constantly in mud, so trench foot (or immersion foot) would have affected them. This results in a loss of sensation in the feet and an abnormal sensitivity to cold. Their poor physical state would have engendered depression. Every morning they would have woken up and thought, 'What obstacle will we have to face today?', knowing that every step on the journey would involve pain.

From his long experience of walking in this type of country, Geoff Law describes how you begin to feel as you try to get through the bush the escapees were facing: 'Often the problem is that you have little choice, and the only option is to go forward. But by doing so you face a ravine full of horizontal. Then you have these route-finding difficulties: often the easiest way is in the completely opposite direction to the one in which you need to go. The right way is to push straight ahead, but it is the hardest option of all. This is frustrating and depressing. So you have to slow your brain down. Instead of deciding that you have to get to this or that point by the end of the day, you have to modify your expectations. That's fine if you've got plenty of food on board, and you're actually doing it for fun anyway. But these men in the Pearce party were starving to death, thinking how much longer will this go on? It must have been a hideous prospect.' Their physical and no doubt psychological state would have made it difficult to think clearly, and this led directly to the next crisis.

Mather had been entrusted with the task of carrying the tinder that was used to light the fires at night. He had it in his shirt to keep it dry, but somehow it dropped down his trousers. Searching for it frantically – dry tinder was vital if they were to have a fire at night – he couldn't find it. Watching him looking for it, Travers raised his axe in a sudden fit of violence and said he would kill Mather if the tinder wasn't found immediately. Fortunately Mather managed to find it down his trousers and a fire was made that night under a cliff. But the men were scarcely able to rise the next morning because of starvation and the cold, wet weather. This incident also illustrates the problem they must have had throughout the trip trying to carry things. They had set out inland almost impulsively and, unlike contemporary bushwalkers, they would have had no backpacks in which to carry food and other necessities. Even carrying an axe tied up one hand and left the man unbalanced as he struggled through the bush.

Up until now we can be generally sure of the route that they took. But once they descended the Deception Range and emerged onto the buttongrass of Lightning Plains they were faced with a choice of route.

In describing the landscape of the south-west there is one element that I have omitted. Much of the area is flat, open, buttongrass plains. Buttongrass, which can also be found in valleys and on mountain slopes, is a kind of reddish-brown-green in colour, growing up to about a metre in height, and it can be found in many environments, but usually on waterlogged plains and in and around eucalypt forests. Growing in peaty soil, it is unsuitable for cattle, and this has fortunately protected the south-west from a destructive invasion of hard-hoofed animals. Buttongrass is extraordinarily hardy; it is fire- and drought-resistant, and regular burning promotes its growth. The extent of buttongrass across the south-west indicates that there has been a regimen of regular burning in the whole region over a long period, resulting either from lightning or regular Aboriginal burning. Dr Jon Marsden-Smedley, an expert on the fire regimen in the south-west and fire officer for the Tasmanian Parks and Wildlife Service, says that the evidence is that the Aborigines mostly used low-intensity fires on the moorland when forested vegetation was too wet to burn. Their aim was to flush out game and make access tracks.

The choice the Pearce party faced at the Deception Range was simple: should they head east–north-east or east–south-east? They had had a chance to survey the country from the ridge-line of the Deception before they descended, and they would have seen that directly across their path to the east was the central section of the King William Range, with peaks like Mount King William II rising to 1359 metres (4460 feet). To the north was Mount Arrowsmith (981 metres/3180 feet) and the 1324-metre (4300-foot) Mount King William I, and to the south Mount King William III (1172 metres/3800 feet). This range has a steep escarpment on the western side and an average height of 1200 metres (3900 feet) at the ridge-line. Given their experience, they obviously decided not to tackle the range head-on. We are not certain if they headed east–north-east or east–south-east to try to find a pass through the mountains or a way around them.

Personally, I think that they headed east–north-east because they could see the seemingly easy-to-traverse buttongrass of the Lightning and Loddon plains, intersected only by a low range of hills. To the east–south-east they would have seen the southern end of the King William Range and its apparent continuation in Algonkian Mountain. However, before explaining the east–north-east route which I favour, I will set out the case for the alternative one.

Jon Marsden-Smedley and Sue Rundle, also of the Tasmanian Parks and Wildlife Service, both experienced bushwalkers, favour the east–south-east route. Their argument is that the Pearce party would have been naturally funnelled straight across the buttongrass of Lightning Plains following the course of the Jane River, turning slightly more south-east to Stannard Flats, crossing to the north of Algonkian Mountain (1073 metres/3490 feet), and then eastward to the south of Mount King William III, the southern extreme of the King William Range. They would have headed due east, crossing the Frith River, the upper reaches of the Gordon, and through beautiful forest country to the Derwent River around the area of present-day Wayatinah. Marsden-Smedley says that this country is 'pretty awful now, but it was not too bad then. The country was much more open as a legacy of Aboriginal burning'. Geoff Law agrees that the area south of Mount King William III would have been easier to traverse in 1822 because of Aboriginal burning, but he points out that the country around the northern reaches of the Gordon is terrible. He walked there in December 1987 and says that 'it carved my legs to shreds . . . The upper Gordon breaks up into channels and you have these primeval-seeming streams choked with moss-covered logs. Even when you get down to the rivers you don't get any sense of space; it can still be very claustrophobic. East of the river is a cutting-grass sort of scrub'.

I quote this because I don't think there is anything in either of the detailed accounts by Pearce that corresponds chronologically with the type of country on the east–south-eastern route. This is not to say that I think those who favour this route are wrong. In a situation like this you can never be certain. The best argument for this route is that the natural lay of the land would funnel the escape party in this direction. Viewed from the Deception Range, this way would have seemed fairly open. I would just say that, following Dan Sprod and others, it is my interpretation of the Pearce texts that the party actually took the east–north-easterly route.

If this is correct, what happened was that they descended from the Deception Range onto Lightning Plains. They then turned north-east and somehow continued on for four more days across the northern section of these plains, which was largely buttongrass and swamp, turned east–north-east, crossed a low range with a 600-metre (1950-foot) ridge and entered more dense forest until they came to the Loddon Plains, another area of buttongrass swamp where, Pearce says, they stopped for the night. Terry Reid says that a virgin buttongrass plain is 'quite reasonable to cross', but it is often bordered by bauera, horizontal, tea-tree and cutting grass. Geoff Law is not so sanguine about buttongrass. He says that 'it looks easy, but the clumps grow up to one metre tall and then in between them you get scrubby tea-tree and other heath-type species . . . It can be frustratingly slow. You think you'll walk across in one hour and it takes two. It is demoralising'.

As they came to the Loddon Plains they were again suffering from severe hunger, having eaten all that was left of Dalton's flesh. The problem with human flesh, especially that of men, is that, while rich in protein, it lacks the carbohydrates needed for energy. Desperation in the face of starvation meant that someone else would have to be killed.

The two main narratives give different accounts of what happened next. The Knopwood narrative says that they sat down famished and exhausted, and they 'began to intimate to each other that it would be much better for one to be sacrificed as food for the rest' – a kind of 'custom of the sea' discussion. They agreed that someone would have to die and a 'horrid ceremony' began. They cast lots to see who it would be and the lot fell to Thomas Bodenham, who did not beg for mercy or ask to be spared. 'The only request he had to make was that they would allow him a few minutes to implore pardon of his offended Maker for past offences' before they killed him. They gave him a half hour for prayer. Then Greenhill again volunteered to be the executioner; he said that he had been in a similar situation before – presumably at sea. He and Travers then politely asked Pearce and Mather to go off some distance to gather wood to light the fire. It was only when the pair were out of sight that Greenhill killed Bodenham with a blow to the head and then, assisted by Travers, cut up the body.

There is something rather contrived about this account. You have the feeling that much of the detail is from Thomas Wells, writing with his respectable London readers in mind. Given the physical state the five men were in, it is psychologically unlikely that they would have been able to sit down and calmly and rationally decide who was to be butchered next. Further, the ceremonial quality of the occasion, with the submissive passivity of Bodenham, the prayer for divine forgiveness and the polite way that Greenhill and Travers asked the others to absent themselves while they killed and butchered Bodenham does not tally with what we have seen of these men. One suspects that in his evidence to Knopwood, Pearce was busy casting himself in the best possible light, fearing that he might eventually be committed for trial for murder. Wells, conscious of the need to soften for his readers the appalling brutality of the murder, has injected an almost liturgical quality into the execution. The sermon-like feel of the narrative is reinforced by a short homily that follows the butchering of the body. It is attributed to Greenhill, but it does not sound like the words of a sailor who has already killed two or more men. It was most likely composed by Wells or whoever the editor was. It could almost have been Knopwood himself, given the way it focuses on how Bodenham had fallen 'a victim to his own folly'.

A very different account of the murder and butchering of Bodenham was given by Pearce to Cuthbertson. It bears the hallmarks of a man who, knowing that he is doomed and that he will hang because he has been caught with human flesh in his pocket, has nothing to hide. It is probably much closer to the truth.

According to this version, by the time they reached the Loddon Plains the remaining five men were desperate with hunger, and Travers, Greenhill and Mather began to discuss who should be killed next. Conveniently for Pearce, he intimated that he was not privy to this discussion and that he and Mather were sent off by Greenhill and Travers to get some more firewood while Bodenham was left standing at the fire, warming himself. Again it was Greenhill who acted as executioner by suddenly attacking

Bodenham, and Pearce made sure he let Cuthbertson know that he was not present when the deed was done and that he did not know what was going to happen. He said, 'In about two minutes I heard a blow given and Mather said "He is done for"'.

As the sole survivor Pearce was in an ideal position to justify himself in these narratives, and one must always bear that in mind while reading the account. It seems most unlikely that Greenhill would send him and Mather off to get firewood just when the deed was about to be done, because from the beginning they had agreed that they were all in it together. While it is probable that Greenhill was again the killer, it is also likely that they were all present for Bodenham's murder and indeed colluded in it. Travers cut the victim's throat, bled him and acted as butcher. Pearce reported that 'Greenhill took his shoes being better than his own'. They only ate the heart and liver that night but, feeling that they now had plenty of provisions, they feasted on the body and rested for the whole of the next day.

Before resuming their journey, they divided the remains into equal parts and then set off 'thro' a marshy ground' for three days, once more in an east–north-easterly direction. This is most probably what is now called 'the sodden Loddon' plains. The Tasmanian Parks and Wildlife Service warns bushwalkers on the nearby Frenchman's Cap Track, which traverses the western sector of the Loddon Plains, that deep mud is often to be expected, illustrating the warning with a photo of a bushwalker almost up to his waist in mud. Terry Reid maintains that this is more the result of thousands of people trudging across the plains toward Frenchman's Cap, although others disagree and feel that these plains have always been very wet!

The first professional explorer to investigate this area was the surveyor William Sharland, who came a decade after the Pearce party in March 1832. On the plains near the confluence of the Adelaide and Loddon rivers, just south-west of the Franklin Hills,

Sharland found human remains, which he took to be those of a convict. He commented, 'They may probably be the remains of some of those unfortunate wretches who have absconded from Macquarie Harbour to seek this melancholy termination of their existence'. From the accounts we can assume that the heap of bones found by Sharland was all that was left of Thomas Bodenham.

While Cuthbertson probably gives a reasonably accurate account of the murder of Bodenham, the Knopwood version is much more believable in its depiction of the party's psychological dynamics after that killing. The dependence of Greenhill and Travers upon each other deepened. Pearce says in an oddly convoluted way that 'they had a respect for each other which they often showed to each other' in many ways. This may or may not be a roundabout allusion to a homosexual relationship, common among convicts in Van Diemen's Land and New South Wales, as indeed they are in prison life today. Ernest Augustus Slade, the superintendent of the Sydney Convict Barracks, told the British Parliamentary Select Committee in April 1838 in his usual blunt way that among certain convicts 'sodomy is as common as any other crime'. The reason, he said, was that the men were not able to consort with women. Slade also had a simple solution for any suspected acts of buggery: he ordered a summary flogging when men were caught 'in an improper, indecent position, with their trowsers [sic] down'. The Catholic Vicar-General of New South Wales, the Reverend William Ullathorne, told the same Select Committee that homosexuality was often practised on the convict ships, and was common in the Convict Barracks in Sydney, where certain boys and men were given female names. It was also prevalent on isolated farms, among stockmen, among the men working on road gangs, and particularly in the places of secondary punishment such as Macquarie Harbour, Moreton Bay and Norfolk Island. Much of what happened in those places was a form of sexual degradation and control, as it usually is in a prison environment. Ullathorne agreed with Slade that the problem would not cease while men were crowded together and the ratio of men to women in the population of the colonies remained so unbalanced.

However, Greenhill and Travers's friendship went back to their time in the frontier country beyond New Norfolk, and it seems to have been sincere for they certainly looked out for each other. Whether their relationship was sexual or not we cannot, of course, know. Preoccupation with sexual relations is very much a post-Freudian, twentieth-century psychological fixation; in the nineteenth century people were less centrally focused on genitality. But Greenhill and Travers's closeness inevitably threw Pearce and Mather together as temporary allies, at least in order to guard against any attempts by the two friends to murder either of them for food. In short, the two sets of men were now pitted against each other as they trudged across the Loddon Plains. It was not long before violence broke out again.

After the slaughter of the young Englishman, the four walked on for three more days, 'subsisting on nothing but the carcass of unfortunate Bodenham which scarcely kept the faculties in motion'. At this point Pearce reports that they again lost the tinder they used to light their camp fire at night and had to go back to search for the tinder, but eventually found it. They would have been in terrible trouble if they had lost it for they would have no means of lighting a fire, their only source of warmth in what was still very wet, cold country, especially at night. To have lost the ability to light a fire would have, quite simply, meant death. Starvation and exhaustion were affecting their judgement and perception and they were dropping and mislaying things with increasing frequency.

They continued in an east–north-easterly direction toward what is now called Mount Arrowsmith at the northern end of the

King William Range. Just to the east of Mount Arrowsmith is the King William Saddle, which is actually the ridge connecting Mount Arrowsmith with Mount King William I. It is crossed nowadays by the only sealed road in the whole area, the Lyell Highway from Hobart to Queenstown and on to the town of Strahan on Macquarie Harbour. At the King William Saddle the modern motorist travelling north-westward from Hobart crosses the boundary between the flatter, drier plains in the centre of Tasmania and enters the wetter rainforested and wilderness area of the south-west.

Starving, exhausted and suspicious of each other, the four began their ascent of the northern end of the King William Range near Mount Arrowsmith – an area, Pearce reports, 'covered with brush and that so extremely thick [that] it made it very bad walking'. From the top of the range Pearce says that they were able to see marshy ground below them with a large river in the middle of it and very fine trees growing on the banks. This was doubtless the lush King William Valley, now submerged in a lake created by the Tasmanian Hydro-Electricity Commission, and the upper reaches of the Derwent River as it began its long journey south-east to Hobart Town. Pearce also says that they saw plenty of kangaroos, emus and other fauna in the valley, the first time in the entire journey that he mentions native animals. But they were unable, or did not try, to catch any, for Pearce says that they had run out of food again. Although they had assured each other that 'they would all die than any more should be killed', when they were alone Pearce says that Mather said to him: 'Let us go on by ourselves . . . You see what kind of cove Greenhill is. He would kill his father before he would fast one day'. Pearce's response is not recorded.

It seems that they wandered around Mount Arrowsmith for a couple of days. At one time they were in a small valley full of ferns. Here Mather made some type of concoction out of fern roots which he boiled and drank, perhaps again as a purge. It made him quite sick and he began to vomit, at which point, according to Pearce, Greenhill 'still showing his spontaneous habit of bloodshed seized the axe and crept up behind him [and] give him a blow on the head'. Mather must have seen it coming and it can't have done much damage because he shouted, 'Murder, you will see me killed'. There was a struggle and the younger and stronger Mather grabbed the axe from Greenhill and threw it to Pearce. Oddly enough, Mather did not seek revenge, perhaps because of his natural disposition. Pearce reports that he was a peaceful type who 'wished to enjoy tranquillity'. Possibly it was also because they all realised that without Greenhill, their navigator and guide, they had no hope of reaching the settled districts. Whatever the reason, it turned out to be a bad mistake on Mather's part not to kill Greenhill.

When it comes to the murder of Mather, there is again a significant divergence between the two narratives. According to the Cuthbertson version, after the first attack on Mather the men walked on a little further to a creek where they decided to camp for the night. Pearce then says that he wandered away from the others for a short time 'and on looking around saw Travers and Greenhill collaring Mather who cried out "murder" and when he [Mather] found that they were determined to have his life, he begged they would give him half an hour to pray for himself'. A prayer book that they just happened to have with them was produced and, after he finished his prayers, he handed the book back to Pearce and laid down his head. Greenhill immediately took up the axe and killed him. After that the three men remained two days camping by the creek and then continued their journey, 'each taking a share of Mather's body'. This time it is the Cuthbertson narrative that seems very contrived, especially in the depiction of Mather's apparent surrender, the convenient absence of Pearce when Greenhill's second attack on Mather occurred, and the sudden and extremely unlikely appearance of a prayer book. However, I think this narrative is believable in saying that Mather was killed on the night after the first attack on him when he was vomiting and at his weakest.

The Knopwood narrative describes a much longer and more complex interaction. After he is attacked the first time while vomiting, Mather understandably becomes more and more fearful and defensive. It is the intimacy between Greenhill and Travers that especially worries him. Mather tells Pearce that he is convinced that Greenhill and Travers are determined to kill him and says it would be wise for Pearce and himself to be on their guard and 'make each other acquainted with whatever they perceived in any way treacherous or deceitful in either Greenhill or Travers'. Although the weather had now improved considerably, they walked on for two days 'in a far worse state than before'. By now Pearce's loyalties were shifting, and though he had sworn 'to be [Mather's] confidential friend' and warn him if the other two were plotting anything, he begins to associate more with Greenhill and Travers and to abandon his erstwhile ally. It did not take Mather long to work out that Pearce had withdrawn from him and had joined in a coalition with the others to kill him.

They made camp and sat around the fire 'in a very pensive and melancholy mood'. The young baker from Dumfries only had one option: to try to keep some distance between himself and the other three. But he could not keep up his guard forever, and eventually one of them crept up on Mather 'under the pretence of gathering wood for the fire'. All three jumped him, dragged him to the ground, 'striking him with the axe on the head and soon terminating his existence'. The body was then dissected 'and having appeased their cannibal appetites [they] laid themselves down by the fire'.

Eighteen years later, in December 1840, the explorer and Deputy Surveyor-General James Erskine Calder discovered items that indicated that escaped convicts had been in the area in a small, open valley through which the modern Lyell Highway passes, which was later named Wombat Glen, just to the west of Mount Arrowsmith. Calder, an experienced bushman and a big man with a strong physique, reports that he found 'in the last stages of decay, several articles which indicated that a party of runaway convicts from Macquarie Harbour, had, many years ago, passed this way. They were placed in the hollow of a fine old tree, which had been the means of preventing their entire destruction. They consisted of an old yellow jacket, a pea jacket, a blanket, and a pair of boots. On searching about we found a large gimblet [a tool for boring holes], a hammer and a broken iron pot. Several trees had been marked'. These may or may not have been Mather's belongings and Calder does not indicate the state of the convict remains. But it does indicate that it was possible for a party of convicts to have got this far from Macquarie Harbour. Wombat Glen is at the northern end of the Loddon Plains and right at the base of Mount Arrowsmith, and it makes sense for the party to have rested here before pushing on over the Saddle and down into the King William Valley.

At this point the Knopwood narrative has Greenhill delivering a monologue justifying their actions in killing Mather. Even a superficial reading indicates that Wells or the editor has taken over – this was written with a reading audience in mind and Wells could not resist the temptation to moralise. From this narrative it is clear that they did not have the means to survive, and that once they had chosen cannibalism as a means of sustenance, there was no turning back. Perhaps Pearce's betrayal of Mather was merely a recognition that his only chance for survival lay in throwing in his lot with Greenhill and Travers. Of course, by doing that, Pearce was running a terrible risk. Given that the other two were so close, he was setting himself up as the next victim. But, as he saw it, he had no other viable choice.

The clue to Pearce's decision can be found in Greenhill's comments after the 'sumptuous repast' following the slaughter of Mather. Greenhill says that they 'must be drawing very near to some settlement or habitation'. In fact, they still had some considerable distance to go to reach the settled districts, but all three men had worked in the back country near the centre of the island and the landscape they had seen across the King William Saddle was beginning to look familiar to them. If they were as close to the settled districts as they thought they were, Pearce no doubt reasoned that he could make a run for it on his own and leave the other two to their own devices. Greenhill also said that he feared that as soon as an opportunity offered, Mather would have gone to Hobart Town to 'give information against them for the murder' of Bodenham, another indication that they thought that they were near the end of their journey.

Once they crossed the King William Saddle the feel and shape of the country changed significantly. They had entered into what are now called the Navarre Plains. Here the country was more open and easier to traverse, and the weather was improving because it was less under the influence of the Roaring Forties. At the Saddle you cross what today is called the 'quartzite line'. Here the structure and geology of the landscape changes and you leave behind the predominantly dolerite mountains of western Tasmania and enter a flatter, drier, semi-alpine landscape. Pearce, Greenhill and Travers found themselves traversing the more open and rather beautiful eucalypt forests that predominate in the high plains of central Tasmania. The dominant trees at higher altitudes were the 20-metre (65-foot) Eucalyptus pauciflora, which are usually known as snow gum, and at the lower levels they encountered the straight and tall alpine ash (Eucalyptus delegatensis). Throughout, the undergrowth was much more open and there were many native animals.

There were also humans – the Aborigines. Once they had

crossed the Saddle, the local clan of the Big River tribe, the Larmairremener, would have begun to observe them, although the three escapees were oblivious to this. While there is evidence from burning patterns that the Aborigines ranged across the whole of the south-west, they did not live in the difficult landscape of the far west permanently. But once the escape party entered Big River land they would have been carefully watched and their behaviour monitored. It is probably only because they were in such poor shape and were perceived as posing no threat that they were not killed.

Four days after the slaughter of Mather, Pearce reports that 'Travers had his foot stung by some venomous reptile'. Snakes hibernate between April and October, so the one that got Travers must have just been coming out of hibernation and was probably fairly lethargic. It would have been either lying in the sun or else looking for a sunny spot. Tiger snakes are quite territorial and, except during the breeding season in January when males are looking for a mate, they are shy of humans, so it is likely that the sluggish snake was slow in getting out of Travers's way. The bite incapacitated him, thus holding the party up for another four or five days.

Australia is famous for having among its 760 known species of reptiles the most venomous snakes in the world. Only two of these are to be found in the south-west of Tasmania: the white-lipped whip snake and the Tasmanian tiger snake, both of whose venom is highly toxic. However, the men were also close to the border of the range of the lowland copperhead, another deadly species found in central, eastern and northern Tasmania. The Navarre Plains is a place where you are likely to encounter snakes, including the copperhead.

Terry Reid and Geoff Law think that it is most likely that Travers was bitten by a tiger snake. The Tasmanian sub-species can grow up to 2 metres (6 feet) or more in length, and manifest considerable colour variation from black to brown, yellow or cream. The predominant colour in the south-west is jet-black, which is an adaptation to its environment that allows the snake to absorb light and heat more effectively in the cold, wet climate. Tiger snakes love frog-infested swamps, although they also eat birds, lizards and small mammals. While its bite is potentially fatal, the tiger snake is well down the evolutionary scale and its fangs are small and underdeveloped. Thus the venom is not injected efficiently into the limb, much of it being lost on the skin surface. Today if the bite is dealt with quickly with the antivenenes that have been available since the 1920s, survival is likely, especially when the victim is an adult. No such antitoxins were available in 1822.

The bite of the tiger snake has a neurotoxic effect and can cause a range of reactions, but usually the first symptom is a massive frontal headache. Vomiting can quickly follow, and the victim lapses in and out of consciousness. The poison flows through the lymphatic system and the nerves controlling the heart and lungs can be adversely affected. It can also cause paralysis and respiratory failure. Bleeding often occurs from both nose and ears, blood clots occasionally form and a heart attack can result. In the Knopwood narrative, Travers is convinced that he is dying – a reasonable supposition given the symptoms – and he exhorts Greenhill to leave him behind. He appeals to their friendship: 'That as they had been companions for so long a time both in days of prosperity as well as in the present days of adversity, where they had always communicated to each other . . . on every subject and had entrusted each other with the most guarded secrets . . . He trusted and hoped that they [Greenhill and Pearce] would not delay time in waiting for him, but to proceed on their journey and leave him where he was that he might have an opportunity of making peace with his Maker'. Despite being very moved by Travers's heroic speech, Greenhill refuses to leave him, convinced that he would recover. Travers soon becomes delirious, although he is 'apprehensive that Pearce would instil into the mind of Greenhill the thought of murdering him', a not unreasonable fear. In response, in an unusual show of emotion, Greenhill tells his mate that 'he would never think of leaving him', that he would carry him all the way, if necessary, because the tie of affection between them was so strong.

So Greenhill and Pearce wait with Travers for five days. It was the correct decision because rest is the best way to deal with tiger-snake bites. Eventually Greenhill felt that Travers had recovered sufficiently for them to proceed. So they set off again, Greenhill and Pearce half-carrying, half-dragging Travers, whose foot was very swollen. They crossed another mountain range, probably the Wentworth Hills, and on the eastern side they came to a large river, the Nive. Travers, as we have seen, was a non-swimmer, so Greenhill swam across carrying the axe and Pearce crossed with the scraps of Mather's flesh that remained. They then cut a long wattle pole and pulled Travers across, camping on the east bank of the Nive River that night. Now in flatter, much more open forest country, they struggled on for two more days eastward from the Nive.

At this stage the inflammation in Travers's foot was turning black, a sign that gangrene was setting in. Pearce states that on the second night after crossing the river, Travers, who was now in great pain, said again that it would be better for them to abandon him and go on. When the sick man eventually fell asleep, Pearce and Greenhill went off to get some wood for the fire and discussed what they were going to do. According to Pearce it was Greenhill who took the initiative again. He now comes across as appallingly objective and callous about the fate of his friend. The narrative claims that Greenhill said, 'Pearce, it is of no use being detained any longer by Travers, and we will serve him as the rest'. According to the Cuthbertson narrative, Pearce refused to play any part in this murder, but in the Knopwood account 'they unanimously agreed to act by him as they had done by the other two' – actually three, if you count Dalton.

When they returned to the camp fire, Travers was awake because of the pain, and he begged them to kill him and be done with it. Soon afterwards he fell into a deep sleep. 'One of them took the axe [most likely Pearce] being driven by the greatest distress and hunger and gave him a blow to the head which soon terminated his life.' Pearce had no doubt that if the tiger snake had not intervened, it would have been he who would have been killed at this time to provide food for the other two. Despite his earlier callousness, Greenhill 'was much affected by this horrid scene and stood quite motionless to see one who had been his companion . . . compelled to be slaughtered as food'. They cut Travers's throat and dissected his body, cooked parts of it on the fire and ate them. 'Having appeased their appetite they lay themselves down to sleep.'

For two days Greenhill and Pearce remained where they were and did nothing 'but gorge themselves on the carcass and sleep'. They then took as much of the body as they could carry and continued on 'through a very fine country'. Throughout the journey Greenhill had used the sun and moon to maintain an easterly direction, and now they were confident that they were somewhere near the settled districts, or at least close to an isolated stock run.

From this point the Cuthbertson narrative becomes increasingly sparse in detail, whereas the Knopwood account becomes almost lost in minutiae and editorialising, although in my view maintaining more verisimilitude. The Knopwood text describes a dramatic and increasingly tense interaction between Greenhill and Pearce as they run out of food again and begin to eye each other off as a source of sustenance. By this stage they were probably somewhere west–north-west of the present-day town of

Ouse. If this is correct they were actually 16 to 18 kilometres (10 to 12 miles) from the nearest isolated sheep run.

The place that they were trying to reach, the 'summit of their hope', as Pearce calls it, was Table Mountain, a 1095-metre (3350-foot) peak immediately south of Lake Crescent, and at the southern end of the tiers that border the central mountain plateau of the island. This was about 40 kilometres (about 24 miles) east–north-east from where they were, but they did not know that. Pearce knew the Table Mountain area because he had ranged through this country after absconding from his assignment and before being sent to Macquarie Harbour. He knew that there were Irish convicts around that region who would help them. But Table Mountain proved peculiarly difficult to find, probably because by this stage they were unable to think straight and maintain a steady direction. Throughout this period the Aborigines would have continued their observation of the two white escapees.

Pearce says they left the place where they had slaughtered Travers, protesting to each other 'the greatest fidelity and friendship, and as they had always travelled by the sun or moon they were confident that they could not be very far from some settlement or stock run'. But despite finding some very good country, any traces of white settlement or even of sheep or cattle runs proved elusive. Pearce then reported that he and Greenhill saw smoke, which turned out to be coming from an Aboriginal camp. He says that knowing that the Aborigines usually have freshly caught game, they decided to charge into the camp brandishing the axe and a large stick, flaying anyone who got in their way. Pearce boasts that the two of them chased off forty to fifty men, women and children, then destroyed the Aborigines' spears and made off as quickly as possible, 'for although these natives are not cannibals, there has been several instances of people being barbarously murdered by them in several parts of the colony'. Pearce claims that a few days later they repeated the performance with another group of between eighteen and twenty Aborigines.

These stories of attacks by two half-starved white men on large groups of Aborigines seem most unlikely and were almost certainly invented by Pearce. The clans and warriors of the Big River tribe would not have tolerated such behaviour.

Knowing their home ranges well, the Aborigines would have had no trouble quietly observing the activities of a couple of escaped convicts wandering directionlessly through them. Aborigines were constantly astonished at what they considered the gross ignorance of Europeans. They saw the whites not only as violent people, but also as amazingly stupid when it came to surviving in what they experienced as a plentiful land. The Big River people did not perceive Pearce and Greenhill as a threat, or else they would have been killed, quickly and efficiently. Given the way in which the Tasmanian Aborigines were being dispossessed of their land and abused by well-armed settlers, they would have felt justified in giving short shrift to two half-crazed escapees encroaching their hunting grounds. The most that the two of them probably ever did was to scavenge some remnants of food from abandoned Aboriginal camps, or search for small reptiles, or even look for edible grubs under fallen trees or by tearing off rotten bark. They were perhaps inspired by the yellow-tailed black cockatoos, which tore bark from trees in an attempt to find the larvae of the wood-boring insects that lived underneath.

Their state was accurately described by Pearce when he says that the two of them 'were terribly reduced in strength and their constitutions dreadfully impaired by the fatigues of this distressing journey. Being exposed to the night dews and cold, they being nearly naked and quite barefoot, their flesh was dreadfully lacerated and torn by the rocks and briars, [with] ulcers showing themselves in several parts of their bodies'. More and more the journey seemed endless. They were probably not making much headway and wandering around in circles. Also as the days went by they became increasingly suspicious of each other, with a dreadful hopelessness setting in and psychologically sapping the little energy they had left. Greenhill always kept the axe in his possession, which made Pearce wary and edgy. They kept their distance from each other during the day and at night Pearce always made a fire 'at such a distance from Greenhill as he considered far enough to prevent an attack that might be made by him'. Greenhill always slept with the axe under his head. Pearce became more fearful than ever. He seldom slept. 'I acted with the greatest precaution never trusting myself near him particularly at night.'

One night they were both pretending to be asleep when Pearce realised that Greenhill was getting ready to attack him. 'I immediately rose as though out of a slumber, [pretending] I had not perceived him.' Greenhill backed off and Pearce reflected that he was lucky he was not really asleep, or else he would have shared the same fate as the other men. So he says he resolved to try to give Greenhill the slip. But this was easier said than done in the country through which they were now travelling. Pearce then decided that he had to get the axe and kill Greenhill in self-defence. He says that they continued along, 'watching each other'. He also claims that Greenhill made several attempts to kill him during this period, but 'I always guarded against such attempts'.

In the end this cat-and-mouse game became a test of who could stay awake the longest. It was Pearce who had the staying power. 'One evening while he was asleep I crept slyly to the brush where he lay and took the axe from under his head, gave him a severe blow on the head which deprived him of his life'. It was as simple as that. He was alone and safe from his companions at last. Pearce bluntly told Cuthbertson that after killing Greenhill 'I cut off part of his thigh and arm which I took with me, and went on for several days until I had ate it all'.

But he had still not found Table Mountain. He was soon starving again and struggled on for several more days, when he was lucky enough to catch two ducks which he ate raw. But the end of the journey was near. 'On the seventh day after leaving Greenhill while travelling through a large marsh I was suddenly surprised at hearing the noise of a flock of sheep, I could not believe my ears.'

He had not exactly arrived at Table Mountain, the 'summit of his hope', but as it turned out he was about 30 kilometres (about 18½ miles) to the south-west of it. Not bad, given that he had been walking through some of the most difficult country in the world for at least forty-nine days. Pearce's feat in surviving such a journey, by whatever means, was remarkable.

•

Pearce's time of freedom started at that moment at the end of his trek from the harbour. He had been walking for so long that he had lost all sense of time and direction and he feared that he would never get to Table Mountain. It was a hot day and he was in a large, flat, marshy, open plain, bordered on either side by stunted trees with pale cream trunks. His figure was gaunt, his beard long, his whole body covered with cuts, sores and festering wounds. He was hungry again, as it was about four days since he had caught and eaten the ducks. At this stage he felt he was going batty because he had this feeling that someone was always watching him. The feeling had first come upon him after he killed and ate Greenhill, and over the last days and nights he had become absolutely convinced that there was always somebody observing his every move. Several times he had screamed, 'Come out you bastard and face me', but no one appeared and all he ever heard was the echo of his own voice.

When he suddenly heard the familiar plaintive bleating of the sheep from over in the trees, he started to shake and felt like crying. Somehow, he had made it to the settled districts. He had beaten all that the bastards had thrown at him, and he had got through to where other white men lived.

It did not take him long to find the sheep. At one end, the marshy plain narrowed into a rocky crevice. Beyond that the ground dropped away sharply down a forested hill to a river in a deep, narrow valley. He had always been good at herding sheep; he had once got into a fight because some stupid cove had said it was because he had a lot in common with them! He positioned himself so that he could corral the sheep into the rocky crevice. Despite his hunger, he slowly manoeuvred the mob into place. When frightened, sheep tend to crowd in together, and then jump on and over the top of each other. He quickly spotted a large, well-fed one and grabbed it. The animal was smart enough to turn away from the area into which he had herded the flock, and it dragged him twenty or thirty yards over rocks toward the wooded hillside down to the river. In the end he had to let the sheep go because he was badly cut and bruised. He had also bashed his head severely on an overhanging rock as he tried to stand up to get a better grip on the animal.

He lay where he fell until the pain cleared a little, and then slowly dragged himself to his feet again. Most of the herd were still standing close by. Sheep are such stupid buggers, he thought, so he tried again to drive a group of them back into the crevice. He cornered about a dozen of them, and grabbed a lamb, dragged it aside, quickly slit its throat and carved it up. The other sheep had scattered in the nearby undergrowth.

He had hardly started eating when he heard the noise of dogs. He looked up, and a man appeared from behind him and held a musket to his head. With a strong Irish accent he said, 'Leave the bloody sheep alone, you bastard, or I'll blow yer brains out! I've been tryin' to find this mob all day, and now, by God, you've frightened 'em off again.'

Looking up at the man Pearce realised that it was one of the McGuire brothers. Pearce smiled and said, 'I'll help you find 'em, Paddy.'

McGuire recognised Pearce's voice immediately. He dropped the musket. 'Well, fuck me, if it isn't me ol' pal, Alex Pearce. What are you doin' here, me lad? Last I heard you was at Sarah's Island. What's wrong wit ya? You look shockin'.'

As quickly as he could Pearce told McGuire the story of the escape, and of the trek across the wilderness. He did not say what had happened to the others.

McGuire took pity on him and assured him that he would look after him. There was some honour, after all, among thieves. They slowly walked to Paddy's nearby hut at Mosquito's Creek close to the high plains, crossing both the Ouse and Shannon rivers on the way. McGuire explained to him that while he was officially assigned to a drunken idiot, George Salter, who had a run nearby on the Derwent River, he had actually been hired out to that mean bastard Tom Triffett, whose sheep Pearce had cornered. His brother, Michael McGuire, was also assigned to Salter and he was still at the Dunrobin run looking after Salter's sheep.

When they got to the hut, Paddy McGuire nursed him as best as he could. It took Pearce some time to get used to ordinary food again, and all he did for several days was sleep and eat. He stayed five days with Paddy, who treated him very kindly, and once he was able to walk he moved on again, as there was always the danger that an unexpected visitor might arrive who recognised him.

Supplied with provisions by McGuire, he headed south, following the narrow valley of the Ouse River to its junction with the Derwent. Near here he stayed for another eleven days with Mick, Paddy's brother. Once he was restored to full health at

Mick's hut, he moved on to his own secret hut, which he had built while he had last been on the run. From there he could range right across the country, knowing the lay of the land exactly. He stayed in his own place for seven days and then returned to Mick McGuire's while Mick was away in Hobart Town.

Late on the second night at Mick's he heard a repeated whistle from outside the hut. When he went out to investigate he found two armed men with several kangaroo dogs. They thought he was a military spy of some sort and threatened to kill him. Eventually he was able to persuade them that he was who he said he was. As he suspected, the men were also escaped convicts on the run. Their names were Ralph Churton and William Davis. The long and the short of it was that he threw in his lot with them. His experience on the run was that he was always better off with a couple of others than on his own. He stayed with them for about seven weeks. Once they had nearly been caught by a party of soldiers from the 48th Regiment when they were droving 180 stolen sheep. They just managed to escape, but they had to abandon the sheep and all their belongings.

On the early morning of Saturday, 11 January 1823, they were near Lake Tiberias with some ex-convict mates who did a lot of sheep-stealing. They were sleeping in a rather out-of-the-way and narrow valley just to the west of Jericho, sheltering under a tree from the rising sun, when a party of red-coated soldiers from the 48th appeared. Davis saw them coming and made a run for it but he was shot and wounded. Pearce and Churton were caught sitting under the tree. It was obvious that someone had dobbed them in. Honour among thieves was not absolute, especially if a reward of £10 was involved – the price on the heads of Davis and Churton.

They were marched back to the barracks at Jericho and by Monday night they were secured in Hobart Town jail.

5

The Sudden Death of a Shropshire Lad

It was the suddenness and sheer violence of the axe attack that took Thomas Cox completely by surprise. He did not even see it coming, so he had no chance to shield himself, let alone offer any defence. Pearce had been standing about a metre away from him, looking out across the river, an ugly scowl on his face. Cox was bending over and blowing on wet sticks and wood, trying to get a fire alight to cook some of the food that they had stolen from the officers' hunting party the previous morning. The two of them had just had a raging argument. It had arisen because Cox had mentioned that he could not swim, and that he thought they should try to take an inland route so that they would not have to cross all of the rivers that flowed into the sea along the coast. Pearce demanded to know why he had not told him this earlier. The northern Irish accent was very pronounced.

'I'd never have bolted wit ya if I'd known dat, and I'm fuckin' not goin' over the mountains agin,' he screamed in Cox's face.

The words were accompanied by a spray of spittle. Cox was tempted to lash out in response, but he backed off; he was suddenly genuinely scared of the older man. The stories that the soldiers and other prisoners were telling about him being a 'man-eater' flashed through his mind. For the first time he felt it might have been a bad mistake to have bolted with the Irishman. He decided that silence was probably the best course he could take.

Cox was anxious to get the fire going because he was very hungry and wanted to cook the fish they had caught as well as eat the rest of the pork and bread they had stolen from the officers. All the convicts at Sarah Island knew that the Commandant, soldiers and other officials often went hunting in the forests around Macquarie Harbour to supplement their own food supplies. Two days previously Pearce and Cox were in thick rainforest inland from Sophia Point on the eastern shore when they had heard shooting in the distance and, guessing what was going on, they crept up and hid in the thick bush to see if they could filch anything to eat from the hunting party. The shooters were Spence the surgeon and Lucas the pilot, assisted by the convict John Douglas, who acted as the Commandant's secretary and commissariat clerk. Lucas shot at a pademelon, which the convict clerk had first spotted in the dense, wet undergrowth, but missed. Spence, who was carrying a large, leather shoulder-bag, absent-mindedly put it on the ground. He told Douglas to remember the spot so that they could come back for it. Both of the officers said they were determined not to return to Sarah Island empty-handed and, telling Douglas to look sharp, they handed him their guns. As they moved on, leaving the leather bag behind, both Pearce and Cox could have sworn that Douglas looked in their direction and with a slight nod of the head indicated that they should take it. He then led the officers off over a slight rise and further on into the thick forest, well away from the hiding convicts. The two escapees quickly nabbed the bread and pork in the bag and headed off in the opposite direction.

They had already eaten some of it, but when they reached the King River, Cox was looking forward to finishing it with a feast of cooked fish. After the violent words about his inability to swim, he decided to busy himself preparing the fire, hoping that a good meal would distract Pearce and bring back his good humour.

But behind his back the Irishman was still fuming. The idea that he was stuck with another blockhead like Travers and Bodenham who could not swim and who would hold him up and put him in danger at every river they came to utterly frustrated him. He felt himself becoming more and more angry. But beyond the anger, and somewhere just beyond the edges of his consciousness, he knew he was going to kill the young man for another reason: he wanted to taste human flesh again. He knew he liked the flavour, but most of all he wanted the feeling that he could do what he liked with the body after he had killed the bastard. He could still remember the taste of the meat of Greenhill's arms. In the end he felt the joke was really on Bob Greenhill because he was the one who told Pearce that the thick part of the arms was the best meat on the human body when they were eating Travers.

A violent paroxysm of both anger and hunger possessed Pearce and he could contain himself no longer. He turned. Cox was kneeling beside the fire, his head bent over it. Pearce picked up the heavy, blunt axe and without a sound hit out at the young man's head, but his aim was bad and he only hit him a glancing blow. Cox rolled over screaming, trying to cover his head, and twice more Pearce lashed out at the young man with the axe. Then suddenly, without really knowing why, he turned away, walked toward the river and prepared to swim across. Cox was still alive and conscious, but badly injured and in unbearable pain. He called out in a faint voice, 'For mercy's sake come back, and put me out of my misery!' Again without thinking, Pearce turned back and obliged him by smashing the axe into his head a fourth time, killing him instantly. He then laid down the axe, turned away from the dead body and focused his attention on getting the fire going.

It was early in the evening of Sunday, 21 November 1823 when the attack occurred. The two escapees had arrived at the King River about half an hour before, and had begun to make camp on the sand near the edge of the forest bordering the south bank of the river, some 360 metres (400 yards) upstream from where it flowed into the northern end of Macquarie Harbour. They had worked out that at this spot the fire would be well hidden by a headland and a small island from any passing boat that might be heading up or down the harbour. They were also pretty sure that the soldiers from the 48th Regiment had given up looking for them because it was nine days since they had escaped from Constable Logan's work gang in the rainforest near Kelly's Basin, and for the last few days they had seen no sign whatsoever that anyone from the Sarah Island penal settlement was actively looking for them. Pearce had laughed a lot about escaping a second time from Logan. He hoped the fucking bastard would cop a 'bull' (seventy-five lashes) from the Commandant for letting him bolt again.

However, Cox had noticed that for much of this particular Sunday his mate was not his usual jocular, garrulous self. Somehow he seemed to have withdrawn into himself and gone quiet, but Cox put it down to the older convict's exhaustion; he was known by all the men back at the island as a moody mongrel. Right from the beginning Pearce had been adamant that they were not going to try the inland route. He insisted to Cox that it was far too arduous and that once was enough; he was not prepared to try it again. So they had remained in the Macquarie Harbour area working their way slowly north, not trying to cover too much territory, always on the lookout for an opportunity to steal food from the stores at the mines, or anywhere else that provisions might be taken. They had had no luck except with the hunting party. Some of the territory they had traversed was dense and hard to penetrate, but other parts were more open. It had been raining for the last day and a half and they were wet and cold. When the rain finally stopped, they came out of the forest and made camp on the small beach on the southern shore of the King River.

Their intention was to make a fire, dry out their clothes, rest overnight and then try to catch some more fish. After that they hoped to begin their trek northward along the west coast, intending ultimately to get beyond the reach of British justice. Not that Cox had thought it out very carefully or talked with Pearce about where the two of them were actually going. Their escape was guided more by impulse than forward planning. Their primary aim was to escape from the penal oppression of Sarah Island and Macquarie Harbour. The general idea was that after they had made their way up the coast to the north, they would cut across toward Port Dalrymple or even Launceston, and then work out where to go from there. Beyond that, Cox and Pearce largely trusted to instinct and luck.

Pearce was a hero for young Cox, as he was for many of the other 230 prisoners at Sarah Island in November 1823. Everyone knew about his feat in getting through the wilderness of rugged mountains and dense rainforests to the settled districts in the centre of Van Diemen's Land. After a two-month period as a bushranger and outlaw on the edges of the settled areas north of Hobart Town, Pearce had been recaptured and interrogated. The 33-year-old Irish thief from County Monaghan was then shipped to Macquarie Harbour to serve out the rest of his sentence.

When he got back to Sarah Island in November 1823, Pearce relished the role of convict celebrity, much to the frustration of Commandant Cuthbertson, who cursed the idiots in Hobart Town who foisted more and more troublesome no-hopers like No. 102 on him. The Lieutenant wished that they had hung him, or at least kept him in Hobart Town, where stories of escaping and making it through to the settled districts would not have created so much expectation among the prisoners. At night in the penitentiary Pearce told wild stories about the escape to anyone who would listen, and he often had an enthralled audience. He boasted how Greenhill and Travers had killed the bastard Dalton who had volunteered to be a flogger, and how Greenhill had suggested that they eat his flesh. He made sure that everyone knew it was Greenhill who was the prime mover in the killing and subsequent cannibalism. He told his fellow prisoners that the authorities were lying when they said that you could not escape from the harbour, and he assured them that strong men could make it through to the settled districts. He suggested that they ought to plan some type of mass break-out. At least some of them would make it back to the grog and fleshpots of Hobart Town. When they asked him what had happened to his other mates, he became vague and confused and said that the old fool parson, 'Bobby' Knopwood, had treated him as a liar and had told everyone that his testimony about Greenhill and Travers killing people was merely a concocted and 'depraved' cover story for his mates, who were probably still alive and at large in the bush. As he recounted the story he imitated Bobby's upper-class, high-church accent, much to the amusement of everybody.

When pushed on what had really happened by a couple of the more intelligent prisoners, Pearce simply replied that he had become separated from the others and that he did not know where they were or what had transpired. The story was hopelessly inconsistent, but most of his fellow prisoners did not spend a lot of time analysing it. The fact that he had 'made it through' to at least a brief period of freedom gave them hope. Hope was what they needed most, that there was something beyond the slavery of Sarah Island. Anyway, what if there had been a few murders? Here at the harbour they were treated as government chattels and most of them felt that it was every man for himself. At least Pearce showed what could be achieved by a strong man with a determination to gain his freedom.

The prisoners also soon heard that there were stories circulating among the soldiers and officers that Pearce was a 'maneater' and that you needed to be very careful of him. As a punishment and warning to others who might be contemplating escape, Cuthbertson ordered that Pearce be given a period in solitary, and that he then work in the penal settlement's logging operations in heavy leg irons. He hoped that this would serve as an example to the others and that it would make it much more difficult for him to abscond a second time.

Among the many 'new chums' that Pearce met on his return to Sarah Island was the young, Shropshire-born Thomas Cox, who had been sentenced to transportation to Van Diemen's Land for life for robbery. He had been shipped to Hobart Town with 369 other English male convicts on the Royal Navy ship Dromedary, arriving on 10 January 1820. The convict conduct register, appropriately called the 'Black Book', shows that Cox had kept out of trouble for two years after arrival, until a minor misdemeanour concerning leave passes landed him in the public stocks in Hobart Town for three hours, to be humiliated and jeered at by the passers-by. A month later he was back in court because he tried to pass himself off as a free man and assaulted the constable who challenged him, for which he received twenty-five lashes. Three months after that he got twenty-five more from the Hobart Town magistrates for attempting to escape from lawful custody. Finally, in late August 1823, he absconded from the Hobart Town prisoners' barracks, headed 200 kilometres (125 miles) north to the settlement at Launceston, was rearrested, and then escaped again from the local jail with another convict named Abner Smith. They were quickly recaptured. By this time the magistrates of Van Diemen's Land had had enough of Thomas Cox, so he was given fifty lashes and sentenced to be transported to Sarah Island.

Cox worked in the same logging gang as Pearce, and he 'constantly entreated' the Irishman to escape with him, but initially Pearce was having none of it. He had seen too much of the wilderness to want to try his luck again. However, when Cox secretly 'procured fishhooks, a knife, and some burnt rag for tinder', the basic wherewithal for an escape, Pearce began to be persuaded that they might have a chance if they headed north together up the coast toward the settlement at Port Dalrymple. Both men were impulsive, and Cox was inexperienced and immature. The clincher for Pearce came when another convict stole his shirt. Although it was not his fault, he knew he would get a Botany Bay dozen (twenty-five lashes) from Cuthbertson for the loss of any item of slops. Pearce was not prepared to cop twenty-five for something he had not done, so he eventually agreed to attempt the escape with the enthusiastic Cox, who had probably only been at Sarah Island for a couple of months.

Having heavy chains and irons attached to both legs made it difficult for the men to run, but given the darkness of the rainforests in which the logging gangs worked around the shores of Kelly's Basin, escape was not impossible, even for a man in chains. Both the rainforest and the nature of the logging operations made it very difficult for any overseer to keep check on where each of the eight men in the work-gang was at any given time, especially when the overseer was as careless as Constable Logan, to whom Pearce had again been assigned. So Cox and Pearce were able to exploit his negligence, and the two men quietly slipped away into the dense forest. As soon as they were out of Logan's earshot, Cox used his axe carefully to 'oval' the Irishman's ankle-fetter ('to oval' was convict slang meaning to bend the round ring) and draw Pearce's foot through it, heel first. It was a delicate and perilous operation using the blunt end of the axe as a hammer, but eventually he was successful.

Once free, it took Pearce several hours to be able to walk normally. Because he had dragged around such a heavy weight for months, he had to remember to control his legs' tendency to over-compensation; otherwise they shot up in the air in a kind of goose-step.

A couple of hours elapsed before their disappearance was noticed and communicated to Sarah Island, and two or three soldiers and some trusted convicts were dispatched to the eastern shore to search for them. But by then they were well away into the forest, which Pearce had come to know fairly well. In his later confession the Irishman says that 'for the first and second day they strayed through the forest' and 'on the third made the beach [on Macquarie Harbour] and travelled . . . until the fifth, when they arrived at King's River'. They remained near the river for three or four days, hiding 'in an adjoining wood to avoid soldiers who were in pursuit of them'. They robbed some hunters on the seventh day, and by day nine they were satisfied that the authorities had given up looking for them, and that it would be safe to emerge from the depressing wetness of the thick rainforest around the banks of the King River near where it flowed into the harbour.

They talked a lot in the course of their time together. Cox was eager to hear all the details of Pearce's escape. He asked what Dalton's flesh tasted like and Pearce said that it was like pork. For the first seven nights they had not lit a fire, and the couple of fish they had caught were eaten raw. They were too close to Sarah Island and were never sure if there were soldiers still lurking around who would spot the fire in the dark. Even though it was early summer the nights were cold, and they slept huddled together to try to keep warm.

On two of the nights Pearce had groped the younger Cox and then buggerised him. Although this had happened quite often to Cox since he had entered the prison system and he was getting used to it, he did not enjoy rough sex with a man, especially because he was always used as a passive partner. He had never approached another man himself, although on one occasion when he could pay he had been with a female whore in Hobart Town. What he particularly resented was being treated like a 'punk' and a 'molly'. He had been shocked when it first happened to him on the ship out to Van Diemen's Land. Other stronger men had grabbed and penetrated him in the Hobart Town convict barracks, and later at Sarah Island. Afterwards Cox always felt humiliated and powerless, especially because he knew it showed where he belonged in the pecking order.

He resented Pearce doing it to him because originally he had felt safe with him, having heard that the Irish were hardly ever involved in buggery, and so he had assumed that Pearce was not a 'shirt-lifter'. But the instinctively intelligent Cox soon realised that Pearce was an old hand who had adopted convict ways. He also knew that he would have to put up with it because the Irishman was much stronger than he was, and he had much more experience of the bush.

•

The prosecution later asserted at Pearce's trial that after he had killed the young man 'he then cut a piece [of flesh] off one thigh, which he roasted and ate . . . [and then] he swam across the river with an intention to reach Port Dalrymple'. This is a summary account, and the actual butchering of Cox's body took longer, which, as the *Hobart Town Gazette* of Friday, 25 June 1824 put it, was 'a thrilling tale of almost incredible barbarity'. What happened was that after killing the young man, Pearce stripped the body naked, got the fire going, cut off the hands, decapitated the body and placed the injured head in a nearby tree. He carved up the torso and ate parts of it, including the flesh of the underarm, and fell asleep on the south bank of the King River.

He awoke early the next morning while it was still dark, ate some of the fish and had a little bread, then changed into Cox's clothes, which were in better shape than his own. He gathered up his odds and ends, as well as the remains of the bread and pork they had stolen earlier from the hunters, and wrapped everything in a swag made from his own shirt, adding what he could carry of Cox's flesh. As an afterthought he also shoved a sizeable piece of flesh into his pocket. As the dawn appeared, he swam across the mouth of the river and headed northward along the beach and sand dunes. With a full belly he walked quickly, and after about 5 miles (8 kilometres) he came to the upper end of Macquarie Harbour, passing by the little bay where the present-day town of Strahan is situated. His main aim was to avoid going anywhere near the pilot's station at Hell's Gates. Once he got to the northern end of the Harbour, he turned north-west across flat, sandy country behind the thick scrub and coastal tea-tree, hoping to reach the ocean beach and the Southern Ocean beyond the entrance to the harbour. Then he intended to head up the beach, sticking very much to the coast. He had no idea of how far he would have to travel to get anywhere near a settled district.

But as he walked across the flat land toward the ocean beach, something started to trouble him. It was a confused mixture of feelings. Perhaps it was that he just did not have the physical or psychological energy to push on much further, and could not face the prospect of an endless, lonely trek. Now that he was on his own he knew that once he had consumed what was left of Cox and the other food he had, he would be hungry again. Perhaps he also realised that there was a chance that he would be killed by Aborigines, as he guessed had happened to other convicts who had escaped from Macquarie Harbour. If he was going to stick to the beaches he knew that constant walking in soft sand is a demanding exercise. It also could have been that, at a deeper level, he realised that he liked human flesh and he began to feel something like remorse. These were new feelings for him. Whatever his reasons, he decided to return to the Macquarie Harbour area and try to survive somewhere near the King River by stealing whatever came his way. Perhaps he could attach himself to another party of escaping prisoners.

By late morning he had turned back and was heading again toward the scene of the murder at the King River.

•

As he walked back Pearce began to recall all that had happened to him. He suddenly felt that the only time he had been free and happy was the period he had spent on the run up-country, after he had killed Greenhill and reached the settled districts at the end of the nightmare journey from Macquarie Harbour. There he was with his old boon companions and there was rum, tobacco, food and the occasional woman to keep him warm at night. Once he regained his strength, he had been able to range freely over the country from hut to hut. He was confident that his mates would look after him if any bosses or soldiers came snooping around. He felt safe in this back country; he knew where he was, he could do what he wanted, and no man stood over him. There was one white woman who said she fancied him, but he did not really want to get stuck with her. As far as he was concerned you had your way with them, and then you left and looked after yourself. He did not want to get tied up with anyone, especially now that he was on the run. A woman could become a burden.

When Pearce got to the northern bank of the King River, he had to decide what he should do. Eventually he swam across to the south side, still carrying his supplies, and, skirting the remains of Cox, he began to head south across the sand dunes and coastal scrub to the medium-density forest that reached right out to the edge of Macquarie Harbour at Pine Cove Point. Here he could watch activity on the harbour and give himself time to decide what his next move should be. He had already gathered some dry driftwood for a fire which he would light later that night further back in the forest. He sat in the shade at the edge of the trees looking out over the harbour. It was the first time he had been alone and away from other convicts for months.

By now it was getting toward late afternoon. Although he did not spell it out for himself explicitly, he was shocked by the violence of his attack on Cox. He had almost torn up the body. He was also uncertain of what he should do. How long would his liberty last if he hung around the harbour? There was always the danger of wandering into a party of soldiers, or his being seen by someone who would report him in order to curry favour with Cuthbertson. He felt hungry and took out a piece of Cox's flesh, but the scene at the King River came back to him and he was unable to eat it and put it back in his pocket. He felt exhausted and he dozed off to sleep where he sat. At least when he was asleep he did not feel so terribly alone.

When he awoke about twenty minutes later he looked idly across the water, and there was a ship! It was the pilot-schooner *Waterloo*, sailing toward Hell's Gates from Sarah Island with James Lucas in command. It was just north of Liberty Point, about 5 miles (8 kilometres) away. Impulsively, and without thinking of what he was doing or what he would say, Pearce ran out onto the beach and was eventually successful in getting the dry driftwood to catch alight. Soon a good fire was burning, and by pouring some water on the fire he created a lot of smoke. Now at least he would have company and not be alone with his frightening thoughts. As he waited for the pilot-boat he reflected that he was a tough and strong survivor, and that he had talked his way out of lots of problems before. He had even convinced old Bobby Knopwood that he was innocent of all the killings on the terrible journey across the wilderness, and he hoped he would be able to do something similar with Cuthbertson. He would simply say that Cox had drowned in one of the rivers and leave it at that. He would cop a hundred and that would be that!

As soon as the smoke began to rise from the shoreline of the harbour it was spotted from the schooner's deck, and Lucas ordered the *Waterloo* to change tack. As the schooner came close to shore, a boat was dispatched to pick up the lone figure on the beach at Pine Cove Point. As it approached the beach, Pearce was recognised, and William Evans, a tall seaman from the *Waterloo*, was sent ashore by Lucas. As Evans neared him, Pearce blurted out, 'Cox was drowned in the King's River'. Evans replied that he should tell that to the Commandant. The able seaman tied Pearce's hands behind his back and marched him out to the boat. It was rowed back to the *Waterloo* and Pearce was brought on board.

Lucas ordered that Pearce be placed in leg-irons and searched. The piece of human flesh was found in his pocket. Lucas demanded to know what it was.

'It is a piece of Cox, and I brought it to show that he is lost', Pearce said, making up the story on the spot. Knowing his reputation as a possible man-eater, Lucas ordered that the *Waterloo* turn around and return to Sarah Island. It was the only safe place for a man like Pearce.

However, an observant guard at Sarah Island had also seen the smoke, and Cuthbertson immediately ordered out a whaleboat, boarded it and went up the harbour to investigate. It was nightfall when the schooner and Cuthbertson's whaleboat met. The Commandant went aboard the *Waterloo* and, after conferring with Lucas, he confronted the escapee. He asked Pearce about the human flesh in his pocket and demanded that he explain why he was wearing Cox's clothes. Immediately Pearce started fudging. He said he had cut off the piece of flesh to show that Cox really was dead, and that he was wearing the young man's clothes because he would not be needing them any more. Cuthbertson could tell he was lying and asked him directly: 'Tell me, Pearce, did you do the deed?'

Without thinking, the Irishman replied, 'Yes, and I am willing to die for it'. For the moment Cuthbertson was satisfied, but later while the officers were having a quiet drink together, Able Seaman Evans asked Pearce why he had killed Cox who, after all, had been his mate. By now Pearce had had time to think about his situation and had again become cagey. He said, 'I'll tell no one until I am going to suffer for it'. As time went on, he began to make all types of excuses for his behaviour. Perhaps this is because he found it hard to concede, even to himself, that he had been guilty of such sheer violence.

They all slept on the *Waterloo* that night, Pearce firmly chained to a bulkhead, and early the next morning Cuthbertson sent the whaleboat under the command of his coxswain, Thomas Smith, with Pearce aboard, in leg-irons and his hands firmly tied behind his back, to recover what was left of the body of Cox.

When they reached the King River, an appalling scene awaited them. This is how Smith described it to the Supreme Court in Hobart Town at Pearce's trial for the murder of Cox. He told the court that when his party found the body 'the head was away, the hands cut off, the bowels were torn out, and the greater part of the breech and thighs gone, as were the calf of the legs, and the fleshy parts of the arms. Witness [Smith] said to the prisoner, "How could you do such a deed as this?" he answered "No person can tell what he will do when driven by hunger". Witness then said, "Where is the head?" The answer was "I left it with the body". Witness searched for and found it a few yards off, under the shade of a fallen tree; witness then picked up what appeared to be the liver of the deceased and an axe stained with blood, on which prisoner was asked "if that was the axe with which he killed Cox?", and he answered "it was". The fragments of the body were quite naked . . . There had been a fire near the body, and not far from it lay a knife which the witness picked up . . . Prisoner on being asked "where Cox's hands were" said "he had left them on a tree where the boat landed"; a search was made for them but they could not be found'.

Because this is a disinterested, eyewitness testimony given under oath at a murder trial in the Supreme Court, we can accept it as pretty close to the truth, at least as the witness saw it. The remains of the body were then wrapped in two rugs, and the whaleboat, with Pearce and Cuthbertson aboard, returned to Sarah Island. The *Waterloo* continued on its journey to the pilot-station just inside Hell's Gates.

Back at the penal settlement Commandant Cuthbertson felt that he had to interview Pearce and get to the bottom of what had happened to Cox so that he could send a coherent report back to the Lieutenant-Governor. It was clear that the Irish convict was a murdering man-eater, and that what he had told Knopwood about the first escape was substantially true. Cuthbertson was convinced that he should never have been sent back to Macquarie Harbour, but hung in Hobart Town. So the Commandant set up a formal interview with Pearce, with John Douglas, his convict clerk, recording Pearce's responses. At this stage Pearce was in the convict hospital, such as it was, in fear of his life but probably suffering from some type of food poisoning.

The original manuscript of his statement to Cuthbertson is now probably lost. However, the narrative may have come down to us in a long-hand version that is held in Sydney's Mitchell Library and is headed 'Pearce's Narrative'. Dan Sprod considers that this Mitchell Library narrative is very early and may be either a direct copy of Pearce's confession to Cuthbertson, or may even be a portion of the original. Another version of this interview with Cuthbertson comes down to us in summary form from a later surgeon at Macquarie Harbour, John Barnes. He gave evidence fourteen years later to the 1838 House of Commons Select Committee into Convict Transportation, chaired by the radical member of parliament, Sir William Molesworth. Barnes told the

Select Committee that he had taken his information about Pearce from the Sarah Island records but, as with other witnesses who testified before the Molesworth Select Committee, the evidence given was sometimes exaggerated, and Molesworth himself was determined to paint the convict system in the worst possible light. So Barnes's testimony needs to be balanced by the evidence taken at Pearce's trial, which occurred only seven months after the actual events.

Surgeon Barnes shortens the time scale that the escapees were at large by saying that Cox and Pearce absconded on 16 November 1823, not 13 November as in the evidence given at the murder trial. But the most interesting extra detail that Barnes provides is that as well as having half a pound of human flesh in his pocket, Pearce also had other food with him when he surrendered. 'Pierce [sic] could be in no want of food when he committed this horrid deed . . . [W]hen he was taken there was found upon his person a piece of pork, some bread, and a few fish . . . but which he had not tasted, stating that human flesh was by far preferable.' When asked why he murdered Cox, Pearce said that 'they quarrelled about the route they were to pursue, and Cox being the strongest man, he [Pearce] was obliged to take up an axe, with which he knocked him down and killed him'. Barnes says that the two escapees had stolen the food Pearce had 'from a party of hunters two days before'.

Barnes's description of the butchered body of Cox generally concurs with that given by Thomas Smith to the Supreme Court at Pearce's trial, although there are some minor differences. Barnes says that Cuthbertson sent a boat over to the King River to collect the remains of Cox, that Pearce led the recovery party to a site about 400 yards up-river, and that 'the body was found and brought to the [Sarah Island] settlement in a dreadfully mangled state, being cut right in two at the middle, the head off, the privates torn off, all the flesh of the calves of the legs, back of the thighs and loins, also off the thick part of the arms, which the inhuman wretch declared was the most delicious food; none of the intestines were found; he said that he threw them behind a tree, after having roasted and devoured the heart and part of the liver; one of the hands was also missing'. The Barnes account concurs with the Supreme Court evidence that Pearce gave himself up because he had no hope of ultimately escaping, 'that he was . . . horror-struck at his own inhuman conduct', and 'that he did not know what he was about when he made the signal upon the beach' to the passing schooner.

As long as he remained at Sarah Island, Pearce was kept in close confinement and separated from the other convicts. He finally left the penal settlement in heavy chains and carefully confined aboard the government vessel the *Duke of York*. As the signal came back from Hell's Gates that the ship had cleared Macquarie Harbour and was underway for Hobart Town, the Commandant breathed a sigh of relief. His man-eater was gone. Pearce would soon be dead and all respectable people would sleep more soundly in their beds.

•

Ironically, Lieutenant John Cuthbertson himself was to die some seven months before the Irish cannibal was hung. The Commandant drowned on Christmas Eve, 1823. There was a gale blowing and Cuthbertson was concerned about what might happen to the first Sarah Island-built schooner, which was moored offshore. He was watching it from his verandah when he realised that it had slipped its moorings and was beginning to drift toward the mouth of the Gordon River. He immediately ordered out his whaleboat and went after the drifting ship. Eventually he and his crew secured the new boat. Cuthbertson and his men then turned to row back to Sarah Island. Ignoring the advice of a convict overseer who had been a ship's mate, he ordered that they row straight through a high surf breaking on the flats at the mouth of the Gordon. They were tipped over in the heavy sea, and despite the desperate efforts of Smith, his coxswain, the Lieutenant and all but two of the crew were drowned. Cuthbertson was about thirty-eight at the time and had almost finished his tour of duty at Macquarie Harbour. Sorell, who respected him a lot, would have made sure he was promoted to captain on his return to Hobart Town. Instead, after temporary interment at Sarah Island, his body was brought back to the tiny colonial capital and was buried with due ceremony on 19 April 1824. So he was in his final resting place even before Pearce was executed.

After being shipped in late November or early December, Pearce had to wait six months for his Supreme Court trial. He was to outlive his Commandant by seven months.

6

The Death of a Cannibal

Fully wigged and robed, the 31-year-old, newly appointed Chief Justice of Van Diemen's Land, John Lewes Pedder, strutted onto the exalted and uncomfortable bench of the Supreme Court in Macquarie Street near the corner of Murray Street in Hobart Town, on the very cold morning of Monday, 20 June 1824. There was a heavy covering of snow on Mount Wellington, and it was particularly chilly in the courtroom. Given the inadequate heating system, both judge and legal officers needed all the layers of court costume they could muster to keep warm, as did the respectable jury of seven commissioned officers.

Pearce's trial would be the thirty-third case to be held before the Supreme Court since it had opened on 10 May 1824. Chief Justice Pedder, who had arrived in the colony just two months before, direct from the mother country, was a careful legal scholar who was sometimes tediously slow at arriving at what he considered a just verdict, no matter how depraved the malefactor before him. His enemies said that he was a high Tory with a lofty view of the divine right of government and the courts. As a convinced member of the established church he was profoundly opposed to aid of any sort being given to Roman Catholics and other sectaries, such as Methodists, and he certainly did not believe in the right of Catholic convicts to be exempted from compulsory attendance at Anglican services. Pedder often hectored condemned men and women from the bench at length, telling them that they should not complain about the harshness of the law when the penalties for crime were well known to everyone.

Before the learned judge that June morning were two accused. The first to come before the bench was a free man, William Pilinger, who was arraigned on the charge of having stolen a bull and an ox on 15 August 1823. The animals belonged to the wealthy capitalist and often absentee landlord Edward Lord, Esquire, and the animals were valued at £10. Pilinger was well represented by Mr Solicitor Ross who, in an acute cross-examination, soon bamboozled the only witness, the stock-keeper Thomas Burrell. The jury felt that the evidence was insufficient to establish Pilinger's guilt and had no hesitation in acquitting him.

The second accused man had no such accomplished defence attorney. In fact, he had no one at all to defend him and the case was a lot more serious than stealing a bull and an ox. Alexander Pearce 'was arraigned for the murder of a fellow-prisoner named Thomas Cox, at or near the King's River in the month of November last'. When asked what he pleaded, Pearce defiantly said, 'Not guilty'. It was the only plea he could make if he wanted to save his life. But it was inconsistent with the admissions that he had already made to Cuthbertson.

The reporter for the *Hobart Town Gazette* was present in the courtroom for the whole of Peace's brief trial, and he did not hesitate to make his feelings about Convict No. 102 known to the *Gazette*'s readers: 'The circumstances which were understood to have accompanied the above crime had long been considered with extreme horror. Report had associated the prisoner with cannibals; and recalling as we did, the vampire legends of modern Greece, we confess, that on this occasion, our eyes glanced in fearfulness at the being who stood before a retributive Judge, laden with the weight of human blood, and believed to have banqueted on *human flesh*' (his italics). In other words, there was no presumption of innocence in the small community of Hobart Town, and by now everyone knew about Pearce's admissions to Bobby Knopwood concerning the first escape.

Thomas Wells's 'exclusive' story was dead in the water in Van Diemen's Land. The respectable people of Hobart Town were horrified because it was presumed that Europeans could not possibly be guilty of such cannibalistic deeds. You might occasionally expect to encounter man-eating among the non-white races, although the especially well informed were no doubt not surprised that if any European did indulge in such a practice it would be an Irishman! Apparently they had forgotten the Englishman Robert Greenhill and the Scotsman John Mather.

The prosecutor in the Pearce case was the newly appointed 38-year-old Colonial Attorney-General, Joseph Tice Gellibrand. Gellibrand himself was to become lost in the bush near Melbourne in 1837, and was almost certainly killed by Aborigines close to the present city of Geelong. His body was eventually found and buried in Sydney Town.

Both judge and prosecutor were scrupulously anxious to quash all talk of man-eaters and to focus the prosecution case on the explicit charge that Pearce faced: the murder of Cox. The jury were instructed by His Majesty's Attorney-General to achieve the impossible: they were asked 'to dismiss from their minds all previous impressions against the prisoner' and 'however justly their hearts must execrate the fell enormities imputed to him, they should duteously judge him not by rumours – but by indubitable evidence'. Everyone had heard about the eight white cannibal escapees of Macquarie Harbour and, while the authorities now believed Pearce's tale to Knopwood about all that had happened during the first escape, a charge of murder requires a body for it to stick, and Cox's remains were the only evidence the authorities had. Hence Pearce was not charged with the deaths of his companions on the first escape; this was supposed to play no part in the trial at all. Of course, if Pearce had been thinking straight he would have disposed of Cox's remains before surrendering, which would have been easy enough to do, and then made up a story to cover the young man's disappearance. Since there was no body he might have even escaped the murder charge altogether. However, given his personality, there is no doubt that he would have provided the authorities of Van Diemen's Land with the opportunity to get him on some charge in the end. Perhaps in his heart of hearts he really wanted to die.

Prosecutor Gellibrand detailed Pearce's confessions for judge and jury, firstly to 'the much-lamented Lieutenant Cuthbertson', and secondly his admissions under examination by the Reverend Robert Knopwood. His Majesty's Attorney admitted that these confessions, 'although in some respects inconsistent', would 'when coupled with all the facts, merit the most serious attention'. Gellibrand then turned to the known facts about the Pearce–Cox escape. He told his rapt audience that having absconded from the work gang at Kelly's Basin, they wandered about for eight days, hiding in the rainforest before arriving at King River on the Sunday evening. In a curiously telegrammatic fashion, the *Hobart Town Gazette* summarised Gellibrand's description of what happened after that: 'A quarrel then arose because the deceased could not swim, and after the prisoner had struck him on the head three times with his axe, the deceased seeing him about to go away . . . said, in a faint voice, "For mercy's sake come back and put me out of my misery!" Prisoner then struck him a fourth blow, which immediately caused death'. Pearce then proceeded to butcher the body and eat parts of it. The next morning, according to Gellibrand, he set off northward, but soon became 'so overwhelmed by the agonies of remorse' that he resolved to return and give himself up to the authorities. Knowing what we do of Pearce it is hard to imagine his level of remorse. His motivations were more complex, but mention of 'remorse' satisfied the moral sensitivities of the time. Gellibrand concluded by saying that the accused publicly owned up to the murder and admitted that he was 'willing to die for it' on the way back to Sarah Island.

This 'thrilling tale of almost incredible barbarity', as the *Gazette* writer called it, was confirmed by the evidence of several reliable witnesses, among them Thomas Smith, the Commandant's coxswain, and William Evans of the *Waterloo* pilot-schooner, who had gone ashore to take Pearce captive. The *Gazette* reporter, with a plethora of commas, then summarised the rest of the evidence: 'Many other witnesses were called, who corroborated the above depositions in every essential point; and proved, that the clothes and hat, worn by the deceased, when he absconded, were those which the prisoner wore when he was taken on board the pilot boat'. They even found a hat-cover near Cox's body that matched the one worn by Pearce when he was captured.

The case against the Irishman was strong. Besides openly confessing to the Sarah Island Commandant that he had killed Cox in a fit of rage, he had admitted the crime before several other reliable witnesses. His captors repeated the testimony that when he surrendered, Pearce was dressed in the murdered man's clothes. And he knew exactly where the body was to be found and led witnesses straight to it. Thus there was no doubt in anyone's mind about his guilt. There is no record that Pearce said anything on his own behalf.

However, this did not stop the Chief Justice addressing the jury at 'considerable length' and 'with much solemnity' as to 'whether or no it was fully proved that the deceased had died from blows inflicted by the prisoner? And as a quarrel had been stated to have occurred before death, was the prisoner was guilty of the crime charged, or of manslaughter?' In other words, perhaps he was so angry he did not know what he was doing? It was a nice distinction and an important one, and it might have made the difference between life or execution for Convict No. 102. However, the jury did not have much difficulty distinguishing between murder and manslaughter in Pearce's case. They 'retired for a short time and found a verdict of – *Guilty*' of murder.

The guilty verdict gave Pedder an opportunity to indulge in some gratuitous comments from the bench about the horrible events that had been described in the confessions and evidence, and about the need for the miserable culprit to prepare himself to appear before the one divine tribunal where mercy could be obtained. Then, without wasting any time on reflection about the sentence, Pedder solemnly put on the black cloth sentencing-cap over his horsehair wig and passed sentence upon Pearce immediately. 'Your sentence is that you be removed from this place to the gaol, and (when the supreme authority shall appoint) thence to the place of execution to be hanged by the neck until you are dead; afterwards your body to be delivered over to the surgeons for dissection' – or as the Criminal Record Book of the Supreme Court puts it: 'His body [is] to be anatomized'. Apparently God was not requested to have mercy on Pearce's soul. This was to be left up to the Catholic chaplain. Dissection was a humiliation reserved for the worst murderers and was not common, even in early nineteenth-century Van Diemen's Land. However, in the case of the Irishman from County Monaghan, there is a curious resonance between the crime and the punishment: the body of the cannibal was to be cannibalised for science.

After the drama of the trial, the judge, prosecuting attorney, legal officers and jury retired to lunch, and Pearce was led back to jail. The intrepid reporter from the *Hobart Town Gazette* gave full vent to his rhetoric in the paper of 23 July 1824: 'We trust these awful and ignominious results of disobedience to law and humanity will act as a powerful caution; for blood must expiate blood! And the welfare of society imperatively requires, that all whose crimes are so confirmed, and systematic, as not to be redeemed by lenity, shall be pursued in vengeance, and expiated with death!'

Now a condemned felon, Pearce began to reflect on his situation. That night he talked at length to the Keeper of the Hobart Town Jail, John Bisdee, who also acted as a chief constable and as the keeper of the local animal pound. Bisdee was a likeable, reliable and just man, and there were few escapes during his decade-long tenure as jail-keeper. He was also a successful farmer and fine-wool grower. Since Pearce had apparently had no opportunity to say anything in his own defence at his trial, he confessed to Bisdee all that had happened to him since he had arrived in Van Diemen's Land and he asked the keeper to write it down. He obviously wanted to get his side of the story on the official record somewhere.

Bisdee's account of Pearce's confession has come down to us in an article entitled 'Horrid Cannibalism' in a short book printed in London in 1825 with the title *Tales of Today*. Again this shows how interested people in the United Kingdom were in the story of antipodean cannibalism, and how right Wells had been about the possibility of selling the story to newspapers and magazines in the home country. The Bisdee 'confession' is brief, factual and to the point. This probably reflects Bisdee's tidy mind rather than Pearce's brevity. It does not tell us anything particularly new, but it has the importance of being an account in the Irishman's own words.

No date had been set for the execution, and Pearce was to wait another month before being hung. He was only told on Friday 16 July that he was to die the following Monday morning. Knopwood happened to be at the jail when the sheriff informed Pearce. Four other convicts – John Butler, John Thompson, Patrick Connolly and James Tierney – condemned by the Supreme Court three days after Pearce to be hung for sheep-stealing and highway robbery, were told they were to die later in the week.

Pearce had another visitor after he had been sentenced to

death – the Roman Catholic chaplain of Van Diemen's Land, the Reverend Mr Philip Conolly. (The title 'Mr' was generally used in the period before diocesan priests were given the title 'Father', which for several centuries had applied only to priests who were members of religious orders.) Part of Conolly's ministry, as well as that of Knopwood and Bedford, was the care of men condemned to death. Conolly was an intelligent man, devoted to his ministry, with a cynical and dry sense of humour. While most of his ministry was subsumed by his convict chaplaincy – convicts, after all, made up the majority of the population – the priest also regularly visited Launceston, George Town, Campbell Town, Ross and Longford. During his latter years, Conolly's pioneering ministerial work was spoiled by internal strife in the Catholic community, and there was much criticism of him from the newly arrived Irish free settlers. A disagreement over church property led him to criticise the new Catholic bishop in Sydney, John Bede Polding, which in turn led to his temporary suspension from priestly functions. No such criticism came from his civil superiors. Lieutenant-Governor George Arthur told Earl Bathurst that 'The conduct of this gentleman was very favourably spoken of by my predecessor, and . . . he has always merited my approbation . . . In my opinion it would not be possible for any person to perform the duties required by his office, which in a Protestant community are often of a delicate nature, with more satisfaction to the government'.

Conolly had come to Van Diemen's Land in mid-April 1821 and had worked hard building up the Catholic community in both Hobart Town and Launceston. He also built good social relationships with important people in government, no doubt helped by his closeness to Knopwood. This was not mere snobbery. It was the period before Catholic Emancipation (1829) when Catholicism was still a proscribed religion and bigotry toward priests was widespread, especially among Evangelically inclined government officials. Part of his task as a chaplain to convicts and to the Catholic community was to make sure that he built bridges with those in power. Sorell had been particularly helpful to him and, like many in Hobart Town, Conolly regretted his departure. However, as the report to Bathurst showed, he would also get on well with Sir George Arthur.

The reverend gentleman had a busy time throughout June and July 1824. Three of the other four men to be hung had Irish names, so the priest would probably have been looking after them as well as Pearce. During this period Conolly and Knopwood would have talked to each other about the most onerous of all their duties, ministering to those condemned to death, for parson and priest knew each other well. In what was a quite remarkable 'ecumenical' friendship, especially for its time, Knopwood and Conolly spent a lot of time together, talking, smoking a pipe, eating dinner or sharing a drink of wine or liquor. Their closeness had begun at about 1822, the year after Conolly's arrival, and lasted until Knopwood's death in 1838. Both men were criticised by their respective ecclesiastical superiors and members of their own churches for their intimacy, and many subsequent writers, including the distinguished historian Manning Clark, have taken the scuttlebutt of the time as true and accurate. They have been accused of being a couple of lazy boozers who failed in their pastoral duties. Knopwood, as we saw, was also maliciously labelled a 'womaniser', largely because of his kindness to an orphan girl whom he adopted as his ward. In a small community, the peccadilloes of parson and priest would have been eagerly seized upon and exaggerated by scandal-mongers and the rumour-mill.

While they certainly did enjoy a few creature comforts and neither of them was a saint, these men spent almost their entire pastoral lives ministering in a brutalised and isolated penal environment, often having to deal with men and women in the most terrible circumstances. Conolly particularly spent a lot of time travelling all over the colony on horseback, often in extreme weather conditions, most of the time ministering to a jail population that showed little interest in religion. Many of the free settlers were engrossed in the pursuit of mammon. It is no wonder that Conolly and Knopwood sought some solace in each other's company.

Back in the jail in Hobart Town it was an important part of the priest's duties to care especially for those condemned to death. This was not because the government was particularly concerned about the salvation of those who were to die, but because the judicial authorities wanted the hangings to take place in a way that reflected well on the righteousness of the law and the integrity of the court system. There was a ritual to be gone through, and the priest played a key role in this. It began with the religious and moral preparation for the execution.

Pearce and Conolly both came from County Monaghan, and no doubt the priest was able to use this in building a relationship with No. 102. Conolly was about four years older than the man-eater, but they had arrived in New South Wales within five months of each other in 1820, although Pearce was the first to reach Van Diemen's Land. Also they could both speak Irish (they had grown up at a time when the language was still reasonably widely used), and conversed in their native tongue. Through the language they built up a rapport. Given Pearce's opportunistic personality, he was quick to embrace the consolations of religion when Conolly offered them to him. This is not to say that he was insincere, but simply that he was easily influenced. Catholicism provided a good sacramental preparation for death via confession and absolution, followed by Holy Communion. No doubt the priest counted Pearce as a successful penitent. At the end of 1823 Conolly wrote to tell Bishop William Poynter, the Vicar Apostolic of London, that while the behaviour of most convicts was 'depraved', he was bringing some to repentance. 'There is every day some one presenting himself, full of afflictions for his misfortunes, and professing himself ready to follow any course of amendment that might be pointed out to him.' So probably well before the Lieutenant-Governor had set the date for Pearce's execution, Conolly would have heard his confession and given him sacramental absolution. He would have then brought him Holy Communion. Once the date for the execution had been set, the priest spent a lot of time with Pearce, praying and getting him to admit his guilt. Late in the afternoon of the day before execution Conolly read him the 'condemned sermon', delivered in Pearce's cell, which would have contained an exhortation to throw himself upon the mercy of God.

Executions were normally carried out in the precincts of the jail in Macquarie Street, but they were visible to the large crowds that gathered outside to witness the spectacle. The hanging of Pearce was a special occasion, given the notoriety of his crimes, and the authorities were always pleased when a good crowd gathered. It was seen as Conolly's task to prepare the condemned man psychologically and religiously by getting him focused on prayer, repentance and divine judgement in order to keep him under emotional control as he went to his death. The government did not like impromptu speeches from those to be executed, and especially not the utterance of any critical comments. While most felons who were executed in Arthur's time in Van Diemen's Land went to the scaffold either resigned to their fate and asking for God's mercy, or shaking with fear and sometimes screaming, there were also a number of very flash, indecorous executions, at least from the point of view of the legal establishment. The bushranger Matthew Brady, attended by Conolly, was cheered by the crowd as he went to the scaffold and died more of a martyr than a convicted criminal and murderer. His Irish colleague, Patrick Dunne, again led by Conolly, approached his execution blessing the cheering crowd. Most convicts did not have the theatrical talent of Brady and Dunne to turn the execution into a show, and occasionally a malefactor refused the ministry of the chaplain and had to be dragged to the gibbet, screaming and cursing God and the legal system. This was the kind of spectacle that the government wanted to avoid at any cost.

As far as the legal authorities were concerned, an important part of the process was a public confession in which the malefactor admitted his crimes openly, so that the judicial system could be seen to have acted correctly and justly. The dignity of the law had to be upheld. In all of this Conolly was successful with Pearce. It was the chaplain's job to offer the *quid pro quo* of eternal salvation to the malefactor who confessed his guilt. Ironically, in a way, this was theologically more in tune with the more tactile and realistic Catholic sacramental system than with the Protestant emphasis on abstract notions of repentance, conversion and faith. While the modern secular mind might have difficulty accepting the sincerity of a conversion induced by the immediate prospect of execution, this was not such a problem for unsophisticated people of the early nineteenth century. For them, last-minute conversions were not unusual. As long as there was life, there was hope of God's mercy, and they depended on this. While this might have what we would call a kind of 'magical' element in it, they were more convinced of God's direct intervention in human affairs than we are, and the division between good and evil was much more tangible for them.

Pearce's execution almost did not happen that Monday morning. On the day before the hanging the Acting Sheriff, John Beaumont, was unsure that he had the proper authority to proceed. Possibly the problem had something to do with the fact that Pearce was the first man executed under the authority of the newly set up Supreme Court. Before Beaumont could go ahead he felt he needed the authority of the Lieutenant-Governor. He was reassured by Arthur's secretary, John Montagu. Whatever the legal problem, it was quickly sorted out and Beaumont, his scruples allayed, went back to preparing for the hanging.

On the day of the execution, Monday, 19 July 1824, Pearce was woken very early, if he had slept at all. His fetters knocked off, he went to confession again and was given sacramental absolution and Holy Communion by Conolly. Following more prayers, he sat down to a good breakfast. Some time after 8 a.m. the cell door was opened onto the jail-yard. The Acting Sheriff, the Deputy Sheriff, jail-keeper Bisdee and a group of convict constables marched into the yard. Pearce was led out of the cell and toward the scaffold by Conolly. When they arrived, Conolly addressed the crowd of convicts and men from the chain gangs who were forced to be present, as well as onlookers. He took his theme from the Book of Genesis (9:6): 'Whoever sheds the blood of Man, by Man shall his blood be shed'. No doubt he felt it was a good opportunity to use Pearce as an example to all sinners and malefactors present.

Some days before, Conolly had written out a long confession dictated by Pearce, but presumably with lots of additions and embellishments by the priest. There is some evidence that it was originally written in Irish, although, of course, it was delivered in English! Long, drawn-out confessions were not unusual at executions in the early nineteenth century. Addressing the crowd, Conolly said that since Pearce was 'standing on the awful entrance into eternity ... [he] was desirous to make the most public acknowledgement of his guilt, in order to humble himself, as much as possible in the sight of God and Man'. Pearce had admitted that he had murdered Cox, and the confession went on to tell the story of the first escape. However, compared to the other versions, this was a rather sanitised account of events. Perhaps Conolly was unconsciously willing to a certain extent to collude in Pearce's exculpation because they were both from the

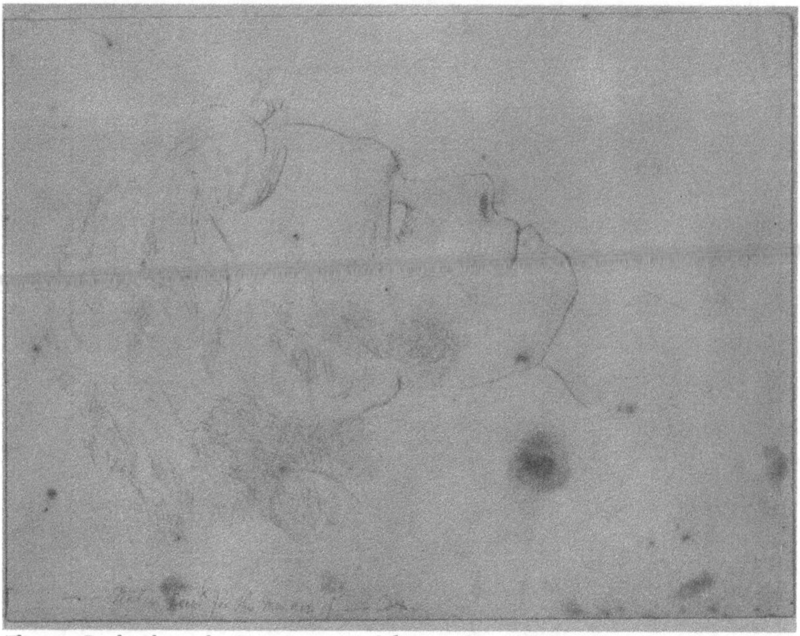

Thomas Bock, Alexander Pearce executed for murder, 19 July 1824. Crayon on paper. (Courtesy Dixson Library, State Library of New South Wales.)

same county. Whatever the reason, Conolly concluded by stating that 'the unfortunate Pearce was more willing to die than to live . . . [and he entreated] . . . all persons present to offer up their prayers, and beg of the Almighty to have mercy upon him'.

An intriguing incident was recorded about the confession some seventy years later by Cardinal Patrick Francis Moran, then Archbishop of Sydney. Moran says that in preparation for the execution Conolly wrote down Pearce's confession in Irish and that when he delivered the speech at the scaffold on behalf of the man-eater, he freely translated it as he went along. Later Lieutenant-Governor Arthur sent for a copy and, unthinkingly, Conolly gave the orderly the Irish version he had in his pocket. When it was delivered to Government House everyone thought it was written in Hebrew! Conolly had to be summoned to translate it for them. Moran does not say where he got this story.

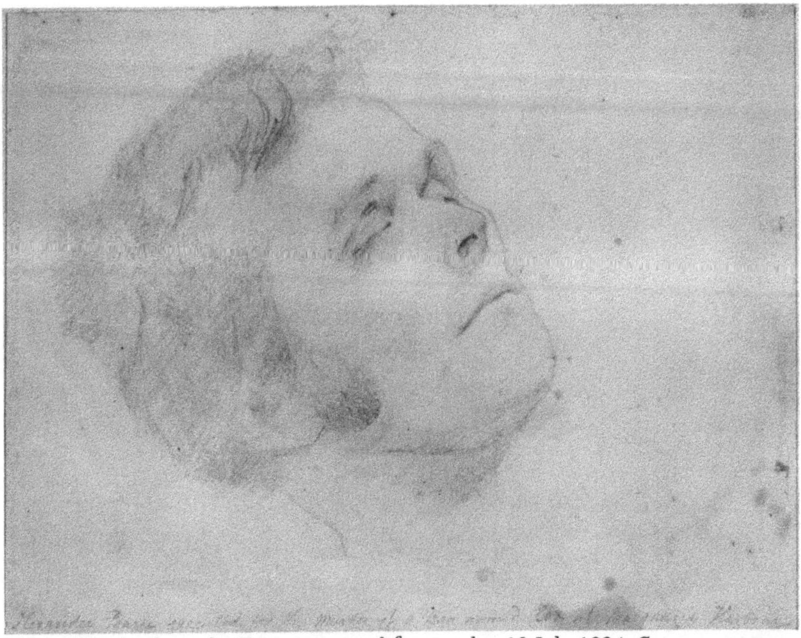

Thomas Bock, Alexander Pearce executed for murder, 19 July 1824. Crayon on paper. (Courtesy Dixson Library, State Library of New South Wales.)

Perhaps this also explains the delay in getting a copy of the confession speech into the *Hobart Town Gazette*. It did not appear there until six weeks after the execution.

The speech concluded, Pearce stepped onto the trapdoor (the 'drop', as it was called), and the white cap was placed over his head. The noose was adjusted around his neck by the executioner, who made sure that the thick knot was placed at the side of Pearce's head so that it would be jerked sideways as the rope suddenly took the full weight of the body. The executioner's aim was to break or at least fracture the first three cervical vertebrae with the knot to damage the spinal cord and bring about immediate loss of consciousness. Pearce was given a couple more minutes of private prayer with Conolly, who then stood back and nodded to the executioner. He reached over and released the trap. Pearce's body dropped out of sight of the spectators. It was 9 a.m.

Death occurred, either immediately or slowly, by strangulation and asphyxiation.

As soon as Pearce's body was cut down by the executioner and laid out on the wooden trolley, Conolly administered conditional extreme unction, the sacrament reserved for the very sick and the dying. In those days recently dead bodies were anointed on the assumption that there still may have been some life remaining. No one knew exactly when the soul left the body. So the priest would not have missed this final opportunity to assist his convert on his ultimate journey to God. After that, all that would be left for Conolly to do would be to bury Pearce's remains after the dissection.

However, another man was also waiting in the wings to deal with the body of the man-eater. His name was Thomas Bock and he was to assist in assuring Pearce's subsequent fame. He had only arrived in Hobart Town seven months previously as a convict, transported from Birmingham for trying to procure an abortion by 'administering concoctions of certain herbs to Ann Yates, with the intent to cause miscarriage'. Apparently Bock had had sex with the nineteen-year-old Yates and she had become pregnant. Bock was also a talented artist and engraver, and on arrival in Hobart Town he was soon employed in various official capacities. Since Pearce's body was being handed over for dissection, the Colonial Surgeon, James Scott, whom we have already met as the surgeon on the *Castle Forbes*, officially requested that Bock do a sketch of Pearce's head. Nineteenth-century men of science were particularly interested in craniology, the study of the size, shape and type of skulls possessed by different races and different categories of people. Some scientists took this further and were fascinated by the heads of notorious criminals like Pearce. The theory was that the shape of the skull gave a clue to character and mental faculties. This was the so-called 'science' of phrenology.

So it was natural that an amateur phrenologist like Scott would have wanted to study Pearce's head as closely as possible. A kind of death-mask drawing by a good artist in crayon was the first step in preserving the record of Pearce's skull and Bock's drawings are quite remarkable. Bock did not have much time to do his work, and he was surrounded by the noise of the crowd and the distractions of all that was happening in the jail-yard after the execution.

As soon as Bock had finished, Pearce's body was wheeled on the trolley down to the hospital for the final disgrace ordered by Chief Justice Pedder – dissection. Scott handed this task over to his assistant, Henry Crockett. Like Wells and other minor officials in the colonial service, Crockett was not above keeping a little souvenir on the side for himself. So he took the liberty of appropriating the skull of the man-eater as a keepsake. Perhaps he, too, was a man of science interested in research, like his superior, Colonial Surgeon Scott, or perhaps he just saw an opportunity to make some money by selling the skull to some other phrenologist. Whatever the motive, he took Pearce's skull home and hung on to it for quite some time.

The chance eventually came for him to sell it to an agent who collected skulls for American scientists interested in phrenology. William Cobb Hurry, from Calcutta, was collecting skulls for the Philadelphia phrenologist, Dr Samuel George Morton. Morton was the author of *Crania Americana, or a comparative view of the skulls of various aboriginal nations of North- and South-America*, published in his home city and London in 1839. Pearce's skull was clearly identified in his collection, and by 1849 Morton was busy embellishing the cannibal story. In his *Catalogue* of skulls, where Pearce is numbered No. 59, Morton presents the Irish convict as a kind of spider luring victims to his web in the forests: 'He [Pearce] succeeded repeatedly in persuading his fellow prisoners to escape with him, for the sole purpose of killing them and devouring their flesh. He used to return secretly to the depot and persuade a fresh victim that he had been sent by others who were waiting in the woods'.

In 1853 Morton handed over his collection of skulls, including that of Pearce, to the Academy of Natural Sciences in Philadelphia, and in 1968 they were moved to the University of Pennsylvania Museum of Archaeology and Anthropology, where they still reside. In March 2002 the keeper of skeletal collections at the museum, Dr Janet Monge, reported that the skull is perfectly intact and in good condition, but that the mandible (lower jaw) is missing, as are most of the teeth. She reports that virtually none of the skulls in the Morton collection have mandibles.

Thus, by an extraordinarily roundabout means, Pearce has attained some physical as well as narrative immortality. If he had just been hung but not dissected, we would have no physical remains, as he would have been immediately buried in an anonymous grave.

•

At the end of it all what are we to make of Pearce? Is he a serial killer in the tradition of the psychopathic Dr Hannibal Lecter in the Thomas Harris novel *The Silence of the Lambs*? In this story Lecter is made to appear almost attractive by his intelligence and penetrating psychological insight. He is played in the film dramatisation by the wonderful Anthony Hopkins, who succeeds in eliciting from the viewer both repulsion and fearful horror, while at the same time we are drawn into his world as we watch the almost spider-like web that he weaves around the young female trainee FBI agent, played by Jodie Foster. We can identify with her fear and uncertainty because we feel her attraction to him. Lecter's cannibalism, while appalling, remains intriguing, because you find yourself asking, 'How could a man with so much psychological insight and intelligence be so mad and perpetrate such terrible crimes?'

But Pearce has nothing like that going for him. He has none of Lecter's intelligence and insight. He killed and ate his companions out of necessity. He showed no sadistic tendencies whatsoever; if anything, he suffered from a poverty of emotion. He was not clever. But he was manipulative, and seemed to lack any emotional response to other people. As a rural labourer in northern Ireland he probably lived a nomadic life, moving from community to community, never forming lasting links with others, let alone any real friendships. He was probably promiscuous, sexually aggressive and untrusting, quickly abandoning relationships that demanded any commitment. While he was emotionally stunted, he did his best to seem normal, and he probably formed superficial relationships easily, but there was no sense of lasting commitment to anyone. While there is something almost humdrum about him, we have seen that remorse was not something he allowed himself to feel very often, if at all. His attack on Cox shows that he had great difficulty controlling his anger and that he did not deal at all well with frustration of any sort. While there is evidence that he understood the difference between right and wrong, he seemed to have a chilling capacity to shut off his conscience and do whatever he needed to do in order to survive.

Pearce was a classic psychopath. Nowadays, when we like to categorise forms of aberrant behaviour, we have a psychiatric category in which to fit him: he is someone suffering from what psychologists would describe as 'Dissocial, or Anti-Social Personality Disorder' (ASPD). In ordinary speech we generally call such people 'psychopaths' or 'sociopaths'. The symptoms of ASPD are a very low tolerance of frustration and being thwarted, which quickly and often suddenly leads to responses of aggression, anger, fighting or violence. People with ASPD are impulsive and cannot maintain a steady job or consistently honour personal or financial obligations. They have a callous lack of concern for other people; while able to form human relationships, they are unable to maintain them. They disregard their own safety and that of others, and lack respect for societal rules and obligations as well as the law. They have no sense of guilt and seem unable to learn from experience and especially from arrest or punishment. They blame others for their own faults. Generally, if a person has three or more of these symptoms to an abnormal and marked degree, they can be diagnosed as ASPD.

Yet while it is easy to talk about him as a 'psychological type', and while we have a good idea of what he looked like physically, it is still very hard to come to grips with him personally. What was he like? Would the real, living Alexander Pearce stand up? Who was he? It is difficult to answer these questions. The problem is not just paucity of historical sources. In fact, historically we know more about Pearce than we do about the vast majority of other convicts transported to Van Diemen's Land. But even allowing for the fact that he is mediated to us through the opinions and views of other people, it is still hard to get a firm sense of his personality. Perhaps this is where we run up against the essential problem of anyone suffering from ASPD. There are no firm delineations of who they are as people; they are chimeras who give expression to their 'personality' essentially through violence, instability, impulsiveness, deception and manipulation. As those who deal with psychopaths report, when you look into their eyes you discover the awful reality that there is virtually nothing there. They are essentially empty; there is no one at home. Sadly, this is the truth about Alexander Pearce.

Psychiatrists involved in the study of psychopathy, as the study of ASPD is called these days, point out that much in modern culture encourages psychopaths. They are often quite successful in corporate structures, especially where there is an ethical and moral vacuum, and the ethos of 'eat or be eaten' rules supreme. Bret Easton Ellis's novel *American Psycho* describes this world to a T. A lack of moral and emotional effect is dominant in vast swathes of culture today. There is a sense in which Pearce's personality has oddly modern resonances, and if he had lived today he might well have inhabited the lower levels of the corporate or business world, or perhaps more likely, the borderline between legal business and shonky dealing. His stunted emotionality and superficial social skills would have remained hidden behind a mask of normalcy, although he would have probably eventually ended up in prison. If he had not been transported, there is every chance Pearce would have settled down in Ireland stealing the odd sheep or personal item, but never getting caught; an unattractive person but not a monster. So we have to ask what the effects of transportation, especially his stints at Macquarie Harbour, had on him. Did the system that was supposed to 'reform' him actually make him worse? The answer is probably yes.

•

Back in the mid- to late-1820s Pearce himself was dead, but his example of escape and survival was not forgotten by other convicts at Macquarie Harbour, just as Commandant Cuthbertson had feared. From the beginning of 1823 until early February 1827, we know that ninety convicts bolted from Macquarie Harbour. Of these, perhaps twenty-four escapees may have survived and reached the settled districts. Fourteen of them, under the leadership of the charismatic Irishman Matthew Brady, were in one group. They seized a whaleboat on 7 June 1824 on Macquarie Harbour and made it to the Derwent River, south of Hobart Town. From here they turned to bushranging. For two years they made fools of the military sent in pursuit of them.

Brady himself gained a reputation for courtesy to women and was only violent when necessary. Eventually the gang was recaptured, tried and executed, but not before they had won enormous popularity among the lower orders. In response to Lieutenant-Governor Arthur's offer of a reward for their capture, Brady insolently issued a 'proclamation' offering twenty gallons of rum for the capture and incarceration of 'a person known as Colonel George Arthur'! Such impertinence would not have gone down well with His Honor.

About seventy-six escapees from Macquarie Harbour are supposed to have 'perished in the woods' or died 'on their way across the interior', and for some of those who are thought to have made it to the settled districts there is no clear confirmation. A few managed to retain their sense of humour. Timothy Crawley, Richard Morris and John Newton seized a boat at the lime-kilns (the lime was used for building at the settlement) up the Gordon River. While they probably perished trying to cross the inaccessible country we have already traversed with Pearce, according to the official report 'the boat was afterwards found moored to a stump about twelve miles above the Lime Burners and written upon her stern, with chalk, was "To be sold"'!

By far the most successful escapees from Macquarie Harbour were James Goodwin and Thomas Connelly. When they planned their escape in March 1828, they had a lot in their favour. Both had been in the colony for eight or more years so they were well acclimatised to conditions in Van Diemen's Land. Goodwin also had the advantage of possessing a superior knowledge of the country, having worked with Thomas Scott of the Survey Department, from which he had stolen and kept a compass. Unlike most convicts, he understood how to use it. He told the authorities later that he only threw it away on the day before he was recaptured. Goodwin, who turned out to be a natural bushman, had arrived in Van Diemen's Land on the ship *Lord*

Hungerford in 1821 on a thieving charge. Connelly, who was from Dublin, had arrived in 1819. Both had seven-year sentences. Connelly had spent time in the New Norfolk area before he and Goodwin were sent to Macquarie Harbour. They arrived there in early 1827, and eventually found themselves working together with a logging party up the Gordon River.

During their time at Macquarie Harbour they would have learned from the convict scuttlebutt that possibly as many as seven men had already made it to the settled districts between 1822 and 1827, in addition to Pearce and the Brady gang. At the time of their escape in March 1828, Goodwin and Connelly had spent enough time in the slave labour conditions at Macquarie Harbour to have been toughened up for their stint in the bush. Men working up-river were not brought back to Sarah Island at night, but more or less lived on the job. They had the added advantage that they were given their rations in bulk, and thus could secrete them away in preparation for an escape. While the convicts up-river were supervised by constables, there was also a small contingent of soldiers in a blockhouse at Lime Burners.

The two men planned their escape well. They picked the best time of the year and made a wise decision in choosing to go by river rather than over the mountains. In his later statement to the police, Goodwin says that he had hollowed a canoe out of a Huon pine log with an axe. He says that while he worked on it periodically over two weeks, it took about a day altogether to carve it out, and that 'it would have carried four people'. As with the Pearce accounts, there are difficulties in pinning down the exact route of the two escapees. But we can probably make a good guess at it from the comments in his police statement. As with Pearce, the problem is that most features in the landscape had not been named, but Goodwin was an observant man and his account shows that he did not miss much.

Based on the evidence in the statement, they took one of two possible routes. Either they turned up the Franklin at its junction with the Gordon and then, abandoning their canoe, headed generally eastward across country on a trajectory to the south of that of the Pearce party, eventually emerging at the northern end of the Vale of Rasselas. Or they continued south down the Gordon to its junction with the Denison River, and then followed the Denison heading north-east until they left the canoe and trekked eastward across country to near the southern end of the Vale of Rasselas. The two routes then come together, with the men emerging from the northern end of the Vale of Rasselas and passing Wyld's Craig, eventually reaching the Ouse River, where they parted company. The escape had taken just over four weeks. They had subsisted on the food they had been able to take, on part of a possum that they scavenged from the Aborigines, and on grass roots, mushrooms and berries, and they were in very poor condition when they reached the edges of the settled districts. They were quickly recaptured, Goodwin in the area to the south of Launceston. The authorities had enough good sense to make the most of his knowledge and skill and, rather than incarcerating him, they made him a guide on a number of exploratory parties. However, he was eventually sentenced to seven years for stealing in 1835 and sent to Norfolk Island specifically 'by the Lieut. Governor's orders'. Both he and Connelly then disappear from the historical record.

Two and a half years later two other men who escaped from Macquarie Harbour made it through to the settled districts. They were the Englishman Edward Broughton and the Irishman Matthew MacAvoy. On 8 October 1830 they emerged from the bush close to Pearce's old stamping ground at McGuire's Marsh, near the confluence of the Ouse and the Shannon. Here they walked right into a military party under the command of Captain Wentworth. These soldiers were part of the notorious 'black line' designed by Lieutenant-Governor Arthur to try to force the

Aborigines eastward toward round-up parties in the more open country north of Hobart Town. The news that the two men had absconded from Macquarie Harbour had not yet even reached the capital, but it was quite obvious that they were escapees, so they were returned to Hobart Town and incarcerated. When the Muster Master, Josiah Spode, who from 1827 onwards was the immediate supervisor of all convicts in Van Diemen's Land, finally received a report in November about the escape from Macquarie Harbour, he discovered that Broughton and MacAvoy had actually absconded with three others – William Coventry, Patrick Feagan and Richard Hutchinson (the latter went by the nickname of 'Up-and-down Dick'). When questioned about the others, Broughton and MacAvoy denied any knowledge of the fate of their companions, so it was assumed that they were still at large.

The regime of Arthur was a lot stricter than that of Sorell, so the two escapees were committed for trial in the Supreme Court for absconding. In the rough and unequal justice of the time, the men were sentenced to death by the Supreme Court on 27 June 1831. The Executive Council ratified the sentence that they were to be hung on 2 August 1831. Right up until the last couple of days before their execution they rejected the ministry of the clergymen, Bedford and Conolly, and in the words of the *Hobart Town Courier* (6 August), 'they both persisted in the most hardened and audacious conduct obstinately turning a deaf ear to the benevolent exertions of the clergymen to awaken their seared consciences to a sense of the awful precipice to the brink of which their crimes had brought them. Broughton, in particular, who was a Protestant, took every occasion to insult the Reverend Mr. Bedford in his visits to him, and to express his utmost contempt of religious duties'.

However, two days before their execution one Thomas Jones was executed for robbery with violence and, while he died very penitent, he had also refused the ministry of the clergymen right up until a couple of days before the execution. This seemed to have a sobering influence on Broughton and MacAvoy and 'roused from their apathy . . . [they both] made . . . confession of the horrid crimes they had committed'.

Broughton made the most detailed confession, and what a story he had to tell. Like the Pearce party, Broughton and MacAvoy had killed and eaten their fellow escapees. Probably because it was a last-minute confession, written up by Bedford and later published in the *Colonial Times* (10 August 1831) and the *Hobart Town Courier* (13 August 1831), there are no geographical details or any descriptions of the actual journey. All that we have are vivid accounts of the men, the murders and cannibalism. Broughton, like Pearce, was probably a psychopath and a hardened criminal, although he does eventually show some sense of guilt and repentance for his crimes. The confession was witnessed by the Keeper of the Jail, John Bisdee.

As Broughton tells the story and Bedford takes it down, it is clear that the details of what happened are very similar to those of the Pearce party. There were five men making up a regular logging gang, working in timber operations on the mainland of Macquarie Harbour. Besides the 27-year-old Broughton from Dorking in Surrey, who had run away from home and had a long criminal record, and the Irishman, Matthew MacAvoy, the party was made up of three others. 'Up-and-down Dick' Hutchinson from Lancashire was a tall man for the early nineteenth century at five foot eight inches. The other two were a sixty-year-old Donegal-born man named William Coventry, and an eighteen-year-old, pock-marked native of Liverpool, Patrick Feagan, described as 'a boy of the most depraved character'. All were under the sole supervision of Constable Bradshaw. Broughton admitted that the overseer had been kind to him, but confessed that he had participated in attempts on Bradshaw's life, including planning to let a tree fall on him. Again, as in the case of Constable Logan, they hated Bradshaw because of his power to report them, which would usually result in a summary flogging. Like Greenhill, Broughton seems to have taken the lead in the escape plans.

They overpowered the constable and left him in the forest without food and virtually naked. Broughton gives no details of their route across country, nor do we have any sense of the time-span involved. What the Englishman from Dorking does tell us about are the details of the murders and the cannibalism; it is clear that with death imminent he needed to talk about it. Like the Pearce party before them, the five escapees had reached the point of starvation when a plot was hatched to kill the middle-aged Hutchinson, the biggest man among them. They drew lots while he was asleep as to who would murder him, and the lot fell to Broughton who, without warning, 'killed him with an axe, which we brought with us'. He then confesses to Bedford that 'He was cut to pieces, and with the exception of the intestines, hands, feet and head, the body was carried with us. We lived some days upon his flesh; we ate it heartily. I do not know how many days it lasted'.

But the problem was that the murder of Hutchinson made the men pathologically suspicious of each other. Broughton tells Bedford: 'We each of us feared that on going to sleep we would be dispatched by the others – we were always in a state of dreadful alarm'. But, as it turned out, the next victim was not asleep, but cutting timber for the fire, which indicates that they had some other wood-cutting instrument besides the axe. The 'depraved' Patrick Feagan attacked William Coventry. Perhaps the reason was that the older man was slow, like 'Little Brown' in the Pearce party, and delayed the group. Whatever the reason, Feagan attacked him with the axe, but Coventry saw him coming and partially dodged the blow, which struck him just above the eye. He cried out for mercy, but Feagan was apparently unable to go on with the deed, so MacAvoy and Broughton had to move in and finish him off. Broughton told Bedford: 'We lived upon his body for some days; we were not starving when we killed Coventry, we had only consumed the remains of Hutchinson the same day. We were not at all sparing of the food we obtained from the bodies of our companions; we eat it as if we had abundance'. Perhaps, like Pearce, they were starting to enjoy eating human flesh.

They certainly seem to have been much better equipped than the earlier escapees. They had knives and razors, and snares to catch small animals. Broughton claims that he was on very friendly terms with Feagan; he says, 'I could trust my life in his hands'. This must have worried MacAvoy and one night he took Broughton aside on the pretext of setting a snare to catch a wallaby. Broughton claims that he was hesitant to go off with MacAvoy because the Irishman was bigger and stronger than himself. But MacAvoy only wanted to persuade the man from Dorking to join forces with him against the Liverpool lad. He claimed that the long and the short of it was that if they got caught they could not trust the young man. 'Feagan', he said, 'was young and foolish, people will frighten him, and he will tell what has been done; now the only thing we can do to prevent it is to kill him'. Broughton argued that Feagan would not 'rat' on them, but MacAvoy claimed that if they were recaptured Feagan would give evidence against them to save his own life. He insisted that they should kill Feagan and suggested that if they make it to the settled districts that they ought to both say that the young man drowned crossing the Gordon River 'at the back of Frenchman's Cap'. Here he is probably referring to the Franklin. Remember, it is Broughton who is telling the story, and he says he replied that it was well known that the youngster was a good swimmer and claimed that people 'would also know that I will not go away and leave him'. The matter unresolved, they returned to the camp where Feagan was warming his bare feet in front of the fire.

Broughton claims that he felt sleepy and that as he dozed off he heard Feagan screaming out. 'I leaped up on my feet in a dreadful fright, and saw Feagan lying on his back with a terrible cut in his head, and the blood pouring from it; MacAvoy was standing over him with the axe in his hand. I cried to MacAvoy "You murdering rascal, you blood-thirsty wretch, what have you done?" He said, "This will save our lives". And then he struck him another blow on the head with the axe. Feagan then groaned – and MacAvoy cut his throat with a razor, through the windpipe.'

It was as simple as that. Broughton calmed down and they stripped the body, cut it up and started arguing over who would have Feagan's red shirt. Broughton had stolen it from Constable Bradshaw in the first place. It 'occasioned words and ill-feeling between MacAvoy and myself . . . Feagan's body we cut up into pieces and roasted it; we roasted all but the hands, feet and head'. He says it was a lot easier to carry roasted and not so easily discovered. They then went on their way and after about four days he says they gave themselves up to the military party at McGuire's Marsh.

Apparently MacAvoy had also undergone a before-death conversion and he had given a similar account to the Reverend Mr Conolly. Bedford and Conolly accompanied the two man-eaters to the scaffold on Thursday, 5 August 1831.

No doubt Conolly relayed all the details of the story that night to his old friend Knopwood over a quiet drink and a pipe.

7
A PERSONAL POSTSCRIPT

I did not set out to write a book about Alexander Pearce. His story is fascinating in its own right and his determination to survive against overwhelming odds is remarkable. And the story includes a feat of cross-country navigation by Robert Greenhill that is extraordinarily impressive. However my original interest was not primarily in the history of Pearce and the other convicts and their stories, but in the natural wilderness in which these events are set.

In January 1970 I first went to Tasmania, Australia's southernmost island state, as an assistant priest in a largely working-class, urban Catholic parish in Hobart's northern suburbs. Public debate over the destruction of Lake Pedder, one of the most exquisite lakes in the world, was then in full swing. In a wry twist, the Lake was named after the Supreme Court judge, Sir John Lewes Pedder (1793–1859), who presided at Pearce's trial. The lake, with its dark water, beautiful beach and many rare species of animals and plants was first sighted by a party from the Survey Department led by John Helder Wedge and James Erskine Calder on 11 March 1835.

At first I took little interest in the arguments of either side of this environmental debate – the natural world seemed irrelevant to me. As a young priest my interests were anthropocentric, focused on the people of the parish and ministry. As I idly watched the debates on TV, it seemed that never the twain would meet. The environmentalists claimed that the lake was unique and should be preserved at all costs. The then Labor state government and the local Hydro-Electricity Commission maintained that another power scheme was needed so that Tasmania could be further 'industrialised' and 'employment' guaranteed. Never mind that almost all the rivers on the island were already dammed, most of them in a couple of places, let alone that Tasmania was remote from the industrialised centres of the world. Lake Pedder was perceived by both major parties as a useful political issue with popular appeal, and the arguments had little to do with logic or common sense. The government's basic assumption was that the natural world's primary function was to act as a source of energy for industrialisation, so that employment could be created. In order to achieve this it was decided that an area that had previously been set aside as a national park in 1955, which included Lake Pedder, was to be drowned behind a massive dam.

The then Premier of Tasmania was an ex-miner and union official named Eric Reece. His argument for the flooding of Lake Pedder is revealing, for it gives insight into the minds of those who believe in development at any cost. Explaining his position in a later book he said: 'God gave us the earth to use and care for. I think that is a reasonable summary of why we are here . . . There is plenty of room out there, in that [wilderness] area, for people to get lost in, to be rescued from and in many instances to die in. People have been lost in there and have never been discovered . . . They [the conservationists] have taken away more than twenty per cent of Tasmania's surface just to be a wilderness and they are now claiming that there should not be any interference with it in any way. This to me is quite wrong'.

This is a fascinating statement. Reece, whose nickname was 'Electric Eric', is revealed as a man of simplistic, almost naive views, who nevertheless was determined to impose his own will on the whole community by damming a river and flooding Lake Pedder in a national park that had already been set aside for permanent preservation because of its unique natural values. Significantly Reece sets up the argument in an explicitly religious context, and was perhaps drawing consciously on the text of the Book of Genesis where humankind was told to 'be fruitful and fill the earth and subdue it; and have dominion' (Genesis 1:28). This widely misunderstood text has been used often over the last century to justify all types of destructive human behaviour toward the natural world and its animals and plants. For 'Electric Eric', 'subduing the wilderness' by harnessing natural resources through modern technology was important because it fulfilled the human need to use the natural world 'to create jobs'.

For the Premier the natural world was 'out there', alien, separate from 'normal', constructed, human life. It was a foreign, dangerous place where people got lost and died. They even sometimes had the cheek to expect to be rescued from it! In other words, conservationists were a selfish and wrong-headed minority, in contrast to normal people like himself who were concerned about 'jobs' and the public good, which Reece identified with the industrialisation that would flow from the electrical power that would be generated. If pressed, he was willing to admit that it was unfortunate that it was the natural world that would have to bear the brunt of this 'progress'. But as far as he was concerned there was lots more 'natural world' out there, so the loss of a bit of it was not so very important, even if it included Lake Pedder. The long and the short of it was that, despite massive public protests in Tasmania and across Australia and the wider world, the federal government refused to intervene, the dam went ahead and Lake Pedder was drowned in 1972. It was an act of enormous vandalism.

Understandably, in the working-class parish where I ministered there was not a lot of sympathy for those who were trying to prevent 'development', denying ordinary people jobs and forcing young Tasmanians to go to the mainland for employment. Some of the parishioners took the same aggressive stance as the Premier. There was an important branch of the Hydro-Electricity Commission just a few blocks away from our church. At first I remained a neutral onlooker, vaguely on the side of the conservationists, but keeping my own counsel in public. As it happened, however, just before the dam was completed and the whole area was flooded, I had a few days off, and I joined a group walking into Pedder to take one last look at the doomed lake. It was in the centre of the remote south-west of the island, which had largely remained a wilderness area, accessible only to walkers up until the early 1970s. Walkers, of course, were seen by the Reeces of this world as an effete 'intellectual elite', in contrast to real 'workers' who were the practical people who kept the world going. As Richard Flanagan has argued in his *A Terrible Beauty* (1985), environmentalists themselves must bear some responsibility for behaving in an elitist fashion and allowing themselves to be cast in this role, but it is also true that politicians are much more at fault for deliberately driving divisions through the community for short-term political gain, by derisively casting 'greenies' in a selfish and irresponsible light.

The day I spent at Lake Pedder was one of the most memorable in my life. It was a moment of conversion in the genuine religious sense. Here was a place of extraordinary beauty, a scene that puts you in touch with a poetic and profound spiritual dimension of life. The whole place palpitated with a living but intangible 'presence' that led me toward the Transcendent with a capital T! For me, as a Catholic, the Lake Pedder area was a vision of the magnificent creativity of God, manifested through nature. I was later to discover the words of the great medieval theologian Saint Thomas Aquinas that summed up what I realised existentially that day. He says simply that '*qualibet creatura . . . demonstrat personam Patris*' ('Every creature . . . shows forth the personality of God the Father' (*Summa Theologiae*, I, q 45, a 7). The lake truly was a magnificent cathedral of nature that showed forth the splendour of God. Significantly, what highlighted this transcendent beauty for me was Pedder's vulnerability, and the fact that it was soon going to be destroyed, its unique species lost forever. Something profound changed inside me that day, and I have been going back to Tasmania's south-west ever since.

Since 1972, massive campaigns have been waged to try to save much of the rest of the south-west from political opportunism and the technocratic mania that drove the dam-builders, and that still drives the inane destructiveness of wood-chip loggers. Fortunately, the campaigns have been to some extent successful, and at least some of the great Tasmanian wilderness has been saved from annihilation and from the small-mindedness typified by 'Electric Eric' and those who obliterated the original Lake Pedder. Much, but certainly not all, of the south-west is now preserved in the World Heritage Area that will be maintained for time immemorial, or at least until future human rapaciousness finds some other reason to threaten it with destruction. Nowadays civilised humankind sees this wonderful environment as a kind of paradise, a place for nurturing the mind, and one of the great remaining untamed and remote wilderness areas left on earth.

About a decade after my Lake Pedder experience and environmental conversion, I was studying the convict system for a doctorate in Australian history and came upon the story of Alexander Pearce and his companions. It struck me that almost all of the most terrible aspects of the story were played out against the backdrop of what is now the World Heritage Area. Here was a group of men who had experienced south-western Tasmania in a very different way from how I and other twenty-first-century people know it. If it is 'paradise' for us, it had been 'hell' for Pearce and his companions, and it was to become a place where their judgements became so distorted that they killed and ate each other. It is abundantly clear that Pearce and Broughton and their fellow escapees would never have turned to cannibalism if they had not stumbled into this wilderness.

Paradoxically Macquarie Harbour was called a 'place of secondary punishment' in the early nineteenth century, and the whole of the south-west was viewed at the time not only as the wilderness barrier that would prevent escape, but also as an integral part of the punishment process. This was a place that had been especially set aside for the most recalcitrant of recidivist convicts by the British penal authorities of the 1820s. This all highlights the ambiguity and subjectivity of place in human culture and consciousness. We now regard the south-west as a kind of paradise where our spirits are revived and our bodies renewed by the extraordinary beauty of the rivers, rainforests and mountains. But in the 1820s they saw it as an isolated hell on earth where the bodies of the most recalcitrant could be subdued and their spirits broken so that they could be converted into submissive and useful citizens. The more I thought about this story and place, the more I was confronted with a startling and paradoxical juxtaposition: violence, murder and cannibalism in what we think of as one of the most beautiful and valuable places on earth.

Pearce and the other convicts at Macquarie Harbour were not alone in their view of the Tasmanian south-west. Their negative attitudes were shared by others who tried to penetrate the rainforests at about the same time. The Van Diemen's Land Company surveyor, Henry Hellyer, travelled through terrain like this in 1827. His view is typical of the period: 'The air in these dense forests is putrid and oppressive and swarms with mosquitoes and large stinging flies, the size of English bees'. Here he is describing a period in late summer, and is most probably talking about what today are called March flies, which are persistent flies that can give a nasty sting. He reports that daylight is completely shut out by the masses of foliage, which are impervious to the rays of the sun.

A similar word-picture to that of Hellyer is painted by David Burn, writing in 1842. He travelled with the then Lieutenant-Governor of Van Diemen's Land, Sir John Franklin, who was accompanied on a famous overland trip to Macquarie Harbour by his wife, Lady Jane Franklin. Burn vividly describes the difficulty of traversing 'This dense, dank, unblest forest of live, dead and fallen myrtle and sassafras trees, their trunks and limbs strewed and intertwisted with the most regular irregularity, forming a complication of entanglements, to which the famous Gordian knot was simplicity itself'.

No doubt there are people today who would view these rainforests as 'putrid and oppressive', who still see them as dark, damp, silent, strangely alien places that retain their deep and integral sense of 'otherness'. This response is understandable. Some of the rainforest species date back over sixty million years and, as we have seen, originally evolved from the plant-life of Gondwana. Because they are so different, the experience of these forests can be psychologically destabilising, especially when you are unused to being in them. But once you become used to them they begin to assume transformative qualities that extend your experience of cosmic history and time, and help you break out of the parochial and limited shackles of the present. They put you in touch with an age long before humankind ever evolved. There is an odd feeling of permeability: you sense that the landscape will absorb you, and that you are in touch with a period long before our remote human ancestors emerged.

Pearce, in contrast, had come from the cleared, open, soft, rolling hills of the farming country that constitutes the border between what is now the Republic of Ireland and Ulster.

Certainly the escapees had already had some experience of the bush they would have to pass through on the escape attempt, in their periods at large to the north of Hobart Town, and in their work in the logging gangs on the mainland side of Macquarie Harbour. However, they must have felt these remnant forests of Gondwana were terribly ominous, menacing and destabilising. Even if Pearce had experienced a northern hemisphere forest, it would have had large trees such as oaks, elms and maples, and a more open understorey, and been crisscrossed with established paths and roads that dated back to the Middle Ages or even further.

In some ways what is left of the south-western rainforests of Tasmania has survived precisely because it was so despised as a useless wilderness. Throughout the nineteenth and the first half of the twentieth centuries, with a small number of notable exceptions, people saw the south-west as an unprofitable and unproductive jungle that if possible should be cleared for pasture. But despite desultory efforts to farm it, in the end it was perceived as useless for agriculture. Up until the mid-twentieth century 'piners', as they are called in Tasmania, worked the ever-decreasing supply of Huon pine, and the only other activity of any commercial consequence that developed in the area was mining, which fortunately was largely restricted to the area immediately around Queenstown and Rosebery. But until the development of modern environmentalism, the usual aim of Europeans in Australia was to 'conquer', 'tame' and 'civilise' the wilderness by turning it into productive farmland. There was considerable truth in the Australian quip that 'If something moves, you shoot it; if it is still standing, you chop it down'.

The attitude of the settlers of North America was not much different from that of Europeans in Australia. Many had come to North America to escape religious persecution and had high ideals about themselves and the achievement of a more just society. But their stance toward the natural world was as destructive as that of the first European Australians. William Strickland journeyed up the Hudson River in 1794–95, and he describes the settlers in this part of New York State as having 'an utter abhorrence for the works of creation . . . [they] drive away or destroy the more humanised Savages, the rightful proprietors of the soil . . . [they] thoughtlessly and rapaciously exterminate all living animals . . . then extirpate the woods that cloath and ornament the country . . . and finally [they] exhaust and wear out the soil'. European colonists saw the new worlds of North America and Australia fundamentally as resources to be exploited and, while this was moderated to some extent in the nineteenth century by a growing appreciation of the beauty of the wilderness, largely inspired by the romantic movement, it did not prevent the destruction of many species, including the extermination by 1915 of perhaps the most numerous species of bird ever known, the passenger pigeon, and the slaughter of sixty million buffalo in the period after the American Civil War.

After World War II the ideology of the 'conquest' of nature in Australia was replaced with that of 'development' at any cost, and this quickly came to dominate the consciousness of successive federal and state governments in Australia. So-called 'national projects' that diverted rivers and created hydro-electricity were all the rage. The Snowy Mountains Scheme, for example, has eventually led to the virtual death of at least two rivers (the Snowy and the Murray), and to the illusion that water-intensive crops such as cotton and rice can be grown in the dry Australian landscape. With the development mania that drove successive Australian governments, the natural world was seen merely as a continent-sized quarry for raw materials, and as a playground where technocrats and engineers could 'harness' the forces of nature in vast schemes of 'national development'. The earth was a massive mineral resource to be dug up and exported to Japan and the industrialised world, and the land was to be cleared of its natural vegetation for whatever cash crop that could be grown to feed and clothe the peoples of Europe and Asia, earning 'export dollars'. The rivers were to be harnessed so that marginal land could be brought into production through irrigation, despite the salination that inevitably followed, and the sea was to be exploited for its food resources, long before we even knew anything about the fish or the limits of their breeding cycles. For the last fifty years Australia and most Australians have been on a development binge.

It is only now that this ideology is starting to be seriously questioned. While Australia is a net exporter of food and Australian agriculture is feeding three to four times our population, the country faces massive problems of land degradation, pollution of our rivers, salination and loss of species diversity. Slowly a whole new consciousness is emerging. This involves an ethic of conservation; but we are also beginning to realise that wilderness has a value in itself as a natural icon, a symbol of a deeper presence, a sacrament of what the Judeo-Christian tradition calls the transcendent God. Macquarie Harbour and the Tasmanian south-west have become places where thoughtful people now go for contemplation, for an encounter with that which is other than us. The profound irony is that this 'place of secondary punishment' has now become a 'cathedral of nature'.

Yet, as bushwalkers and those experienced in wilderness will tell you, this is not the whole story. While it is true that there is a lurking and intangible 'presence' in the natural world, people also have to confront the fact that the bush is utterly detached from us, from our petty concerns and relationships, from our often frustrated longings for human fulfilment and the many other absurd anxieties and illusions that we harbour about the world and our place in it. Nature is even indifferent to our worries about the destruction of the natural world, the loss of biological diversity and our efforts to develop an 'ecological spirituality'. It is, in the truest sense, utterly Other. From the point of view of the natural world, humans are merely a tiny part of a vast cosmos. There is a way in which the convict authorities at Sarah Island and Pearce and his companions were absolutely right: when you are cast into terrible isolated objectivity against your will and without preparation, worked as a slave and pitted against the forces of nature, the wilderness really does become so totally Other that it becomes an absolute hell, especially if you are starving and exhausted.

The Pearce story points to an important ambivalence. It takes us into the heart of the wilderness and helps us discover that while the natural world should be preserved at all costs, it is not as benign as those of us brought up in the tradition of Wordsworth, Keats and nineteenth-century European romanticism tend to imagine. It is not some harmless, exotic, picturesque place where we go like new-age dilettantes 'to discover the self' or 'contact the "divine spark" within' and learn 'to feel good about ourselves'. While it is not directly hostile to humankind, the reality of all wilderness is that it is objective, timeless, independent and completely indifferent to the vagaries of the human condition. In fact, it was precisely this stark objectivity of the wilderness, this disdain for the puny affairs of mortals, that most likely contributed to driving the Pearce party over the edge into a kind of madness that made the killing and cannibalism possible. Perhaps it is also the natural world's complete detachment from humanity's puny achievements that most upsets the technocratic control freaks who built the dams and the believers in the religion of development at any cost, like 'Electric Eric'. Certainly, one can detect a kind of alienated hatred for the forest in the continuing destructive behaviour of the present-day wood-chippers.

•

Another question that lurks behind this whole story, and which I constantly asked myself as I was researching and writing the book, was how these men came to the point where they could become cannibals.

Over the whole of the fifteen months I was working away on the Pearce story, I got horrified and bemused responses from people when I first described for them the contents of this book. 'How could anyone kill and eat another human being?' was the usual question. Most people could comprehend the terrible situation in which the Pearce party found themselves, but they could not understand how they could decide to kill a man, cut him up and eat him. To tell the truth, at first I experienced a similar response, but with a slightly different focus. I was struck by how quickly the Pearce party resorted to killing and eating each other – they were only about eight days out of Macquarie Harbour when the first murder occurred, and there was not a lot of discussion about it. At first I put their apparent callousness down to the brutalising process through which they had passed as convicts. Between them these eight men had received at least 1300 lashes over a three-year period – an average of 162 lashes each. In itself this would have had a profoundly brutalising effect. This was compounded by the near-starvation conditions under which the men worked at Macquarie Harbour, especially in the first year. But even that did not fully explain the celerity with which they resorted to murder and cannibalism.

I think the answer can only be found in the fact that in the course of their journey they had become socially and psychologically alienated from normal human conditions, even by the standards of prisoners. They were literally dislocated – that is, totally out of their normal place, physically, mentally and emotionally. They found themselves in a new and alien world and they had no way of comprehending it. They were the first Europeans ever to penetrate so deeply into the south-west, and their only known reference points were Frenchman's Cap and the Gordon River. Everything else in the landscape was a *terra incognita* – an unknown and alien landscape. Even their slave labour in the rainforests of the coast around Macquarie Harbour could not have prepared them for the difficulties they faced. They would have experienced being profoundly and utterly lost. Even if, like Pearce, they had earlier absconded and lived in the bush, or worked on the edges of the settled districts, this would not have offered them any real preparation for the conditions they experienced in the south-west.

At first sight the notion of 'place' seems rather abstract. Yet it plays a central role in our lives. Who we are, our identity, is closely linked with the place from which we come. North-central Ireland was where Pearce was 'at home', the place that constituted the original geographical and social parameters of his life in which he had been born and formed, the locations and landmarks established inside his head. While Hobart Town and the surrounding countryside was a long way from his true 'home', even there he could at least relate to the communal and social structures enacted by the British penal authorities. In fact, some Europeans adjusted well to Australian conditions and became expert bushmen with a sympathy for the landscape. James Erskine Calder is an excellent example. But they were in the minority. Most whites remained detached from the strange southern landscape, and it took a couple of generations for their descendants to feel at home in Australia. This perhaps helps to explain why European people crowded into cities, where most of the population still lives.

Once Pearce was sent to Macquarie Harbour he was beyond the pale. Because there are so few forest wildernesses left on earth, we tend to forget how claustrophobic, destabilising and debilitating a rainforest can be for those who are not used to moving through it. Because it is so alien there is an ever-present

Miller & Piguenit, *Hell's Gates, Davey River,* 1886, wood engraving. Lower right corner was removed to accommodate text. (Courtesy Tasmaniana Library, State Library of Tasmania.)

sense of unspecified threat and unarticulated danger. In such a place we are always unsure of what menace may lie in the thick undergrowth, or behind the trees and tangled jungle-like vegetation. This was reinforced by the propaganda of the prison authorities at Macquarie Harbour, and the office of the Principal Superintendent's Department in Hobart Town, who assured the convicts of Sarah Island that they were surrounded by the most inaccessible forest country in the world, as well as by ferocious Aborigines. They were told that they would surely perish if they tried to escape across country. The simple fact was that this was true, and that Sarah Island was a prison in which nature itself provided the walls. In fact, part of the underlying theory of 'secondary punishment' was to take evil-doers and recidivists out of their day-to-day world into the isolated wilderness, where they could be psychologically destabilised, reflect on their sins, be broken by detachment from normal society and the use of the lash, and ultimately resolve to amend their criminal lives.

But the problem with Macquarie Harbour was that it took many of the convicts too far; it placed them in situations beyond their ability to cope. This was why men were prepared to do anything, including killing each other, to escape. This sense of alienation and the loss of any feeling for normal moral, human parameters certainly affected the Pearce party.

Even those who are experienced and at home in the rainforest landscape still experience something different and destabilising in it. Few people have loved and protected Australian rainforests more than the poet Judith Wright, but even she is aware of their ambivalence:

> To reach the pool you must go through the rainforest –
> through the bewildering midsummer of darkness
> lit with ancient fern,
> laced with poison and thorn.

> You must go by the way he went – the way of bleeding hands and feet, the blood on the stones like flowers . . .

The comparison with Jesus' way of the cross is striking. Just as he was rejected, misunderstood and had to surrender his life to pass through the process of death to come to resurrection, so the rainforest with its 'midsummer of darkness' plunges you into a process that takes you far beyond the experiences of normal life, beyond what can be comprehended and controlled, into a region of vulnerability and mystery where it is so easy to become lost and die. Rainforests are places where our fragile assumptions are exposed, where all the flimsy and superficial foundations of modern, 'civilised' life are challenged, and where in the profoundest sense we are confronted with the Other. So confronting are they that many of our contemporaries feel that the only way to deal with them is to destroy them. In the process they are destroying our profoundest source of spirituality.

But there is also a frightening aspect of otherness that can quickly destroy a person's grip on reality. This is expressed above all in the earth's sheer neutrality, its absolute lack of concern about our personal fate. It is this that can drive you over the edge, as I think it did the Pearce party. In other words, the escapees were literally out of their minds when they killed and ate each other.

•

Throughout the narrative the Aborigines of Van Diemen's Land have stood there, quietly observing the vicious and destructive doings of Europeans in their country. They were to be forced to surrender to the imperialistic whites, and in this they were rather like the natural world. This does not mean that they were passive. As Henry Reynolds has shown in his book *Fate of a Free People*

(1995) the Aborigines of Tasmania resisted white settlement with all their strength. They observed the settlers and the convicts and they could accurately pinpoint the movements of the Europeans. They would have observed every move of the Pearce party, especially once it crossed into the Big River tribal lands to the east of the King William Range.

The British authorities knew that there were Aborigines in the Macquarie Harbour area throughout the 1820s, and it is likely that many of the escapees from the penal settlement were killed by Aborigines, probably members of the South-West tribe who lived right along the south-west coast from Macquarie Harbour in the north around to Cox Bight and De Witt and Maatsuyker islands in the south. Humankind arrived in Australia probably as long ago as 60,000 years, and some scholars say 70,000 years or more. There is good archaeological evidence for human occupation in Tasmania from about 35,000 years before the present (BP). Humans first arrived in Tasmania during the late or terminal Pleistocene era while the land bridge between Bass Strait and the mainland was still open. It was submerged for 9000 years between 29,000 and 20,000 BP, and then reappeared for another 11,000 years until about 8000 BP.

One of the most interesting archaeological sites in Tasmania is Kutikina Cave (formerly Frazer Cave) in the valley of the Franklin River. This cave was saved from destruction by the court decision to prohibit the building of the dam on the Gordon River below its junction with the Franklin in the early 1980s. The rich deposits in the cave show that it was occupied by humans in the depths of the ice age for 5000 years between 20,000 and 13,500 BP, the southernmost human beings in the world in that period. During this time the area was largely a grassy alpine tundra, just like today's Arctic landscape. Australia's greatest historian of the pre-European settlement period, Professor John Mulvaney, told the Senate Select Committee on Southwest Tasmania in 1981 that 'the degree of preservation, the range of artefactual and biological remains and their correlation with environmental data, makes [Kutikina Cave] possibly the most important site yet excavated in Australia'. Mulvaney says that the cave offers a unique testimony to the adaptability and persistence of the human spirit. Subsequently several other caves have been found in the south-west with evidence of human occupation going back to almost 35,000 BP.

There has been an assumption that the Aborigines only occupied the coastal areas and that after the abandonment of Kutikina Cave they never went near the interior of the south-west. Rhys Jones, Richard Flanagan and Jon Marsden-Smedley have all argued that this is incorrect, and that local Aborigines used much of the south-west for millennia before European settlement. Marsden-Smedley shows how they engaged in widespread seasonal burning using low-intensity, self-extinguishing fires, mainly in spring and autumn, in order to flush out the pademelons and other animals on which they lived, and to gain easier access to areas which they wished to penetrate. These fires would burn up to the edges of the rainforests, which were too wet to burn. There is also ample evidence from the earliest European explorers who visited the south-west that the Aborigines engaged in what Rhys Jones calls a form of 'fire-stick farming'.

At the time of white settlement in September 1803 there were nine tribes of Aborigines in Van Diemen's Land, each made up of several separate 'bands' who shared a common language or dialect and who intermarried. Each band was further broken down into individual 'hearth-groups' or perhaps what we would call 'families'. It is estimated that there were between seventy and eighty-five people in each band, and about fifty bands all together, which gives a total Aboriginal population of between three and four thousand. The west coast of Van Diemen's Land was occupied largely by two tribal groups, the north-west people (the Peerapper) and the south-west people (the Toogee). Probably much of the interior of the south-west was not permanently occupied, although there is much evidence that both tribes often crossed the mountains, valleys and plains. The area was also entered from the east by the Big River tribe (the Larmairremener) from central Tasmania.

It was probably not until the escapees had got further east and closer to Big River territory that they came under Aboriginal observation. The fact that they were not picked off and killed indicates either that they had not breached any significant Aboriginal land, or that in their debilitated state they were not perceived as a threat.

In the early 1820s the conflict between black and white had not reached the pitch it did in the latter part of that decade and in the early 1830s. Both Goodwin and Broughton reported seeing small parties of Aborigines, and boasted about stealing food from them. Goodwin also reported that they 'saw a number of native fires on the hills and the grass appeared to have been burned recently and frequently'. As already noted, Pearce's claims that he and Greenhill charged wildly into native camps and scared off large numbers of Aborigines are unbelievable. It is most unlikely that the Big River people would have tolerated such outrageous behaviour. This is the false boast of someone whose story could not be checked and who hoped to gain kudos from suggesting that he was superior in strength and courage to the Aborigines.

But even in Pearce's time the pressure on the tribes was immense. From the early 1820s onwards, European settlement increased as more and more convicts and settlers arrived on the island. By 1826 the European population was about 15,000, of whom 11,700 were males and 3300 females. There were about 7200 convicts, about half the population of the colony. The demand for land for sheep was increasing, and in that same year the British government granted the Van Diemen's Land Company 250,000 acres in the north-west corner of the island. At the time there were about 450,000 sheep and 40,000 head of cattle in the colony. By May 1835 the European population had climbed to 37,779, of whom about 15,500 were convicts.

Inevitably this put enormous pressure on land. Naturally the Aborigines reacted as the Europeans seized their traditional hunting ranges for sheep and cattle grazing. The Tasmanian frontier was violent. Many of the incidents we know about were recorded by George Augustus Robinson, both the conciliator and captor of the Tasmanian Aborigines. The treatment of Aboriginal women was particularly bad. Outrages against the Aborigines increased after martial law was proclaimed by Arthur on 1 November 1828. The proclamation declared that 'the Aborigines have, during a considerable period of time, evinced and are daily evincing a growing spirit of hatred, outrage and enmity, against the subjects of His Majesty, resident in this Colony'. Arthur's purpose was 'to bring about a temporary separation of the coloured from the British population of this territory, and that therefore the coloured inhabitants should be induced by peaceful means to depart, or should otherwise be expelled by force from all settled districts therein'. To achieve this, settlers were permitted to use 'whatever means a severe and inevitable necessity may dictate'. In other words, it was open season on the Aborigines, and the whites on the frontier knew that they were free to do what they liked. However, serious questions were asked, and Chief Justice Pedder recognised that it was white barbarities that had led to the Aborigines attacking the Europeans.

Right from the beginning Aboriginal resistance to white incursions was strong and intelligent and, despite the good intentions of the Colonial Office, which instructed governors to try to protect indigenous populations, guerrilla war was inevitable between the Europeans on the frontier and the Aborigines who were fighting for their lives, as well as their culture and land. Many

Aborigines learned English and observed the customs and habits of the whites. In the early 1820s conflict between Aborigines and whites was sporadic, but by 1828 attacks on both sides had reached the point where the Lieutenant-Governor, George Arthur, instructed the military to protect settlers and martial law was proclaimed. A long drawn-out guerrilla war followed. The Europeans outnumbered the Aborigines six or more to one, and they had guns. But as anyone with any knowledge of both the country and the tribes could have predicted, the Aborigines had the superior tactics. They had already learned much more about the settlers than the Europeans knew about them. Their tactic was to hit and run, and the military found itself engaged in utterly frustrating warfare that drove tidy-minded bureaucrats such as Arthur to distraction. The strong resistance of the Big River tribe was at the centre of white concern. So it was decided that an all-out campaign was needed.

In late 1830 the military campaign took the shape of a massive dragnet organised by the Lieutenant-Governor aimed at pushing all the Aborigines out of the southern half of the island into the Tasman Peninsula, the isolated, south-eastern extremity of the colony. Arthur took personal control of the campaign in the field, and 5000 men, including troops, police, volunteers and armed convicts were used. From 4 October to 26 November 1830 the 'black line' was organised to flush out all Aborigines – men, women and children – and drive them like fish into a net. A picnic atmosphere prevailed as gentlemen of influence and property mixed convivially with the lower orders of settlers and convicts, manifesting an appropriate *noblesse oblige*. It was a great plan on paper, but it bore no relationship to the realities of the bush or the intelligence of the tribes. At night the whites lit massive fires to illuminate the landscape, but the weather soon turned bad, and once the Aborigines realised what the Europeans were up to, they brought all their ingenuity and knowledge of the country into play.

The net result: total failure, with only two Aborigines caught. The whole affair cost the government about £30,000. It was a massive humiliation for the whites generally and Arthur specifically. Nevertheless, good politician that he was, Arthur tried to put the best gloss on the miserable affair by saying that it created 'a cordial and unanimous feeling' throughout every class in the community, and that 'the knowledge which has been acquired of the habits of the Natives' will in the future assist in 'capturing the Savages'. But despite His Honor's spin-doctoring, it was an utterly humiliating defeat and a vast waste of public money. The Lieutenant-Governor was smart enough not to try any more large-scale military adventures.

One of those taking part, the Danish adventurer and one-time 'monarch' of Iceland and, after transportation to Van Diemen's Land, convict constable, Jorgen Jorgensen, spells out why the 'black line' failed so spectacularly. 'The rock on which our expedition split was a dense scrub of vast extent and impervious character. It was found impossible to penetrate it and keep the line of march intact as hitherto. All our efforts to preserve the continuity of the ranks were baffled, and the Aborigines were thus afforded opportunities, which they did not fail to utilise, of noiselessly gliding through the unavoidable gaps in our line.' Anyone with the most basic knowledge of Van Diemen's Land should have been able to work that out!

But where direct action failed, European guile and deception succeeded. Arthur appointed Robinson a 'Protector of Aborigines', who travelled throughout the island between 1829 and 1834, attempting to round up peacefully the remaining people. Robinson was one of the few Europeans who could speak local languages, and by 1835, by dint of hard work and much help from individual Aborigines, he persuaded the 200 or so surviving Aborigines to accompany him to Wybalenna on Flinders Island in Bass Strait where, he promised, they could at last be at peace. These people had survived two decades of guerrilla warfare, murder, a low birth-rate because so many women had been stolen or taken by the whites and, to a lesser extent than on mainland Australia, European diseases. But for most of those who went to Flinders Island the only peace they were to find was that of death. In 1847 a group of forty-seven men, women and children returned to Van Diemen's Land. Wybalenna today is a pro foundly sad place whose feel is reminiscent, on a tiny scale, to that of the concentration camp memorials at Auschwitz-Birkenau. I have visited both places. There is a profound 'absence' or 'emptiness' about them, a sense of loss, forfeiture and failure.

•

This book began with the young warriors of the Braylwunyer and Larmairremener clans of the Big River tribe quietly observing Travis, Greenhill and Pearce from the bush. They had a chance to observe the brutality of the Europeans toward each other and they should have been warned. Within a couple of years they too would encounter, experience and oppose the appalling violence of the convict shepherds and free settlers. Yet, by 1834, all of these warriors were dead, the victims of murder, warfare and disease. A correspondent of *The Times* of London has left a description of the incredibly sad end of the Big River tribe. He describes on 7 July 1835 a small party that had been captured in late 1834. It consisted of 'three women, one man, and some little children, called piccaninnies . . . They inform us that they are the last of their tribe, once 500 strong, which was long dreaded under the name of the Big-River tribe. They say that, by innumerable affrays with the white men, they were at last reduced to three men, exclusive of women and piccaninnies, and that, a few months since, they were surprised and two of the men were killed; that they wandered all over the island for the purpose of joining some other tribe, feeling themselves too weak to exist, and under constant dread that the remaining man would be killed . . . To look on that fine, tall, and somewhat solemn-looking savage, the last of his tribe filled me with emotions which it would be in vain to attempt to describe "*Sic vos non vobis*"'.

These were not people who surrendered their land easily to the white invasion in which Alexander Pearce was a minor player. They fought a long and hard battle for their traditions and their spiritual connection to place, but they were eventually overcome by the sheer weight of numbers of arriving Europeans. James Erskine Calder commented later that 'Whatever the future historian of Tasmania might have to say, he will do them [the Aborigines] an injustice if he fails to record that, as a body, they held their ground bravely for thirty years against the invaders of their beautiful domains'. There is an important coda to this narrative that is hardly ever mentioned or commented on by even the best recent historians. There is good evidence that small groups of Aborigines, perhaps just families or even clans, survived the massacres, diseases and the Robinson clearances, and remained uncontacted and living freely in the bush. The best clue to this comes again from Calder. In 1847 Governor William Denison had decided to bring the remnants of the Aborigines from the Wybalenna settlement on Flinders Island back to Van Diemen's Land. The news of this stimulated Calder to write to the Governor on 8 August 1847 to tell him that 'In my numerous rambles through the unsettled Western districts [of Van Diemen's Land], many circumstances have led me to believe that there still exists at large, at least one tribe of natives who have never been in captivity'. Calder says that he is convinced that this '*is much more than merely probable*' (his emphasis). He gives a series of examples from his own experience and that of other bushmen, of the discovery of individual Aborigines or small groups, well after the banishment of the remnants of the tribes to Flinders Island in 1834.

Most of these encounters occurred in the south-western and northern sections of the colony.

To support his assertion he cites the capture of a small group up at Dee Marsh on the north-westernmost tip of the island near Cape Grim in late 1842 or early 1843. Calder also speaks of his personal experience of clear signs of Aboriginal habitation and presence in1840 in the south-west, and he refers to the observations of other experienced bushmen who saw evidence that Aborigines were still at large. In conclusion, he comments to Governor Denison that 'there can be little doubt that the primitive inhabitants of this island were never wholly removed from it, and that at least a few escaped capture, and while these have had the wisdom to avoid appearing in the settled districts, they have not wholly evaded observation'.

We can only be thankful that a few, at least, escaped for a while what in practice amounted to an attempt, even if unconscious and unarticulated, to remove and even eliminate a group of people from their traditional lands. Nowadays most people would call that 'genocide'.

•

Back on the other side of the frontier, and coming up to the present day, I have to admit that it is a bit of an occupational hazard for me, having spent thirty-two years in priestly ministry, to be always looking for a moral to every narrative, even to our story of Alexander Pearce and his companions.

But the more you think about it, the more you are struck by the eschatological implications of this tale. 'Eschatology' is the particular branch of theology that deals with the 'last things' – death, judgement, heaven and hell. In a way, it is a passion to work out the ultimate meaning of things, to give events their widest context. This narrative is partly about different perceptions of heaven and hell. It is also about the fact that beauty and meaning are both very much in the eye of the beholder. For Convict No. 102 and his fellow prisoners, Macquarie Harbour, the Gordon River, Frenchman's Cap, the remnant rainforests of Gondwana and everything else about south-western Tasmania were infernal. In this place of secondary punishment they experienced the natural world as hell on earth. For some of them, being hung was a better option and they committed murder in order to be taken back to Hobart Town for trial and execution. It was their only way of escaping from Sarah Island.

Yet for many of us today, especially for those of us who have developed an ecological sensitivity, the south-west has become a heavenly natural wonderland where we go for spiritual renewal and refreshment. It provides a sense of meaning and purpose that our debased technological world fails to give us. However, this notion can be very naive and romantic because it fails to take into account the ambivalent character of nature and its brutal objectivity and otherness. It is so easy to forget that we need it much more than it needs us.

But the fact is that there has been a radical shift in human perception about places like the Tasmanian south-west and this has occurred very recently. At the deepest level this points to a much more integrated view of reality, to a much humbler sense of our place in the cosmos, to the fact that we do not define ourselves and stand over-and-against nature, but are actually part of it.

There is another final comment that needs to be made. Like Ned Kelly, Alexander Pearce has entered into Australian popular culture. Perhaps he will never be as accepted and acclaimed as widely as Ned, but his story has been popularised in Robert Hughes's 1987 account of the history of convictism, The Fatal Shore, and in their third album the band Weddings, Parties, Anything have a song written by the band's founder, Mike Thomas, called 'A Tale They Won't Believe'. It recounts the story of the escape and cannibalism, and recalls that Knopwood did not believe Pearce when he told the magistrate the truth. The song has made Pearce accessible to people who would normally never have heard of him.

What has surprised me is that while I have been writing the book I keep meeting people who have heard of Pearce. Perhaps Hughes and 'A Tale They Won't Believe' are largely responsible for that. But it might also indicate that Convict No. 102 is entering into popular consciousness, and that eventually he might even rival Ned as a national icon.

Now, *that* would be an achievement.

Notes and Sources

Abbreviations

ADB	*Australian Dictionary of Biography*, Melbourne University Press [References in this book are largely to Volumes I and II].
AJCP	Australian Joint Copying Project [A National Library of Australia project to copy primary documents of importance to Australia held in UK and Irish archives].
AOT	Archives Office of Tasmania.
BP	Following a numeral it means 'Before the Present', e.g. 10,000 BP = 10,000 years ago.
CON	Convict Department [Van Diemen's Land colonial government].
CSO	Chief Secretary's Office [Van Diemen's Land colonial government].
HRA	*Historical Records of Australia*.
NLA	The National Library of Australia, Canberra, ACT.
PPRST	Royal Society of Tasmania: *Papers and Proceedings*.
PRO	Public Record Office, UK [London and Kew].
Sprod	Dan Sprod, *Alexander Pearce of Macquarie Harbour: Convict, Bushranger, Cannibal*, Hobart: Cat and Fiddle Press, 1977.
SR NSW	State Records Office, New South Wales.
THRA	Tasmanian Historical Research Association.

West John West, *The History of Tasmania with copious information respecting the Colonies of New South Wales Victoria South Australia &c., &c., &c.* first published by Henry Dowling in Launceston, 1852. Republished by Angus & Robertson (Sydney, 1971) and edited by A. G. L. Shaw.

General Sources

Throughout the writing of this work I have regularly referred to Dan Sprod's indispensable *Alexander Pearce of Macquarie Harbour* [details above]. Everyone writing about the Pearce story is in Sprod's debt. Another very helpful book has been Lloyd Robson's *A History of Tasmania: Van Diemen's Land from the Earliest Times to 1855*, Volume I, Melbourne: Oxford University Press, 1983; see also his *The Convict Settlers of Australia: An Enquiry into the Origin and Character of Convicts Transported to New South Wales and Van Diemen's Land, 1787–1852*, Melbourne: Melbourne University Press, 1965.

Other works that I have found extremely helpful are C. J. Binks, Explorers of Western Tasmania, Devonport: Taswegia, 1989; Richard Flanagan's *A Terrible Beauty: History of the Gordon River Country*, Richmond, Vic.: Greenhouse Publications, 1985; Helen Gee and Janet Fenton (eds), *The South West Book: A Tasmanian Wilderness*, Melbourne: Australian Conservation Foundation, 1978; Ken Collins, *South-West Tasmania: A Natural History and Visitor's Guide*, Hobart: Heritage Books, 1990. Many people will have read the account of Pearce in Robert Hughes's *The Fatal Shore: A History of Transportation of Convicts to Australia* [London: Collins Harvill, 1987]. He tells the story of Pearce drawing largely on Sprod.

Prologue

The geographical area that I am describing in the Prologue nowadays still has a rather isolated feel to it. It can be found on the 1:100,000 Tasmap sheets *Shannon* and *Nive*, in the area generally to the north of Brady's Sugarloaf and in the general vicinity of Victoria Valley Road and Four Mile Marsh and Brown Marsh, to the east of Bronte Park and north of the Lyell Highway. I have also used the *Lake Sorell* 1:100,000 Tasmap sheet. In other words, the area described is to the north of the Derwent River and west of the confluence of the Ouse and Shannon rivers.

Something needs to be said specifically about the sources for the Pearce story. There are four distinct narrations of the escape and cannibalism. Two of them are quite detailed. While all of them originate with Pearce himself, since he was the only survivor, none of them was actually written by him. At best he was probably only semi-literate, but without him we would have no idea of what happened on the trek across the wilderness.

The first account is derived from Pearce's responses to the interrogation of the Hobart Town magistrate, the Reverend Robert Knopwood, who examined him following his recapture some four months after his first escape from Macquarie Harbour in September 1822. When Pearce described the nightmare journey and confessed the cannibalism to him, Knopwood did not believe him, thinking it was a story concocted to cover for his mates, whom the authorities believed to be still at large. Pearce was sent back to Macquarie Harbour to serve out his original sentence of seven years.

However, someone else wrote up the narrative in two versions, with the obvious intention of selling the story to the newspapers in Van Diemen's Land and the home country. In the text I have assumed that this person was the clerk of Lieutenant-Governor Sorell, Thomas Wells, who took down Pearce's evidence to Knopwood. Some time later the Bench of Magistrates Book for January 1823 disappeared, never to be found again, which was confirmed for me by the ATO in March 2002. Clearly someone (Wells?) could see a financial reward in the extraordinary story, and by getting rid of the Bench of Magistrates Book he (?) made sure that he had an 'exclusive'. Two almost identical long-hand versions of this narrative have survived. These are usually known as the Knopwood Narrative[s]. One is held in Sydney's Dixson Library (DL MS3, September 1822) and is entitled 'Narrative of escape from Macquarie Harbour by Alexander Pierce', and the other is held in Canberra in the NLA at Ms. 3323, ff. 1–5.

Pearce also told the story of the first escape in detail to the then Commandant at Macquarie Harbour, Lieutenant John Cuthbertson, after his second escape. This account has also come down to us in narrative form and is part of the evidence given by John Barnes, one-time surgeon at Macquarie Harbour, and is part of an appendix to the second report of the *Proceedings* of the House of Commons Select Committee on Transportation – the 'Molesworth Committee' named after its chairman, the Radical MP Sir William Molesworth. See *British Parliamentary Papers – Crime and Punishment. Transportation* (Shannon: Irish University Press, 1968, Vol. III). This is usually referred to as the Cuthbertson Narrative. However, this narrative has also come down to us in a long-hand written version which is held in Sydney's Mitchell Library and is headed Pearce's Narrative (ML A1326). Sprod considers that this Mitchell Library narrative is earlier than the Barnes version, and is either a direct copy of Pearce's confession to Cuthbertson, or may even be a portion of the original.

Two other briefer accounts have also survived. It is clear that stories of cannibalism fascinated people in the early nineteenth century, just as they still intrigue us. The first of the short accounts is in the form of a disclosure or 'confession' that Pearce made on the night he was sentenced to death to the Keeper of the Hobart Town Jail, John Bisdee. The second is the actual scaffold 'confession' read, and probably largely written, by the Reverend Mr Philip Conolly, the Catholic priest who attended Pearce's execution. The 'confession' was reported in detail by the *Hobart Town Gazette* on 6 August 1824. These two brief accounts only add a few details to the Knopwood and Cuthbertson narratives.

Both in the Prologue and in retelling the story of the escape, the epic journey across the wilderness and the cannibalism, I have drawn largely on the much more detailed Knopwood and Cuthbertson accounts. Both of these accounts are reproduced by Sprod, pp. 24–50, as are the Bisdee 'confession' (pp. 51–3) and the scaffold 'confession' (pp. 54–5).

Sprod (pp. 68–81) deals in great detail with the possibilities in the Knopwood and Cuthbertson narratives about the area of central Tasmania from which Pearce eventually emerged into the settled districts. Pearce says several times that the party's destination was 'Table Mountain', which Sprod has identified with a 1095-metre (3593-foot) hill that is still called Table Mountain. It is situated immediately south of Lake Crescent and to the north-west of the present-day town of Oatlands. Pearce got to know this area when he worked briefly as a shepherd for William Scattergood of New Norfolk, and later when he bolted and was free in the bush after he had absconded in early 1821. Table Mountain, significantly, is almost due east of Macquarie Harbour.

But Table Mountain proved peculiarly elusive, largely because it was much further east than Pearce had remembered. After he killed Greenhill he 'proceeded for several days' and then came to a high hill which he climbed, incorrectly taking it to be Table Mountain, which was still well to the east. This may have been Brady's Sugarloaf which is almost exactly the same height as Table Mountain (1023 metres/3356 feet). It was probably after this that he came upon the marsh, the small lake and the ducks.

However, all of this has to be speculation because it depends, as Sprod points out, on which way Pearce and Greenhill came after they crossed the King William Range. The narratives are vague about the exact route taken. Virtually nothing in this landscape was named in 1822–23. Thomas Scott's *Chart of Van Diemen's Land from the best authorities and from actual Surveys and Measurements* (printed in Edinburgh in 1824), representing the situation in about 1822, shows the whole area traversed by the Pearce party to be unknown. Even in the February 1832 map in James Bischoff's *Sketch of the History of Van Diemen's Land and an account of the Van Diemen's Land Company* (London: John Richardson, 1832, and reprinted by the Libraries Board of South Australia in 1967) gives virtually no detail of the area to the west and north of the Ouse River. These areas had not been explored.

According to Sprod, there were two possible trajectories as Pearce moved toward the area of white settlement. One was along the Derwent River, which he struck somewhere in the King William Valley or even further south, and which he followed to somewhere between the present-day Cluny Lagoon and the Dunrobin Bridge. The other route has him heading much more to the north, eventually reaching white settlement somewhere close to the confluence of the Ouse and Shannon rivers, just to the north of Victoria Valley and the Osterley districts. This is the course that I have followed in the Prologue.

For the feel of the landscape and the type of vegetation described in the Prologue I have largely relied on my own observation, but have also drawn on very practical books like Leon Costermans's *Trees of Victoria and Adjoining Areas*, Frankston, Vic.: Costermans Publishing, fifth edition, 1994; Ian G. Reid, The Bush: *A guide to the vegetated landscapes of Australia*, Sydney: University of New South Wales Press, 1994 edition; and James B. Reid et al. (eds), *Vegetation of Tasmania* [Flora of Australia Supplementary Series, Number 8], published by the Australian Biological Resources Study, 1999.

For the Aborigines see Lyndall Ryan's seminal book *The Tasmanian Aborigines*, St Lucia: University of Queensland Press, 1981. See also Henry Reynolds's *Fate of a Free People: A radical re-examination of the Tasmanian wars*, Ringwood, Vic: Penguin, 1995.

1 'I was the convict sent to hell'

The brief quotation which forms the title of the chapter is taken from Dame Mary Gilmore's fine poem. The primary source for all of the details of the journey from Cork to New South Wales and on to Hobart Town is Surgeon-Superintendent James Scott's Diary of Occurrences which can be found in PRO at Admiralty 101/15–17. This can also be found in AJCP at Great Britain. Admiralty. Medical Department's Registers, medical journals [Adm 101]. The Diary gives a daily report on the ship's position, weather conditions, events on board, and detailed medical reports on the health of both convicts and soldiers. Also helpful is the indent of the *Castle Forbes* which has been assembled from the Shipping Indents held by SR NSW by Peter Mayberry on his helpful website *Irish Convicts to New South Wales* 1791–1820.

For detailed information on nineteenth-century convict ships see Charles Bateson, *The Convict Ships*, 1788–1868, French's Forest: A.H. & A.W. Reed, 1974. See especially pp. 83–93. See also David R. MacGregor, *Fast Sailing Ships: Their design and construction*, 1775–1875, Lymington: Nautical Publication Company, 1973. Geoffrey Blainey, *The Tyranny of Distance: How distance shaped Australia's history*, Melbourne: Sun Books, 1966 is a good introduction to the function that enormous distances play in Australian history.

For conditions of convicts on board ship see Bateson, pp. 58–82. For conditions on nineteenth-century ships in the Pacific area and the Australian run generally, see Captain George Bayly's Journals [edited by Pamela Statham and Rica Erikson] in *Life on the Ocean Wave. Voyages to Australia, India and the Pacific. From the journals of Captain George Bayly* 1824–1844, Melbourne: The Miegunyah Press, 1998, pp. 19–29. The English Catholic priest William Ullathorne also describes conditions on board passenger ships to Australia a decade after Pearce. Ullathorne made several trips to and from Australia in the 1830s. See his *From Cabin Boy to Archbishop: The autobiography of Archbishop Ullathorne*, London: Hollis and Carter, 1941.

In his Diary Scott mentions a number of storms, but he does not describe them in detail. So I have constructed an imaginary storm, but have directly drawn on several first-hand accounts of extreme conditions in the Southern Ocean. One source was the journal of James Finucane which has been edited by Anne-Maree Whitaker in *Distracted Settlement: New South Wales after Bligh. From the Journal of Lieutenant James Finucane 1808–1810*, Melbourne University Press, 1998, pp. 3–17 and pp. 31–53, where he describes aspects of the journey to Sydney. Other sources were Andrew Hassam, *No Privacy for Writing: Shipboard Diaries 1852–1879*, Melbourne University Press, 1995, and Liz Byrski, *Spectacular Australian Sea Rescues*, French's Forest: New Holland Publishers, 1997.

For the processes involved in transportation to Australia after conviction in Ireland, but before leaving the country, see The National Archives of Ireland Research Guide, *Introduction to the Chief Secretary's Office Registered Papers*. This is available on the very helpful homepage of the National Archives of Ireland. For Cove (which throughout most of the nineteenth and early twentieth centuries was usually referred to as Queenstown) see Mary Broderick, *History of Cobh (Queenstown) Ireland*, privately published, second edition, 1994.

For the letters of John England concerning the sending of clergy to New South Wales (and Van Diemen's Land) see the *Orthodox Journal*, 7 (1819), pp. 30–40. See also Peter Guilday, *The Life and Times of John England, 1786–1842*, New York: The America Press, Vol. I, 1927.

Susanna de Vries's excellent *Historic Sydney: The Founding of Australia*, Brisbane: Pandanus Press, 1983 is very useful for early Sydney and descriptions of Sydney Harbour and its foreshores. See also her *Historic Sydney. As seen by its early artists*, Sydney: Angus and Robertson, 1983, pp. 6–23.

2 Convict No. 102

For Knopwood's Diary see Mary Nicholls (ed.), *The Diary of the Revd. Robert Knopwood*, Hobart: THRA, 1977. For a biography of Knopwood see Geoffrey Stephens, *Knopwood: A Biography*, Hobart: The Print Centre, 1990. See also ADB, II, pp. 66–7. For Thomas Wells see ADB, II, pp. 576–7. His *Michael Howe, the last and worst of the Bush Rangers of Van Diemen's Land* was published in December 1818 by Andrew Bent, editor of the *Hobart Town Gazette*. It was republished twice in Wells's lifetime and several times in the twentieth century. While its value is small, it was the first literary pamphlet published in Tasmania. The details of the composition of the Knopwood and Cuthbertson narratives are dealt with in the notes on the Prologue. The AOT has confirmed for me that the Bench of Magistrates Book for early 1823 has never been found.

For early Hobart Town see Carolyn R. Stone and Pamela Tyson, *Old Hobart Town and Environs 1802–1855*, Lilydale, Vic: Pioneer Design Studio, 1978, and Cedric Pearce and Ian Pearce [eds], *Hobart Town Album, 1804–1850. By Various Artists*, Hobart: Fullers Bookshop, 1967. For Henry Savery see ADB, II, pp. 419–20, as well as *The Hermit in Van Diemen's Land* (ed. by Cecil Hardgraft and Margriet Roe), St Lucia: University of Queensland Press, 1964, p. 57. For Bedford see p. 50.

Hotels and inns in the 1820s are described by Grace Karskens in *The Rocks: Life in Early Sydney*, Melbourne University Press, 1997, and in Alexander Harris, *Settlers and Convicts, or, Recollections of sixteen years labour in the Australian backwoods*, first published in London in 1847 and republished by Melbourne University Press in 1986. See also Obed West, Memoirs, edited by Edward West Marriot as *Memoirs of Obed West. A portrait of early Sydney*, Bowral: Barcom Press, 1988, pp. 56–9. For the use of rum in the colony see HRA, Series III, Vol. III, p. 225. For the magistrate A. W. H. Humphrey see ADB, II, pp. 565–66.

Pearce's appearance is confirmed by two remarkable images

of him that have come down to us: they are pencil sketches by the talented convict artist, Thomas Bock, who after emancipation became a well-known and very fashionable portrait painter in Van Diemen's Land. See Diane Dunbar, *Thomas Bock: Convict Engraver, Society Portraitist*, Launceston: Queen Victoria Museum, 1991. Bock did two quick but excellent sketches of Pearce's head and face immediately after he had been hung at 9 a.m. in the yard of the Hobart Town jail on Monday, 19 July 1824. Of course, one can read much too much into faces, especially when the eyes are closed, as in a death mask. In Bock's sketches Pearce looks quite a young man in the first drawing, which shows him side-faced. However, he appears much older in the second, almost full-faced drawing. It is a thin face with sunken cheeks and a sharp, prominent nose. Again, it is the ordinariness of Pearce's appearance that strikes you. The original drawings are held by the State Library of New South Wales in the Dixson Library. See also AOT, CON 23/3/102 for the indent of the *Castle Forbes* where Pearce's physical appearance is described. For Pearce's conduct record see AOT, CON 31/34.

For Lieutenant-Governor Sorell see ADB, Vol. II, pp. 459–62. For Kemp's complaints see HRA, Series III, Vol. II, pp. 684, 686 and HRA, Series III, Vol. III, pp. 220–21.

For Pearce's convict assignments in Van Diemen's Land I have followed the order given in Sprod, pp. 16–21. For the widespread drunkenness see William Bernard Ullathorne, *The Catholic Mission in Australia*, Liverpool, 1837, pp. 29–30. For Ullathorne's comments about bestiality, see his evidence to the Molesworth House of Commons Select Committee (1838).

Major Thomas Bell's evidence to Bigge can be found in HRA, Series III, Vol. III, pp. 230–43. For bushrangers see Robson, pp. 78–105. The executions of bushrangers are dealt with in Richard P. Davis, *The Tasmanian Gallows: A Study of Capital Punishment*, Hobart: Cat and Fiddle Press, 1974, pp. 1–12.

Macquarie's report to the Colonial Office on the state of the Van Diemen's Land colony can be found in HRA, Series I, Vol. X, pp. 500–16. For the March 1826 population figures see HRA, Series III, Vol. V, pp. 699–701. For the 1821 Muster see HRA, Series I, Vol. X, p. 578. For the 1835 population figures, see Robson, p. 168.

I am indebted to Sprod's reconstruction of Pearce's career as a convict. See Sprod, pp. 14–21.

For the inconsistencies between Humphrey's and Chief Constable Richard Pitt's evidence concerning the numbers of lashes per floggings see HRA, Series III, Vol. III, pp. 272 and 486. For Ernest Augustus Slade's evidence see the Appendix to the Report from the Select Committee *on Transportation*, in Great Britain, Parliamentary Papers, 1837, Vol. XIX, Paper 518, pp. 89–90. Ullathorne discusses flogging in his On The Management of Criminals, London: Thomas Richardson, 1866, see especially pp. 18–21. Also Ullathorne's *The Horrors of Transportation Briefly Unfolded to the People*, Dublin: Richard Coyne, 1838 discusses the whole general question of transportation. For a present-day discussion of flogging and its effects on nineteenth-century convicts see David Neal, *The Rule of Law in a Penal Colony: Law and Power in Early New South Wales*, Melbourne: Cambridge University Press, 1991, especially pp. 49–53.

For the complex system of barter and exchange as it operated in New South Wales and Van Diemen's Land see the *Sydney Gazette*, 10 October 1812. The complexities of getting some form of stable currency in the colonies is described by Edward Shann in his *Economic History of Australia*, Australian edition, Melbourne: Georgian House, 1948, pp. 51–61.

3 Through Hell's Gates

For Macquarie Harbour and Sarah Island I am deeply in the debt of Richard Davies, whose knowledge of the whole history of the penal settlement and the other historical sites around Macquarie Harbour is unsurpassed. A tour of the island with Richard brings the place alive and he shares his knowledge generously. See also Ian Brand's reliable *Sarah Island: An account of the penal settlements of Sarah Island, Tasmania*, Launceston: Regal Publications, third printing, 1995. Thomas James Lemprière's *The Penal Settlements of Early Van Diemen's Land*, republished by the Royal Society of Tasmania (Northern Branch) in 1954, pp. 9–51 gives an account by an eyewitness who lived at Sarah Island from 1826 onwards. Lemprière has also left a sketchbook of extremely valuable pencil drawings of Macquarie Harbour which is held in Hobart at the Allport Library and Museum of Fine Arts.

Much of the information on the geology, vegetation and weather patterns of western Tasmania comes from various articles in Gee and Fenton's *The South West Book* and Ken Collins's *South-West Tasmania*.

For a detailed archaeological analysis of Sarah Island see Jack McIlroy, *Excavations at the New and Old Penitentiaries, Sarah Island Historic Site*, Hobart: Department of Lands, Parks and Wildlife, Occasional Paper 18, 1989. For the area around Kelly's Basin see David Bannear's *King River to Kelly Basin Archaeological Survey*, Hobart: Department of Lands, Parks and Wildlife, Occasional Paper 29, 1991.

For the dispatches to London concerning Macquarie Harbour see HRA, Series I, Vol. X, pp. 527–8. Sorell's dispatch to Goulburn is in HRA, Series III, Vol. III, pp. 17–20. Arthur spelled out his vision for Macquarie Harbour in a letter to Lieutenant Wright on 16 June 1824 in HRA, Series III, Vol. 5, pp. 630–1. For Kelly's and King's opinions of Macquarie Harbour see HRA, Series III, Vol. III, pp. 464–6 and pp. 506–7. For the rather sketchy biographical details that are available on Cuthbertson, see ADB, I, pp. 273–4. For details of people first sent to Sarah Island see HRA Series III, Vol. IV, pp. 43–4. For Cuthbertson's Commission as Commandant see AOT, CSO 1/134/3229, and for his first report on the settlement and Deputy-Surveyor Evans report on Macquarie Harbour see the *Hobart Town Gazette*, 9 February 1822. For an interesting book on the King River area see Patsy Crawford, *King: The story of a river*, Dynnyrne, Tasmania: Montpelier Press, 2000.

Details of charges and sentences of some of the convicts sent to Macquarie Harbour in the first few months can be found in the court reports of the *Hobart Town Gazette*, 22 December 1821, 5 January 1822, 12 January 1822, 26 January 1822, 9 February 1822.

For information on the seven other convicts who accompanied Pearce on the first escape attempt see Sprod, pp. 56–9. Further information on the escapees can be gleaned from their transportation ships' indents and the convict Conduct Registers held in AOT. Specific information on the charge of larceny against Greenhill can be found in *The London and Middlesex Calendar of Prisoners in H.M. Jail of Newgate for the Session Commencing on Wednesday 28 June 1820* in the London Metropolitan Archives at XO71/039. Surgeon James Spence's 8 February 1823 letter to the Colonial Surgeon, James Scott, can be found at AOT, CSO 1/134/3230.

For flogging rates, see David Neal's *Rule of Law*, pp. 49–50.

4 The Transit of Hell

There are two books that are very helpful for the landscape, flora and fauna, weather patterns and natural history of south-west Tasmania: Gee and Fenton's (eds) *The South West Book*; and C. J. Binks' *Explorers of Western Tasmania*. Chris Binks's book is also excellent and very reliable for the history of the exploration of the region; Ken Collins's *South West Tasmania* is also full of information about the south-west. Leon Costermans, *Trees of Victoria and the Adjoining Areas* is helpful. For the Gordon and Franklin rivers see especially Flanagan's excellent *A Terrible Beauty*. For fauna see

R. M. Green, *The Fauna of Tasmania: Mammals*, Launceston: Potoroo Publishing, no date.

Here I want to acknowledge that some of my most helpful sources for this chapter were the recorded interviews that I conducted with (1) Mr Terry Reid, Senior Ranger (Queenstown) for the Tasmanian Parks and Wildlife Service on 12 November 2001 in Queenstown; (2) with Ms Sue Rundle, Research Officer – Statistics, and with Dr Jon Marsden-Smedley, Fire Officer, Fire Management Section, both of the Tasmanian Parks and Wildlife Service, in Hobart on 14 November 2001; and (3) on 15 November 2001 with Mr Geoff Law of the Wilderness Society, Hobart. (The Parks and Wildlife Service is a division of the Department of Primary Industries, Water and Environment, Tasmania.) All of these people have a vast knowledge and practical experience of walking in the south-west, and they provided me with invaluable material. I have taken the liberty of quoting them throughout the text of this chapter. I have also had helpful discussions with Dr Simon Kleinig of Burnside, South Australia, who is at present completing a history of the Frenchman's Cap region. See his article 'Journeys to the Ivory Tower' in *Wild* magazine, Winter 2000, pp. 28–32.

I have largely followed Dan Sprod's reconstruction of the route taken by the Pearce party in Sprod, pp. 61–81. For the exploration of the area see S. M. Franks, 'The First Track to the West Coast', THRA Journal, 6/3 (December 1957), pp. 65–9.

However, here I must again mention Chris Binks's excellent *Explorers of Western Tasmania*. The book reflects Binks's intimate knowledge of the area, both geographical and historical. He apparently offers a third alternative route for the escapees. It is my understanding from some private correspondence shared with me that he thinks that, despite their toughness, the Pearce party would not have been able to cross such a succession of ranges, gorges, rivers and forests and still survive. His view apparently is that the 'grain' of the country would have deflected them northward right from the start. He sees them crossing the Darwin Range and going north up the King River valley and then heading north of Frenchman's Cap following the natural breaks in the mountains to Wombat Glen. This means that the escape party pretty much followed the course taken by the present-day Lyell Highway from just east of present-day Queenstown to the King William Saddle. If this accurately reflects Binks's view it is an interesting conjecture made by someone who knows the country intimately. This may also fit in with the convict remains found by Calder at Wombat Glen. However, in my view, this admittedly much easier route does not really fit in with the Knopwood and Cuthbertson narratives.

For the quotation from Sharland concerning his finding human remains on the Loddon Plains, see his 'Rough Notes of a Journal of Expedition to the Westward (from Bothwell to Frenchman's Cap)', 1832. *Legislative Council Journals*, 1861, Paper No. 16. For Calder's discovery of convict remains at Wombat Glen see his 'Some account of the country lying between Lake St Clair and Macquarie Harbour' in the *Tasmanian Journal of Natural Science*, 3/6 (1849), pp. 417–29.

For the Aborigine fire regimen see W. D. Jackson, 'The Tasmanian Legacy of Man and Fire' in PPRST, 133/1 (1999), pp. 1–14, and Jon B. Marsden-Smedley, 'Changes in Southwestern Tasmanian Fire Regimens Since the Early 1800s', PPRST 132 (1998), pp. 15–29.

For Australian snakes see H. G. Cogger, Reptiles and Amphibians of Australia, Sydney: Reed Books, 1992. See also Gerry Swan, *A Photographic Guide to Snakes and Other Reptiles of Australia*, Sydney: New Holland, 1995, and Mark Hutchinson, Roy Swain and Michael Driessen, *Snakes and Lizards of Tasmania*, Hobart: Fauna of Tasmania Committee, 2001.

For the Tasmanian Aborigines at the time of white settlement see Lyndall Ryan's *The Aboriginal Tasmanians*, especially pp. 83–100.

Sprod (pp. 68–81) deals in great detail with the possibilities suggested in the Pearce narratives, especially Knopwood and Cuthbertson, concerning the area in which Pearce finally emerged from the bush near the settled districts. The Irishman says several times that his destination was 'Table Mountain' which Sprod has identified with a 1095-metre (3560-foot) hill which is still called Table Mountain, situated immediately south of Lake Crescent and to the north-west of the present-day town of Oatlands. Pearce got to know this area when he worked briefly as a shepherd for William Scattergood of New Norfolk, and during the time he was free in the bush after having absconded in early 1821. Table Mountain, significantly, is almost exactly due east of Macquarie Harbour. But Table Mountain proved peculiarly elusive, largely because it was much further east than Pearce seems to have remembered.

After he had killed Greenhill he 'proceeded for several days' and then came upon the ducks. I have placed this scene in the area to the north of Brady's Sugarloaf. Around about this time also he climbed a high hill which he incorrectly took to be Table Mountain and which was most likely to be Brady's Sugarloaf. At 1023 metres (3356 feet) it is almost the same height as Table Mountain. All of this presupposes that Pearce and the others had continued along a generally westward trajectory from the King William Saddle, down into the now flooded King William Valley to the south of Lake St Clair, and on over the Wentworth Hills. In this scenario, Travis was probably bitten by the snake somewhere in the King William Valley, and Greenhill was killed somewhere near the Wentworth Hills. Pearce then proceeded onward in an easterly direction until he met his shepherd mate around the confluence of the Ouse and Shannon rivers about 24 kilometres (15 miles) north of the present-day town of Ouse.

There is another possibility that Pearce did not come this

way at all, but had followed a more southerly route along the course of the Derwent River. According to this theory Greenhill, Travis and Pearce struck the Derwent after they had crossed over the King William Range and followed the river all the way down to just south of Ouse where the encounter with the shepherd occurs.

The problem is, as Sprod points out, the narratives are so vague that we are uncertain as to the exact route that they took after crossing the King William Range. Virtually nothing in this landscape was named in 1822–23. Certainly, Thomas Scott's chart of 1824 shows no detail for this frontier area except for the general course of the rivers. Even the February 1832 map in James Bischoff's *Sketch of the History of Van Diemen's Land and an account of the Van Diemen's Land Company* also gives virtually no detail on the area west of the Ouse River.

In the text I have not tried to reconstruct the details of Pearce's activities while he was free. Sprod has examined the narratives and all of the possibilities in detail.

5 The Sudden Death of a Shropshire Lad

For a contemporary discussion of homosexuality among the convicts see Thomas Cook's book *The Exile's Lamentations* edited by A. G. L. Shaw, North Sydney: Library of Australian History, published in 1978 from a manuscript in the Mitchell Library.

There is a discrepancy in the dates of the escape of Pearce and Cox from Kelly's Basin. Barnes told the Molesworth Committee that they escaped on 16 November 1823 and that Pearce surrendered on 21 November. However, at the Supreme Court trial the escape date is given as 13 November and the surrender is dated 22 November. I have followed the dates given at the trial for they are much closer to the event.

For the drowning of Cuthbertson see Lemprière, pp. 11–12, and the *Hobart Town Gazette*, 2 January 1824.

6 The Death of a Cannibal

For the fullest report of the trial of Pearce see the *Hobart Town Gazette*, 25 June 1824. For John Lewes Pedder see ADB, II, pp. 319–20. See Also M. C. I. Levy, *Governor George Arthur: A Colonial Benevolent Despot*, Melbourne: Georgian House, 1953, pp. 43–5. For Joseph Tice Gellibrand see ADB, I, pp. 437–48.

For the Rev. Philip Conolly see Father W. T. Southerwood's *Lonely Shepherd in Van Diemen's Isle: A Biography of Father Philip Conolly, Australia's First Vicar General*, George Town, Tas: Stella Maris Books, 1988. See especially p. 75 (for Pearce), pp. 59–63 and 67–8 (for friendship with Knopwood). For Arthur's opinion of Conolly see Arthur to Bathurst, 1 February 1826. HRA, III, Vol. V, p. 93. For the close relationship between Knopwood and Conolly see the parson's *Diary*, passim.

For the story about the Irish version of the scaffold confession see Patrick Francis Moran, *History of the Catholic Church in Australasia*, Sydney: Oceanic Publishing Company, no date but 1894, p. 243. While Moran is not necessarily unreliable, he never quotes sources, so we do not know where he got this story. He is also incurably pro-Irish and anti-English. His anti-Englishness is also directed against any English priests or bishops, including the English Benedictines who put the Australian mission on its feet. For the foundation period of Australian Catholicism see my unpublished PhD thesis *William Bernard Ullathorne and the Foundation of Australian Catholicism* 1815–1840, Canberra: Australian National University, 1988.

For the rituals of hanging see Richard P. Davis, *The Tasmanian Gallows*, pp. 14–25. For information on Bock and reproductions of his crayon drawings of Pearce's head see Diane Dunbar (ed.), *Thomas Bock*, pp. 25–6. For Pearce's skull see Sprod, pp. 127–29. I am also grateful to Dr Janet Monge, Keeper of Skeletal Collections at the University of Pennsylvania Museum of Archaeology and Anthropology, an expert on Neanderthal man, for her email on

29 March 2002 with information on Pearce's skull.

For James Goodwin's statement concerning his 1828 escape with Thomas Connolly see AOT CSO 1/276/6658. I am indebted to Dr Jon Marsden-Smedley for providing me with a copy of this statement. See also Binks, pp. 29–37 for a good discussion of the Goodwin–Connolly escape. It needs to be noted that in a letter from the Police Office at Launceston accompanying Goodwin's Statement, it says that Connolly also came per the *Lord Hungerford*, whereas Binks says he arrived in 1819 on the ship *Admiral Cockburn*. Here I have followed Binks.

For the Broughton escape and cannibalism story see Stephan Williams, *The Awful Confession and Execution of Edward Broughton*, Woden, ACT: Popinjay Publications, 1987. The accounts of the escape, the killings and cannibalism are based largely on the statement of Broughton (written down by Bedford) which is quoted verbatim in the *Colonial Times*, 10 August 1831. The *Hobart Town Courier* (13 August 1831) also pretty much quotes the statement verbatim, but also adds a commentary and a little more information.

7 A Personal Postscript

For the quotation from Eric Reece see Roger Green (ed.), *Battle for the Franklin: Conversations with the combatants in the struggle for South West Tasmania*, Melbourne: Australian Conservation Foundation, 1981, p. 33.

For the Pedder and Franklin campaigns see Roger Green (ed.), *Battle for the Franklin*, and Brian Walters, 'How the Franklin Was Won', Wild, Summer 2002, pp. 46–7. Several useful discussions of the notion of 'place' can be found in George Seddon's interesting book *Landprints: Reflections on Place and Landscape*, Cambridge University Press, 1997.

Henry Hellyer's description is quoted in James Bishoff's *Sketch of the history of Van Diemen's Land and an account of the Van Diemen's Land Company*, 1832. Sir John Franklin's journey is described in florid and at times tiresome detail by a participant in the party that accompanied the Franklins. His name was David Burn. See his *Narrative of the Overland Journey of Sir John and Lady Franklin and Party from Hobart Town to Macquarie Harbour*, 1842, first published in 1843 and edited and printed in full by George Mackaness in Sydney in 1955. For the mountain ash see Tom Griffiths's splendid new book *Forests of Ash: An environmental history*, Cambridge University Press, 2001.

The quotation from William Strickland comes from his *Journal of a Town of the United States of America* 1794–95, reprinted 1971, New York Historical Society.

The quotation from the poem 'The Lost Man' of Judith Wright is taken from *A Human Pattern: Selected Poems* (Sydney: ETT imprint, 1996). Used with permission.

For Jorgen Jorgenson see ADB, Vol. II, pp. 26–8. Also see the section of his memoirs describing the 'black line' edited by J. F. Hogan, *The Convict King, being the Life and Adventures of Jorgen Jorgenson, Monarch of Iceland, Naval Captain, Revolutionist, British Diplomatic Agent, Author, Dramatist, Preacher, Political Prisoner, Gambler, Hospital Dispenser, Continental Traveller, Explorer, Editor, Expatriated Exile, and Colonial Constable*, Hobart: J. Walch, 1891, pp. 193–97. Recently Dan Sprod has published a biography of Jorgenson, *The Usurper: Jorgen Jorgenson and his turbulent life in Iceland and Van Diemen's Land*, 1780–1841, Hobart: Blubber Head Press, 2001. John Connor's *The Australian Frontier Wars* 1788–1838, UNSW Press, 2002, pp. 84–101, also describes the attack on the Aborigines and their response.

For George Augustus Robinson see ADB, Vol. II, pp. 385–87. See also N. J. B. Plomley, *Friendly Mission: The Tasmanian Journals and Papers of George Augustus Robinson*, 1829–34, Hobart: Tasmanian Historical Research Association, 1966. Lyndall Ryan also draws on *Friendly Mission*, pp. 124–73 in her description of Robinson's work. The quotation from Calder is recorded in Reynolds, *Fate of a Free People*, p. 206. Robson (History) deals with the Aboriginal wars and G. A. Robinson on pp. 210–53. See also Reynolds's other books, especially *The Other Side of the Frontier* (Penguin, 1981) and *Frontier: Aborigines, Settlers and Land*, Sydney: Allen and Unwin, 1987.

For the Kutikina Cave see John Mulvaney's letter of 7 December 1981 to the Senate Select Committee on Southwest Tasmania, a copy of which he kindly sent me. See also Mulvaney and Johan Kamminga, *Prehistory of Australia*, Sydney: Allen & Unwin, 1999, pp. 180–88.

For Calder see ADB, I, pp. 193–95. I am indebted to Dr Jon Marsden-Smedley for drawing my attention to the existence of Calder's letter to Governor Denison (21 July 1847) concerning uncontacted Aborigines, and for providing me with a copy of it. It concerns groups of Aboriginal survivors still free in the south-west. It can be found at AOT CSO 24/24/579. It is referred to in passing by Reynolds in *Fate of a Free People* (p. 54).

For a discussion of 'A Tale They Won't Believe' see Jeremy Mouat, 'Making the Australian Past/Modern: The Music of Weddings, Parties, Anything', in *Australian and New Zealand Studies in Canada*, 6, 1991.